A THEORY OF IMPERIALISM

A THEORY OF IMPERIALISM

Utsa Patnaik
and Prabhat Patnaik

WITH A COMMENTARY FROM
David Harvey

AND A FOREWORD BY
Akeel Bilgrami

Columbia University Press
New York

Columbia University Press
Publishers Since 1893
New York   Chichester, West Sussex
cup.columbia.edu

Library of Congress Cataloging-in-Publication Data

Names: Patnaik, Utsa, author. | Patnaik, Prabhat, author.
Title: A theory of imperialism / Utsa Patnaik and Prabhat Patnaik ; with a
commentary by David Harvey.
Description: New York : Columbia University Press, [2017] | Includes
bibliographical references and index.
Identifiers: LCCN 2016014641 | ISBN 9780231179782 (cloth : alk. paper) |
ISBN 9780231179799 (pbk. : alk. paper)
Subjects: LCSH: Imperialism—Economic aspects. | Capitalism—
Developed countries—History. | Developed countries—Commerce. |
Colonies—Commerce.
Classification: LCC JC359 .P37 2017 | DDC 325/.3201–dc23
LC record available at https://lccn.loc.gov/2016014641

Columbia University Press books are printed on permanent and durable
acid-free paper.
Printed in the United States of America

c 10 9 8 7 6 5 4 3 2 1

p 10 9 8 7 6 5 4 3 2 1

Cover design: Diane Lugar
Cover image: © Amy–Iv/Adobe Stock

Utsa and Prabhat Patnaik dedicate their contribution to this book to Malini and Mihir Bhattacharya.

Contents

CHAPTER SEVEN

CHAPTER EIGHT

CHAPTER NINE

Foreword by Akeel Bilgrami

I

The concept of imperialism has been wielded and studied by a wide range of disciplines over the last two centuries or more (History, Political Studies, Political Economy, Cultural Studies) as well as by diverse theoretical traditions (Liberalism, Marxism, Post-Colonialism). For all this varied deployment and a distinguished intellectual history in the writings of Burke, Marx, Hobson, Lenin, Luxemburg, Gandhi, Fanon, Guha, and Said, there remains disagreement about its meaning and relevance; and there is still much confusion about its relationship to 'colonialism'.

On a standard understanding of the distinction between colonialism and imperialism, the latter—deriving in its etymology from the Latin term 'imperium' connoting 'command'—has to do with the domination of one region by another through some form of control whether direct or indirect; whereas the former refers to such a control by a direct and relatively abiding, if not always permanent, settlement of a population or, at the very least, a governing class, by some form of conquest of one region by another. The treatment of the subject in the pages that follow is a variant on the standard view and its focus is entirely on the modern period. A clear claim is made: 'Imperialism' is said to be the more *general* term and it is defined by a form of *economic* domination of one region by another. Colonialism is then treated as an historically special case of imperialism. Historically, imperialism first took a colonialist form. But it frequently survived the passing of colonialism, that is to say survived the withdrawal of a governing class from the conquered region after the latter gained its independence from colonial rule. It shares with colonialism certain properties of economic domination of one geographical region over another, properties that get modified after decolonization, yet at a more general and more fundamental level of description these properties are *invariant* in colonial as well as post-colonial contexts.

Presenting these invariant properties is the large theoretical preoccupation of the book. A specification of these invariant properties may properly be said to be *the theory of imperialism* on offer in it. Presenting the *different* mechanisms by which these invariant properties are instantiated first during and then after the colonial period respectively, is only one of the several illuminating details it presents.

The analysis, though it has some affinities with the Marxist tradition, derives a good bit of its argument by revealing some of the limitations of that tradition. It is a highly original argument made with both a conscientious focus on empirical detail as well as a deep theoretical foundation, building up its case by coming to its main claims from a variety of different angles, fair-minded against the views it opposes, and throughout raising hard questions and objections to its own convictions and responding to them with attentive care. For all these reasons, despite its modest use of the indefinite article in the title of the book, the analysis is as close to a definitive scholarly treatment of imperialism as one can hope for in a book of relatively short length. It takes the concept of imperialism beyond its popular usage today, which only speaks of episodic forms of domination via invasions and wars waged by stronger nations on weaker ones, to a chronic condition of history over centuries down to the present day.

The most general of the book's claims regarding the economic basis of imperialism, is that there is no understanding the nature of *capitalism* as an economic formation of modernity without understanding imperialism as being, not a mere 'last stage' to use Lenin's phrase, but essential to capitalism pretty much from the outset. This means that it is not sufficient to see capitalism merely in terms of the privatization of land and property and the recruitment of wage-labour by its proprietors to work on it with the purpose of obtaining surpluses. If that were sufficient to define the economic formation that we call 'capitalism', then imperialism would be a merely contingent further accrual to it, an expansionist *extra*, as it were, but not built into its essential workings. This would be to view the nature of capital in purely static terms, missing its intrinsically dynamic nature whereby, as a result of the demands forced by the incessantly competitive nature of capital, new and *external* stimuli are indispensable to the reproduction of capital—and one vital such external stimulus is provided by the relations that capital constantly seeks from outside of its initial territorial anchors in more distant regions of the world. These relations are inevitably relations of domination and the features of the relations that specify the exact nature of the domination is what is called 'imperialism'. As I said, these features were first instantiated historically by the mechanisms which colonialism put into place by conquest and direct control, and recurred in a different form after decolonization.

II

What, then, are these features according to the Patnaiks?

They are presented in a theory and, like all theories of this sort, it contains an analytical component and an empirical component.

The analytical component contains a sustained argument which, at the most schematic and general level, exploits three central concepts, with a number of further auxiliary concepts brought in to elaborate the details of the theory and to defend it against possible objections. The three chief concepts are 'increasing supply price', 'the value of money', and 'income deflation'. The general line of argument, taking capitalism to be the prevailing economic formation, is this: Capital accumulation causes increased demand for certain goods, leading to more production, leading in turn to *increasing supply price*. When this happens, there will be a threat to the *value of money*. The actualization of such a threat, given the nature of capitalism, is intolerable. The actualization of this threat to the value of money can only be avoided by enforcing an *income deflation* that imposes hardship on the petty producers and working population.

This theoretical argument, as I have expounded it, is, as I said, general and schematic, so imperialism is not visible in it. When the analytical schema is filled in with elements of the empirical component, the argument becomes an argument about imperialism.

The first and driving empirical observation is that both in the past and in the present some countries have provided certain commodities which other countries cannot really do without and which they cannot produce in their own territories because of climactic and geographical considerations. In fact, very often, as with food crops, it is not merely that countries x, y, z, can produce goods that countries a, b, c, cannot produce but need, it is also the case that x, y, z can produce in the winter the goods that a, b, c produces in the summer. So there is an actual material *asymmetry* induced by climate and geography. This material reality of an asymmetry is exploited effectively by the Patnaiks to expose the fallacious assumptions underlying Ricardo's theory of comparative advantage which could only be true by assuming something manifestly false (the absence of such asymmetries) and which was advanced by him and all of subsequent mainstream trade theory to preach the universal benefits of trade, disguising the historical fact that a great deal of trade had a brazenly coercive dimension to precisely overcome the handicaps bestowed by geography's asymmetries. What was this coercive dimension?

Here we return to the argument of the analytical component applying it now to the empirical component of such a material asymmetry. So: after a point, for the reasons given earlier, the relevant commodities are producible only at increasing supply price. When this happens, the countries which require these goods but cannot themselves produce them are able to acquire them from the countries that produce them only under a threat to the value of money. In order to avoid this threat, which is intolerable, these countries impose income deflation on the countries where these goods are produced causing untold hardship to the poor and working people of those countries. The countries that produce these goods and have this income deflation imposed on them by the countries that need and acquire these goods from them were initially the colonized and colonizing countries respectively, but the same relationship frequently abides between these sets of countries via different mechanisms after decolonization. 'Imperialism' is the name for this relationship between these different sets of countries. Or to put it more specifically, since the beginning of the fault-line is the prospect of increasing supply price of the commodities that are predominantly produced in some countries, imperialism is the set of policies (income deflation) devised by countries that rely on those commodities but do not sufficiently produce them, to prevent that from happening and thereby preventing the threat to the stability of the value of money on which their monetary economy depends. It is these set of policies devised with these anxieties and purposes in mind that amount to the economic domination of one set of countries by another that has always characterized 'imperialism', properly so called, in the modern period.

All this explains more specifically what is meant when I said that capitalism by its nature generates imperialism because it needs an external source to be the very sort of economic formation it is, thereby giving it the spatial dimension that this book stresses. Though there is no doubt that capitalism originated in European nations, it was never really a self-standing system, isolated from the rest of the world and proceeding to become global as a mere and late contingency. Rather, its logic suggests that it did not become capitalism till it found itself (or formed itself) to be centred within a much larger system which contained a vast *pre*-capitalist population of peasants, artisans, etc., (petty producers, to use the Marxist term) in outlying regions which alone produced a range of commodities necessary for the reproduction of capital. This is because, given the dynamic nature of capital, it seeks at the very outset to reproduce itself and so, as capital accumulates in this process, it must seek an external stimulus and one such is the prospect of obtaining external inputs of primary and extractive commodities (at different points in the book there is extensive discussion of a variety of foods, of minerals including oil, of cotton . . .) that are produced in a geographically and climactically distinct region (either exclusively or, at any rate, at sufficient levels and all the year-round). It is thus brought into interaction at the outset with these outlying pre-capitalist populations with which it has a relationship with very specific structural properties. With increasing accumulation of capital, there is a continuous need for these commodities from these regions at non-increasing prices, if the value of money and a monetary system which allows wealth to be stored, is to remain stable, and it ensures that it is stable by rendering the outlying population chronically poor and thereby compresses the population's own demand for the commodities they produce and thus restrains absorption of those products in internal consumption (something it is necessary to do because these commodities are not inexhaustible and the cultivated land mass is neither infinite nor measurably under-used) so that they are available to European nations (and more generally to the capitalist countries of the temperate belt) at a supply price that is not subject to increase. It is that process which is called 'income deflation'.

From a different starting point than the one I have expounded above, one may reformulate the book's argument as follows. Capitalism is centred on money (or assets tied to money) as a *store* of wealth. This is what underlies and makes possible the circulation of money via its function as a medium for transactions. The *value* of money, as we know, is measured by the amount of goods a given amount of money can buy in a given period of time. It is determined, for the most part, therefore, by the general price level—the value of money is high when the general price level is low, and vice versa. If the value of money falls against commodities, there is a danger that citizens will shy away from holding money and move towards holding commodities, thereby undermining money's status as a store of wealth and eventually therefore its status as a circulatory medium. The entire monetary system, under capitalism, is thus jeopardized by the threat of price increases and an increase in supply price of essential commodities needed for the reproduction of capital is a serious source of concern therefor for the stability of capitalism as a system. Citizens must be given grounds to expect that the value of money is going to be stable. To display how well understood this point was among economic thinkers of an earlier era, the Patnaiks unearth a gorgeous quote from Keynes which refers to Lenin: "Lenin is said to have declared that the best way to destroy the Capitalistic System was to debauch the currency . . . Lenin was certainly right. There is no subtler, no surer means of overturning the existing basis of society than to debauch the currency." (*The Economic Consequences of the Peace*).

The point then is that when those essential commodities are not produced by capitalist countries (call them the 'metropole') and only produced in regions containing pre-capitalist populations in outlying lands (call this the 'periphery'), it must be ensured that their supply to the metropole must be at non-increasing prices. How is this to be ensured? If there is no restraint on the demand for those commodities among the peripheral population that produces them, the supply price is bound to rise since there will be decreased availability of these commodities for the consumption of metropolitan capital. So, what needs to be ensured is that that demand itself is compressed. That is done by 'income deflation', a method of reducing the power of these populations to purchase these goods, which then releases them for consumption in the metropole (Or it may take a slightly different form: the suppression of demand for some goods that are not in demand in the metropole via the curtailment of the spending power of these populations may lead to the abandoning of their production for the production of *other* goods that are demanded by the metropole.)

I have given the argument in its most skeletal form. At each step of the argument, the book considers a number of objections to the argument at that stage or considers claims that are alternative to their own claims at that stage of the argument; and it addresses these objections and alternatives before it moves to the next step. This dialectical method not only achieves what it is supposed to—fortification of the book's argument—it provides valuable lessons in the entire field of the political economy of imperialism. Thus for instance, after it is argued that increasing supply price of certain agricultural commodities would cause a shift from the money form of holding wealth to the commodity form thereby threatening the monetary system, it is considered whether this threat can be avoided by something other than the process of income deflation of the outlying populations. Of course, as I implied above, if the commodities were inexhaustible or if the size of the land mass was infinite or if it was highly under-used, there would be no need to compress the demand of the populations of the outlying populations for the commodities they produce by deflating their incomes so as to make the commodities available for metropolitan use in the reproduction of capital. One could just grow more of the commodities both for metropolitan use and for local consumption. But in the absence of such plenitude, are there other possibilities yet? The authors consider one such possibility for agricultural commodities in particular, by considering methods which, even in the face of finitude of land and its full utilization, would increase the output per natural unit of land, methods which are summarized in the book under the label of 'land augmentation' (examples being higher yielding seeds, multiple cropping, more quantities of fertilizer, . . . to name just a few). Could these methods make income deflation unnecessary? The answer is yes they could, but land augmentation of this kind involves all sorts of further commitments. Thus some improvements will involve serious and substantial commitments to technical research, others such as multiple cropping require irrigation on a much larger scale. This will require both new forms of expenditure and a much greater scale of expenditure, which one cannot expect individual petty producers to undertake; so it would depend on public investments of a kind only the state could undertake. And that is precisely what is not countenanced within a capitalist framework, whether out of a consideration of 'balancing the budget' in the earlier colonial form of imperialism (thus, for instance, the British Crown invested next to nothing by way of public irrigation in India during colonial rule) or out of considerations of 'sound finance' in our contemporary neo-liberal version of imperialism. I've mentioned just one such alternative claim to their own that is addressed by them at one stage of their argument. There are, throughout the book, several such self-consciously pursued fortifications of the argument against virtually all comers, in the course of which a wide variety of positions from Ricardo and before to Keynes and after are discussed at length and with an impressive weight of substantial and constructive as well as destructive criticism.

III

During the colonial period of imperialism, the Patnaiks point out, income deflation was imposed partly by the agency of the colonial state and partly by the 'spontaneous' tendencies of trade within a capitalist framework. The former method was basically the colonial state's system of taxation targeting the population of petty producers which resulted in the reduction of their income and a reduction therefore of the domestic absorption of these commodities; and the tax revenues were then largely used to purchase these very goods from the very same producers and send them abroad—basically a case of something for nothing, which is why it was referred to by critics as the 'drain' of surplus or wealth. The second method was a fallout of the imports of manufactured products from the metropole to the periphery, which, as a result of their replacing the products of the local artisans (something that those very same critics referred to as 'deindustrialization'), created a reserve army of labour in the periphery; and to be cast out of work in this way is, in effect, to suffer from an income deflation, again ensuring restraint on the domestic absorption in the periphery of the commodities that are sought cheaply by the metropole so as to maintain stability in the value of money.

In a fine chapter on labour reserves, the authors elaborate in detail how imperialism quite generally, that is to say in both its colonial and post-colonial phase, effect this continuing income deflation by making sure that this army of unemployed and underemployed does not ever diminish *in the periphery*, in particular. In addition to this, there is a strategy of income deflation in the post-colonial period that is more specific to the last four decades or so—familiarly characterized as 'neoliberal'—and this is the strategy of 'fiscal measures'. This period is

characterized by two features: on the one hand, the global flows of capital, including finance capital, and on the other the demands of fiscal
discipline which imposes serious limits to the relative size of fiscal deficits. The first feature surfaces when nations in the peripheral regions,
seeking 'development', are caught in this global network of finance capital
and they competitively seek to lure investments, something that is
bound to be more successful only if there are concessions offered to
capital such as, for instance, tax concessions to corporations. But given
these concessions to capital, the other feature—of fiscal responsibility—
can only be exercised by making sure that there are cuts elsewhere, in
particular cuts in public expenditure, i.e., cuts in all transfers to the
working (and workless) population such as expenditure on health, food
subsidies, education, etc. All of this deflates their income, once again
bringing to effect a restriction of their consumption of the goods
needed for the metropolitan region at a non-increasing supply price. A
similar effect is brought about by yet another familiar strategy of our
time, a revival of what Marx called 'primitive accumulation', the 'em-
inent domain' form of dispossession of the peasantry from their land
(and foresters from the commons) for corporate projects at 'throwaway'
prices as part of this headlong pursuit of 'development', thereby im-
poverishing this dispossessed population of petty producers. I have
named just two of the most prominent strategies for income deflation
in our own neo-liberal time, the book offers more yet in a very thor-
ough treatment and thereby instructs us comprehensively about the
nature of *contemporary* imperialism and its continuities with as well as
differences from colonialism.

In this very brief exposition of income deflation, I leap-frogged from
how it was achieved in the colonial period to how it has been done the
last forty years. I was silent on the period immediately following decolonization, roughly the three decades or so after the Second World
War. There lies a tale of instructive significance.

The Patnaiks view the political economy of these decades as a kind
of caesura in the rhythms of imperialism, which then allows them to
explain the emergence of the neo-liberal strategies for income deflation
of more recent years via the concepts of their own analytical account of
imperialism. As they see it, this period is defined not only by the continuance of constraints first put on the natural (what they call the
'spontaneous') trajectory of capital by the Keynesian policies of demand

management in the metropole to cope with a prolonged and unprecedently deep crisis, but, given their interest in imperialism, it is a period of even more significant constraints coming from policies adopted in the periphery by governments formed through the success of mass mobilizations that led to decolonization. As a result of decolonization itself, the income-deflating strategies of colonialism ('drain of surplus' and 'deindustrialisation' as discussed above) lapsed. That much is obvious. But because the peasantry and other petty producers had extensively participated in these mass movements that led to decolonization, these new governments, out of a sense of obligation to them, not only did not replace them with other policies to the same effect, they in fact adopted polices that pulled somewhat in the opposite direction, against the runaway interests of foreign and domestic capital and—through subsidies and the provision of some essential services—in favour of petty production. Thus capitalism in this period, having lost its colonialist strategies for income deflation and faced with these new constraints from the newly emerging governments of erstwhile colonies, was confronted with precisely the increase in supply price of essential commodities from these ex-colonies that threatened the value of money and its entire monetary system.

The Patnaiks thus reverse the standard accounts of this period. Where the standard account views the increase in commodity prices in the nineteen seventies as a consequence of an extreme and panicky reaction to the collapse of the monetary system of Bretton Woods, their account explains the emergence of neo-liberalism after the re-mantling of the Bretton Woods institutions as a way of coping with the rise of commodity prices that owed, first to the loss of colonialist forms of income deflation and, second to the adoption of these new policies of freshly independent governments that pulled away from income deflation—a neat confirmation of their own theory of imperialism. To repeat in summary, the neo-liberalism of the last thirty years was a way of *returning* to the protection of the value of money against commodities (something essential to the wealth-holding function of money on which capitalism fundamentally depends) by a *restoration* of capitalism's built-in imperialism, i.e. its policy of income deflation in the periphery (but now by different *post*-colonialist strategies of primitive accumulation by land dispossession of petty producers, fiscal responsibility and austerity measures, etc) to counter the increase in commodity prices resulting from the policies of a heterodox interregnum in the years immediately following the Second World War.

IV

The book is primarily a theoretical *analysis* of imperialism and a theoretical *diagnosis* of its persistence throughout the history of capitalist political economy. Despite its wide and humane sympathies, it does not undertake any elaboration of what resistance to imperialism would require nor what a world without imperialism, as they diagnose it, would look like exactly. It is an obvious inference from the analysis itself, which explains how imperialism is a non-cancellable feature of capitalism, that capitalism would have to be, as the title of the very brief last section of the book puts it, 'transcended' for imperialism to be a thing of the past. The details of the analysis, especially of the post-colonial period, logically imply, as the authors briefly hint in various places, that to overcome imperialism the nations of the South would have to mobilize an opposition against the policies adopted by their elites, which acquiesce in imperialist efforts to impose income deflation on their subaltern populations. This implication is obvious not only from the analysis of imperialism itself, but from what the authors say about what I have called the heterodox interregnum in the immediate aftermath of decolonization where precisely such an opposition was fitfully attempted by many ex-colonies. But what such an opposition to compulsory income deflation would amount to once neo-liberal policies set in in the third quarter of the last century is bound to be very different from what was attempted in the preceding decades of heterodoxy.

There are some suggestive hints on offer in the book. The Patnaiks speak passingly of the necessity for nations of the South to 'de-link' from neo-liberalism's globalized financial economy (presumably initially by serious efforts to impose controls on the flight of capital) and elsewhere they hint of a subsequent partial South-South relinking so that the smaller economies of the South can survive with the support of its larger economies. These are only hints of necessary initial steps and it would be an interesting exercise to explore how they may be developed in detail, building on the wealth of detail of their analytic and diagnostic account of imperialism. It seems to me that one thought-experiment to pump our intuitions on the matter might be to ask a question in the subjunctive: if such a de-linking (and partial South-South re-linking) were to occur, would the countries of the South be better off than they are and would the countries of the North and temperate regions be worse off? I realize that terms like 'better off' and 'worse off' are themselves ideologically contested terms since what gets to count as better or worse off will be differentially approached by contesting positions. But assuming some resolution of such disputes, an affirmative answer to these questions would be to confirm one's intuition about the presence of imperialism, while those who are sceptical of the continuing relevance of the category of 'imperialism' for our contemporary world, will give negative answers. These sceptics who intuitively answer in the negative will then have to respond to the entire argument of this book and also particularly to the extensive empirical evidence mobilized in the making of the argument, including in the various tables and in the carefully formulated response by its authors to David Harvey's spirited and challenging comment on their argument (also published here), which, in fact, expresses this scepticism.

I expect that many, even many on the Left, will be made anxious by the very idea of resisting income deflation by some form of partial delinking. Most economists do not want to resist financial globalization, they want to 'make globalization work'. Moreover there is a widespread anxiety among the lay intelligentsia and the cultural Left that such de-linking amounts to some sort of return to nationalism and nationalism, given the history of Europe, understandably fills the Western mind with qualm. But there are fascinating hints in the book that point towards a more subtle analysis, suggesting that a return to greater national sovereignty in the very specific realm of economics (i.e., a return to control of one's economy rather than have it hegemonized by global finance capital) is the best way to resist the *wrong* forms of nationalism all over the world, the rightly feared reactionary nationalisms based on ethnicities and extremist religious elements prevalent in many parts of the world today. These ideas deserve close study and further development.

Though it is not how it is explicitly presented in the book, I have in these introductory remarks right at the outset distinguished between the analytical and empirical sides or components of its theory of imperialism. I have done so deliberately. This is because there is scope for misunderstanding its conclusions, misunderstandings that are avoidable.

There is no gainsaying the importance to the book of the sheer empirical facts about climatic divisions in the world's geography, facts that bring out the spatial nature of imperialism, the domination of one *region* of the world by another. We do not have a completely clean and exceptionless vocabulary with which to distinguish between these two regions, and the authors do the best they can by helping themselves to a variable ongoing vocabulary at hand ('Metropole and Periphery', 'North and South', 'Temperate and Tropical/Sub-Tropical' . . .). But they should not be held rigidly bound to any of these labels, for that would give rise to irrelevant quibbles about whether one or other country in question is properly described by one or other of these terms. As with all such labels, they don't in every single case fit the subject-matter of a complex theory. But the substance of the book's claims should not be held hostage to the shortcomings of an ongoing available terminology. The work is being done by the *theory* and the empirical support for it, not by the nomenclature. Indeed even the term 'colonialism' may not be perfectly sufficient for the authors' purposes since there were colonialisms that were not characterized by the structural relationships that the theory posits. That only shows that the terms 'colonialism' and 'imperialism' are eventually intended to be defined by the analytical and empirical relations that the *theory* proposes, not by some independent criterion. As I said, by the end of the theoretical argument, 'imperialism' is just a term for the features of the economic domination that are invariant in the colonial and the post- colonial era. Once those features are characterized, i.e., once the theory of imperialism on offer is in place, the *exceptions* to a more casually understood notion of 'colonialism' are also *explained* by the *theory itself.* (Thus for instance, once the account of imperialism is in place, those colonialisms that occurred with the settlement of populations within the temperate region itself—North America, for example, more or less replacing native populations or reducing them to life in reservations—are not instances of imperialism but rather of a *diffusion* of capitalism from Europe to other temperate areas of the world. Indeed the theory also explains why such a diffusion did *not* take place to the non-temperate regions of the world since then one would not possess the external element in the form that is essential for the stability of the value of money.) There is nothing surprising or unusual about this method and this way of proceeding. It is how all explanation proceeds: One first identifies an explanandum with a terminology that one has on hand—in this case, by the term 'colonialism' and 'imperialism' and the various labels I mentioned above for the basic distinction between the two geographical regions. One then constructs a theory that provides an explanation of what one has identified. The explanation then retroactively shows the limitations of the initial terminology that identified the phenomenon to be explained and accounts for the exceptions to the terminology. If this is right, nothing deep is at stake if there are exceptions to any bit of nomenclature that is initially deployed.

I am labouring this point as well as stressing in my exposition that the book has a dual aspect—an analytical schema which then gets an empirical filling—because I think there is perhaps less disagreement between David Harvey (who raises some of these exceptions) and the Patnaiks than it might first seem. Apart from pointing to exceptions, Harvey worries about a geographical determinism that pervades the book, a worry that might to some extent subside if one saw the geographical claims as having the role of giving empirical ground to an analytical schema both of which together comprise the theory of imperialism. This is not to suggest that the empirical claims appealing to geographical and climatic differentials are not important for the book's claims. They certainly are. It is just that their importance does not come at the expense of denying that geography itself is deeply integrated with political economy and that the subject of the book is *that integrated phenomenon*, just as Harvey rightly insists work of this kind should be.

V

I could not close these forewords on *A Theory of Imperialism* without expressing a sense of gratitude that I feel, and I expect many others will feel, for what it brings to the peculiar disciplinary pass that we have been landed with in the academy in the past many decades. This book is so welcome today not just for its brilliance and originality, nor just for its depth of insight and its painstaking empirical specifications, but because the discipline of Economics, as it is pursued in departments in universities all over the world, has completely ignored the subject of imperialism for half a century or more. The idea that one can understand the economic conditions of the world without a full comprehension of imperialism both past and present comes close to the proportions of an intellectual scandal. And it is this perhaps that accounts for what would otherwise be a curious development of the last few decades: the recent revival of the topic by the passionate advocacy of a Palestinian *literary* critic whose wide influence made it central to intellectual life in universities. As a result it is English Departments and the modish developments in what has come to be called Cultural Studies that have explored the subject in recent years. Though I suppose we must acknowledge and applaud the generosity and capaciousness of these disciplines for picking up the scandalous slack in other disciplines that have abdicated a theme that should in a sane disciplinary distribution be central to their interests, we cannot also fail to remark that the study of imperialism in our universities in recent years has, as a result, not unsurprisingly, focused primarily on its *cultural* aspects. This is not merely restrictive, it cannot fail to be shallow, since there is no understanding the culture of imperialism independently of an understanding of its political economy (and, to be fair, I don't doubt that the reverse is also true). Utsa and Prabhat Patnaik have performed the long overdue service of returning the subject of imperialism to its economic roots and they have done so with a marvelously accessible argument that non-Economists may also grasp without strain.

Akeel Bilgrami

Preface

THIS BOOK is the result of seeking answers to a number of questions that arose from a study of the origins and functioning of contemporary capitalism and from our failure to find satisfactory answers to these questions in existing theories. One question was why external expansion and trade were historically so important for the rise of the capitalist system at its West European core. Access to energy, food, and raw materials was clearly essential for its development and for industrialization, and evidence shows that internal sources or exchange with sovereign areas alone did not provide the bulk of these necessities for the first industrializing countries. Colonial subjugation of peoples located mainly in tropical and subtropical areas and the large scale transfer of tax-financed or rent-financed goods gratis to the core countries were crucial to the rise of industrial capitalism, but these realities were generally glossed over by existing theory, which located growth and industrial transformation in endogenous factors alone.

This led to the realization that mainstream theories of trade and development ignored the material reality that the production capacities of temperate lands and those of tropical lands were and continue to be vastly different. In fact, despite all technological advances, import substitution is not possible at all as regards a large range of tropical products in the temperate-region advanced economies—where the definition of "tropical products" includes strawberries and roses in December. The products of the tropical landmass, along with energy, are an essential, taken-for-granted part of the daily requirements of advanced countries, both as current inputs into production and for the consumption basket of their populations. But the supply of the tropical landmass and of known, currently exploitable energy sources is inelastic. Ricardo's idea that trade arose because there was mutual benefit from specialization and exchange was not tenable since the basic assumption of the theory, that all countries can produce all goods, was not true. Some countries alone could produce all goods, which all countries required.

The stability of the prewar international payments system based on the gold standard and centred on the world capitalist leader, Britain, and the acceptance of the pound sterling as being "as good as gold" seem to have been crucially dependent on the latter's appropriation gratis of the global export earnings of its tropical colonies. These earnings reached remarkable heights because only these lands could produce a certain range of goods needed by the entire developing capitalist world. The appropriation without any quid pro quo of these export earnings by the world capitalist leader enabled it not only to run current account deficits with, but even to export capital to, the developing areas of recent European settlement, all of which were located in the temperate regions of the world.

The value of money at the core, and hence the entire financial system, rested on the ability to ensure that an uninterrupted flow of these goods could be obtained at nonincreasing prices by the expanding capitalist core. This was made possible by severely limiting the growth of demand of indigenous populations through taxation, through rent extraction, and through the creation of mass unemployment by the destruction of local crafts. And a part of this very same tax and rent revenue was used to pay for the flow of these goods to the expanding capitalist core, which meant therefore, from the point of view of the colonizing power, an appropriation of these goods without any quid pro quo.

In what ways has the present-day capitalist system maintained the most important structural features of the earlier period of imperialism even in the absence of direct political control? This was the main question to be answered, particularly with respect to countering the instability of the value of money at the core, which could destroy the viability of the financial system. As in the earlier period, ensuring that the supply of energy and of goods is kept flowing at nonincreasing prices to meet the growing demand at the core is crucial for maintaining the value of money at the core, as well as to ensure the stability of wealth-holding, which is a central concern of capitalism; but the conditions for doing so are more difficult to establish in the absence of direct political control. How this stability is nonetheless achieved is a major issue that we had to examine.

In the existing literature the question has been posed: What is the origin of third world food dependence? But the even more important question is never asked: What is the origin of the demand for the products of third world land by the advanced industrial nations and how is this demand, which continues to increase, met? And what is the consequence for local populations of meeting this growing demand from the North? The nature of land as a nonproducible resource, and the absence of specific "land-augmenting" economic measures by their states,[1] which were constrained by the system's insistence upon "sound finance" (or its recent incarnation, "fiscal responsibility"), meant that the specialization by southern nations in export crops, rather than benefiting them, entailed certain important adverse consequences: it was always marked by a decline in the production and availability of food grains for local populations owing to the diversion of land and other resources to export crops. This inverse relation, between the growth of export crops and the availability of food for the local populations, is invariably ignored in development theory.

The main economic mechanism for ensuring an uninterrupted supply of these products to the advanced North at nonincreasing prices has been an "income deflation" imposed on the working populations of the South, which restricts their demand for their own products. This has indeed proved to be a highly effective tool and continues to be used even in the absence of direct political control being exercised over southern populations. The resulting decline in the nutritional standards of this population and the rise in the incidence of poverty within it are denied in the existing "mainstream" literature, which follows untenable methods of measuring poverty.

In the process of asking and answering these questions, we found that we had formulated a theory of imperialism that has relevance not only for the past, but also in the present era. This theory is set out in the present book in a brief form. It is not our intention to present this theory as a substitute for, or as an alternative to, the existing theories of imperialism. We are simply attempting to draw attention to certain phenomena that have always characterized capitalism *and continue to do so even now.* These phenomena underlie imperialism but have not received the attention they deserve. They are ensconced within a universe that has been much studied by writers on imperialism; our concentrating on them alone while not discussing these other studies, should not be construed as detracting from the worth of these other studies.[2]

A THEORY OF IMPERIALISM

CHAPTER ONE

Introduction

THE TERM "IMPERIALISM," though still widely used in third world countries, has become rather rare even in radical discourse in advanced capitalist countries. Terms like "empire" have increasingly replaced it;[1] and even when "imperialism" is occasionally used, it is usually taken to merely describe the tendency on the part of the leading capitalist power, the United States, either singly or with the support of other capitalist powers, to exercise political-military hegemony over countries of the third world, without reference to any economic compulsion for doing so. In fact, many well-known Marxist writers today explicitly reject the term "imperialism" insofar as it is taken to mean any systemic tendency for metropolitan capital to dominate the *outlying regions in particular.*

I

Reluctance to Use the Term "Imperialism"

This reluctance to use the term "imperialism" is not surprising. Central to the concept as it was used earlier was a division of the world into two segments, with both workers and capitalists in one of them being better placed than their counterparts in the other. It made sense in that situation to talk of a systemic tendency that could be seen as underlying imperialism. But in today's context, two basic changes have been brought about by globalization. On the one hand, the domestic big bourgeoisie in several third world countries like India not only is closely integrated with international finance capital but has actually prospered and flourished as well: the list of the top billionaires in the world today not only contains, as it used to in the old days, the names of persons belonging to the advanced capitalist countries, but a fair number of Chinese and Indian names as well.

On the other hand, capital is free to move across countries and locate plants in the third world for producing goods not just for the local market but for exports to the entire world market. Since this freedom does not exist merely on paper but is actually exercised by metropolitan capital that is locating plants in China and elsewhere for servicing the world market, the implication is that workers in the metropolitan countries are now competing against low-wage workers of the third world. They are no longer insulated from the low wages prevailing in the third world.

The segmentation of the world economy such that workers in one part of it could raise their wages more or less in tandem with the increase in their labour productivity, while workers in the other part were stuck at a subsistence level (admittedly not a biological subsistence) because of massive labour reserves, breaks down in the era of globalization. Workers in the advanced capitalist countries are now exposed to the baneful effects of the third world's labour reserves on their real wages, as Joseph Stiglitz's finding that the real wage rates of American workers have not increased at all over the last several decades proves.[2] What this means is that the growing divergence in real wage rates over time between the two segments of the world economy has been halted, if not even slightly reversed.[3]

Thus, while the third world big bourgeoisie is coming up rapidly and making common cause with the capitalists of advanced countries, to a point where even the distinction between the two bourgeoisies is getting obliterated, there is also a certain parallel tendency, if not towards an actual obliteration of the wage differences between the workers in the advanced and third world countries, then at least towards a freezing of these differences. The advanced country workers have wages whose ratio to third world wages does not increase no matter how high the rate of growth of their labour productivity.

It follows then that in lieu of the original dichotomy between an advanced capitalist world and a backward capitalist world, which typically underlay the concept of imperialism, we might be seeing the division between the capitalists on the one hand and the workers on the other as an emerging phenomenon, both within countries and also globally. The spatial dichotomy between two parts of the world, or the segmentation of the world economy into two unequal parts, one of which maintains control over the other, as the term "imperialism" implied, appears to be passé.

There is a further point, quite apart from the break-up of the former segmentation of the world economy as a consequence of globalization, which lends support to this view: it has to do with the emergence of *international* finance capital as the new lead actor on the global scene. When Lenin (1977) was writing about imperialism, his perception was of a set of rival imperialist powers, each characterized by a financial oligarchy that presided over a coalition of banks and industrial capital, was closely integrated with that country's state personnel, and was engaged in partitioning and repartitioning the world in the quest for "economic territory."

The three main features of the scenario sketched by Lenin were: first, the *national* character of finance capital; second, a close link within each nation among industry, banks, and the state, which entailed that the quest for "economic territory" (as the strategy of this *national* finance capital that was put into effect by the State and ideologically sustained by a glorification of the "national idea" [as Hilferding noted[4]], also promoted industrial interests and could be presented as a "national strategy"; and, third, the pervasiveness of rivalry among these *national* finance capitals, of an "inter-imperialist rivalry" for repartitioning a world whose partitioning had already been completed.

These features have been largely superseded by the emergence, through further centralization of capital, of *international* finance capital that is globalized, is not tied to any particular nation-state (though it is defended in its global operations by the leading capitalist state with support from the others), is much more financial in nature, and is engaged in massive speculation for capital gains, rather than being concerned with the promotion of industry. (The term "financialization" that is often used in lieu of and as distinct from "industrialization" captures this last point.) It is in the interests of international finance capital, which moves all over the world in quest of speculative gains, *that the world should not be partitioned*, that no barriers should exist in the way of the free movement of capital, including in the form of finance, and of commodities. International finance capital therefore specifically wants a muting of inter-imperialist rivalry, a removal of all barriers in the form of boundaries between "economic territories" of rival finance capitals, which had been a feature of the scenario sketched by Lenin. This, as we know, does not mean an end of wars, or the ushering in of an era of peace, but only the end of wars *caused by inter-imperialist rivalry*.

Two implications of this process of globalization of capital are important in this context. First, while capital is globalized, the states still remain nation-states, which suggests that state policy must, willy-nilly, cater to the caprices of globalized finance. The political and military might of the most powerful capitalist state is proximately used for defending the interests and operations of globalized finance capital, but all states fall in line in concurring with the defence of these interests (with the exception of some "recalcitrant" state, which may be trying to opt out of the globalization arrangement and hence *ipso facto* curbing the free movement of globalized finance, and against which the might of the most powerful state would typically be directed). Second, globalized finance capital does not belong exclusively to any one country; rather, it draws the capital of all countries into the process of globalization. The corporate-financial oligarchies in all countries get integrated into the process of globalization.

In this scenario there is a certain apparent uniformity in the experience of all economies. There is no one economy, no one power aggrandizing itself at the expense of some other countries. Instead, freely mobile globalized finance capital apparently metes out even-handed treatment to all countries. To be sure, not all become equal gainers or losers because of such treatment, but these disparities are determined by a host of factors having nothing to do with the domination of one country by another. And if one argues, with some justification, that being caught in the vortex of free cross-border flows of capital and commodities is *per se* inimical to the interests of the people of the third world, then two kinds of objections would be raised against that argument: first, that the experience of China, India, and several East and Southeast Asian countries proves that there is nothing in the nature of the international economy, as opposed to factors internal to third world countries which they should try to overcome on their own, that hurts the people through such free flows; and second, that there is no coercion being exercised against the wishes of third world governments to make them embrace globalization, so that the blame for the deleterious consequences, if any, of such globalization on the people's living standards should not be laid at the door of something called "imperialism."

Taking all this into account then—quite apart from the fact that the divergences between the advanced and backward countries' bourgeoisies and between the advanced and backward countries' workers no longer operate the way they used to—a spatial perspective on the world economy, such as what imperialism suggests, is far removed from what we have today: namely, a foregrounding of globalized finance capital. It is not "North versus South" or "advanced versus backward countries" or as Lenin (1977, 637) had put it, the "financial strangulation" of the overwhelming majority of the world's people by a handful of advanced countries; it is globalized finance capital, of which the finance capitals of individual countries are component parts and which does not belong to any particular country, operating all over the globe. Even if it immiserates the people, it does so, and can do so, everywhere; it cannot be called "imperialism." Capitalism has the effect of exploiting, oppressing, and immiserating the people; and contemporary capitalism, which is no exception to this, does this in its own way. But calling it "imperialism" is misleading. Doing so gives an impression that what had prevailed earlier continues to prevail today. It analytically obliterates the *sui generis* character of contemporary capitalism and should therefore be shunned.

II

The Object of the Present Book

The purpose of the present book is to argue a position contrary to the one outlined above: namely, that there is an abiding relevance to the concept of "imperialism." It seeks to establish that there is a continuity between the colonial period and now, notwithstanding the fact that countries of the third world now are no longer ruled by foreign powers. This continuity arises from a certain structural relationship that characterizes capitalism but that, surprisingly, has received very little attention until now. Put differently, in addition to the capital-wage labour relationship, capitalism is characterized by an additional structural relationship, and "imperialism" refers to that structural relationship. That relationship necessarily has a spatial dimension and was as much a feature of the colonial period as it is of contemporary capitalism: its essence lies in the fact that capitalism, within which of course metropolitan capitalism has the predominant position, must, in its "spontaneous" operation, act in ways that tend to *immiserate* the traditional petty producers of the third world, who constitute the overwhelming bulk of the working population of these countries.

The fact that big capital *of the third world itself* is complicit in this process of undermining and squeezing the traditional petty producers, viz., the peasants, craftsmen, fishermen, artisans, and so on—is not germane to the argument, just as the fact that metropolitan capitalism also squeezes its own residual petty producers, not to mention the workers directly employed by it, is not germane to the argument. What is important is the fact of this compression of income and livelihoods exercised by metropolitan capitalism upon the traditional petty producers of the third world, especially of the tropics. This occurs for a very specific reason *and must be distinguished from the general tendency of capitalism to destroy the basis of petty production everywhere.*

Not to recognize the *sui generis* nature of this compression, and hence of the structural relationship of which it is an expression, is to miss out on a very crucial aspect of capitalism, which alas has largely been the case until now. We use the term "imperialism" to cover this structural relationship, and not to recognize imperialism in this sense amounts to missing out on an understanding both of colonialism and of contemporary capitalism. The need for metropolitan capitalism to impose income deflation upon the petty producers of the tropics will be discussed at a theoretical level in the next several chapters, after which we shall present empirical data to substantiate our argument.

CHAPTER TWO

The Threat of Increasing Supply Price

I

The Reason for Increasing Supply Price

Capitalism at the core cannot do without access to a number of primary commodities that have the following two characteristics. The first is that they are produced in distant outlying regions and typically by petty producers who, though linked to capitalism and therefore no longer retaining their original character, are nonetheless outside of the capital-wage labour relationship. Some of these commodities, even when produced within the metropolitan core, are nonetheless also imported to the metropolitan core from the outlying regions, so that an increase in the demand for them at the margin requires larger supplies from these outlying regions. But other such commodities simply do not get produced at all within the core and are not even producible within it because of their specific climatic and other natural requirements.

The second characteristic is that these commodities are subject to the phenomenon of increasing supply price, which means that if an increase in the demand for them were to be satisfied by greater production, then even at the existing level of money wage rate *per efficiency unit of labour* at the point of production, or money income of the producers per unit of their labour (measured in efficiency units), their unit prime cost of production would increase.

The notion of the "efficiency unit of labour" may be explained as follows. *If a given output, whatever it is, is maintained over time*, then it is quite possible that either through "learning by doing" or through the use of new technology, labour productivity would increase in the production of this output, which is the same as saying that one labourer would become over time the equivalent of more than one. A doubling of labour productivity for instance means that as a consequence of such doubling, one labourer becomes the equivalent of two—i.e., one "natural unit" of labour becomes two "efficiency units" of labour. To say "at given money wage rate per efficiency unit of labour" amounts therefore to saying: "if the money wage rate per labourer (as a person) increases in tandem with the rise in his or her labour productivity." Obviously, if money wages per person increase in tandem with the rise in the person's labour productivity, then the unit *labour* cost in money terms remains unchanged at any given level of output, so long as the unit labour input (in efficiency units) remains unchanged. And if in addition the non-labour current inputs per unit output also remain unchanged, then there is no reason why the unit *prime* cost of production, and hence the unit supply price, should change over time. There is, in short, a certain supply price associated with that level of output. If the output increases in any period, and if the current input coefficients, including the labour input, which would have prevailed had the smaller output been produced, could be replicated, then there is no reason why the supply price should increase. Put differently (since the other current inputs do not matter so much for our general argument), if the *level of labour productivity per efficiency unit of labour remains unchanged in any period in the event of an output expansion*, then the supply price should remain unchanged for any given money wage rate per efficiency unit of labour. Hence increasing supply price, in the sense of a rise in the unit prime cost (or unit variable cost) of production with an increase in output, arises when this increase lowers the *level of labour productivity per efficiency unit of labour*, i.e., raises the labour input (in efficiency units) per unit of output.

Increasing supply price occurs therefore not because one natural unit of labour becomes *less* in efficiency units (which amounts to technological retrogression). It occurs because of a *decline* in labour productivity per efficiency unit of labour, which means that as more is produced, more labour *in efficiency units* is needed per unit of output. With the money wage rate per efficiency unit of labour assumed to be given, this raises the unit labour cost and hence the unit prime cost, i.e., the supply price.[1] And the only way such an increase can happen is because of transition to inferior quality of land, or because of the greater depth to which the extraction of mineral resources has to be carried, and so on.

The fact that commodities with these two characteristics are required regularly by capitalism is obvious. Mineral resources, in the absence of the discovery of new and more easily exploitable sources, are a clear example of such a commodity. They may not be produced by petty producers, but they are produced in distant outlying regions, and without supplies from these regions, the growing demand for them cannot be met. (Less than one-eighth of remaining known global oil and natural gas reserves lies within the territories of the advanced economies.) The other clear example consists of the products of the tropical landmass. Such products are produced typically by petty producers in outlying regions that are at some distance from the metropolitan core. In fact, most such products are either not producible at all within the core itself for climatic reasons, or are not producible except in a limited season; they can either only be produced on tropical lands or be accessed from these lands to avoid seasonal dearth of supply. And in their case, since uncultivated tropical land scarcely exists any longer, in the absence of "land-augmenting" technological change (on which more later), we do not have just increasing supply price, but actually an almost vertical supply curve, i.e., a steeply increasing supply price.

While the argument of this book will also hold with suitable modification for the case of mineral resources, we shall be concerned in what follows primarily with products of the tropical landmass.

II

The Fallacy of "Mainstream" Trade Theory

The fact that a large range of products of the tropical landmass, *which are not producible at all in cold temperate regions where the metropolitan core of the capitalist world is located*, are essential nonetheless for this metropolitan core has been systematically ignored in economics and continues to be ignored to this day. *In fact, all arguments about the benefits of free trade are fundamentally based on ignoring and glossing over of this material reality.* Since the idea that free trade benefits all trading parties is the core idea of "mainstream" economics, which informs contemporary policy measures like the setting up of the World Trade Organization and was being emphasized during the recent Doha round of negotiations,[2] it follows that such glossing over is central to "mainstream" economics.

This ignoring of material reality, this glossing over of facts, began with none other than David Ricardo himself, whose theory of comparative cost advantage argued that even if the absolute cost of production of commodities was lower in some countries compared to others, all countries would benefit from specializing in producing those commodities in which they enjoy a relative or "comparative cost advantage."[3] Free trade, which makes countries produce in accordance with their comparative cost advantage, is potentially beneficial for all, because with such specialization and exchange through trade, the total world output, taking all countries together, is vector-wise larger than in a pretrade or a nontrade situation.[4] This argument presupposes that all countries can produce all commodities, and in fact do so in the pretrade scenario, so that relative costs can be defined. Only then does trade bring about a situation in which countries benefit when they specialize in particular commodities and exchange, instead of producing everything themselves.

The material fallacy in Ricardo's argument, which renders it an incorrect one, arises from the fact that all countries could not produce all goods: precisely that premise is not true, which is required to reach the conclusion of benefit for all through trade. Ricardo, in short, was ignoring the fact that the cold temperate regions could never produce a large range of crops, which tropical or subtropical countries could, whereas the latter countries (especially the large ones with varying topography) could produce through year-round cropping not only those crops that cold temperate regions could never produce, but also, during their winter months, even the same crops that temperate regions did in summer.[5] With permanently zero output of tropical products in temperate lands, there was no "cost of production" that could be defined there at all for these products, let alone any relative cost (U. Patnaik 2005). Thus, no basis existed for comparing cost advantage.

Even within the temperate region itself production capacities differed between the warm temperate and cold temperate regions. There were two distinct problems with Ricardo's specific example in which he took Britain and Portugal as the two countries and woolen cloth and grape wine as the two commodities to reach the conclusion that even though labour used per unit of output was lower in both goods for Portugal, since relative costs differed, Britain should specialize in producing cloth and Portugal should specialize in producing wine, and thereby both countries would benefit through exchange. First, the premise of the argument was that both countries could produce both goods (otherwise relative cost cannot be defined), but this premise was not satisfied by his own example since cold temperate Britain could not produce grape wine on a commercial basis; this was particularly so when Ricardo wrote, since genetic modification of plants was unknown. Second and much more importantly, even if Ricardo had chosen an example to fit his premise, the argument would not be true because his premise itself was wrong.

While warm temperate Portugal could produce both grape wine and cloth, cold temperate Britain could produce only cloth; and in such a case *specialization does not bring about a vector-wise increase in the output of the two commodities, taking both countries together, so trade is not mutually beneficial.* Since Britain would have already been specializing in cloth production before trade (as it could produce no grape wine) and since Portugal would be producing some cloth before trade, the post-trade specialization by Portugal in wine production would mean an overall reduction in world cloth output and an overall increase in world wine output, but no vector-wise increase in the output of *both* commodities. Ricardo's proposition falls to the ground if both countries do not produce both goods before trade.

Specialisation and trade certainly did take place, but not for the happy Ricardian reason of perceived mutual benefit. Mercantilist policies, the use of a combination of naval force and diplomatic pressure by Britain on Portugal, led to the Methuen Treaty in 1703, a century before Ricardo wrote, which gave nonagricultural market access for English woolen cloth in exchange for the wine it could not itself produce. Portugal shifted a large part of the adverse effect of importing cloth, which displaced its own manufacture, by re-exporting cloth to Brazil, but the historical records show that it did suffer decline in its own grain output as the area under vineyards grew (Boxer 1973). To this day, obtaining nonagricultural market access in the developing world is the mantra for advanced countries, which have written the rules for the WTO. And as we shall see later, the pressure to export primary products the advanced countries cannot produce has led to the same outcome of declining grain production per head in developing countries.

Ricardo's specific example, which did not fit his own premise, was altered without any discussion of why he did so, by Paul Samuelson (1970). Samuelson replaced "wine" with "food" in both text and diagram in his paper on "Market Mechanisms and Maximisation," and this is the form in which modern text books present the theory. But this clandestine alteration to make the example fit the premise obviously cannot address the basic problem that the premise itself—that both countries can produce both goods (and by extension, all countries can produce all goods)—is not true. The type of material fallacy in Ricardo's argument is what logicians call "the converse fallacy of accident"[6] in which, a *specific* and restrictive premise is stated, but the conclusion arrived at on its basis (mutual benefit from specialisation) is improperly treated as a *general* one—namely, the conclusion is asserted to hold in all cases including those in which the premise is not true. But the conclusion of mutual benefit cannot hold when the premise is not true. Numerical examples can be easily worked out to demonstrate this (see U. Patnaik 2005).

"Mainstream" trade theory after Ricardo has followed the same fallacious track. The case for free trade is made nowadays on the basis of the argument that the "utility possibility curve" after trade in each country lies outside (though it may touch at some point) the "utility possibility curve" before trade. For the "utility possibility curves" to have this relationship, the bundle of goods available to each country must be vector-wise larger with trade than without; and for this to happen to both countries, the total bundle of goods available after trade, to both countries taken together, must be vector-wise larger than before trade.[7] *But this is impossible unless both countries were producing both goods before trade.* Otherwise if, before trade, country A produces only commodity x (because it cannot produce y), while country B produces both x and y, then any change in the production pattern as a result of trade must bring about a lowering in the output of x (assuming of course, as "mainstream" trade theory does, that there is full utilization of resources in both countries in both the pretrade and post-trade situations). The basic premise for demonstrating the mutual benefit of trade collapses.

"Mainstream" trade theory to this day has therefore assumed that the temperate countries can also produce tropical products, which is an incorrect statement of fact and renders the theory itself incorrect. But clearly it is an expedient assumption since it leads to the inference of mutual benefit. It has allowed mainstream theory to ignore the real reasons for North–South trade in tropical commodities, as well as the actual methods of extra-economic coercion used for securing the trade. It has also allowed mainstream theory to ignore the economic implications of the limited size of the tropical landmass—implications we discuss later, both as regards adverse effects on the food security of local populations as primary exports grow, and as regards the methods of deflating their incomes both historically and at present to ensure that the supply price of these products does not rise.

Since the tropical landmass is more or less fully used up, and since its products are required in the metropolitan core located in the temperate world, capital accumulation that enlarges the demand for such products must lead to a rise in the price of such products. Such a rise in the price of these products will not elicit larger outputs of these products from the tropical lands (on this more later). But additionally, such a rise has serious implications for the stability of the metropolitan economy.

III

The Threat to the Value of Money in the Metropolis

Even if the output of the products produced by the tropical landmass does not increase because of the fixity of this landmass, which is fully used up, the supplies to the metropolis of these products can still increase as a consequence of the rise in their prices; but this can happen only if the money wages of the workers or the money incomes of the petty producers, including the peasants, who are engaged in producing this output, do not increase in tandem with the rise in prices. For, in such a case there would be what Keynes (1930) called a "profit inflation," giving rise to a forced reduction in the consumption of the fixed money income-earners. This forced reduction in their consumption is often called "forced savings," but this is misleading in an important sense, since the credit for such "savings" does not accrue to those whose consumption is squeezed. What they do not consume accrues to profit-earners who market these commodities and who therefore get the credit for the "savings," even though they are not the ones whose consumption has been curtailed; they in turn make these products available to the metropolis. If the rise in prices also affects the buyers whose money incomes do not rise in tandem in the metropolis itself, then they too are forced to consume less. In such a case, even as the supplies of these commodities increase from the tropical lands through a curtailment in their local consumption, the demand for these commodities simultaneously falls in the temperate regions. The rise in prices works at both ends.

But such a rise in prices runs the risk, at least in the metropolis, of generating demands for money wage increases, in which case the inflation would become more acute and the squeeze on the tropical fixed money income-earners (workers, petty producers, and poor peasants, who constitute a semi-proletariat) even more severe.

But no matter whether the inflation is more or less acute, every increase in demand for such commodities would give rise to a fresh round of price increases, which would come to an end only when the balance between demand and supply has been restored (or excess demand has fallen to zero). And this would happen in every period as capital accumulation in the core proceeded. Such a situation, however, would undermine the value of money in the metropolis and with very serious consequences. Let us see why.

Money constitutes not only a medium of circulation, *but also a form in which wealth is held*. Indeed, even in playing its medium of circulation role, money simultaneously plays the role of being a form of wealth-holding, since in the C- M- C circuit itself (where money is only a medium of circulation), there is a period of interregnum when the wealth, obtained from the sale of commodities, is held in the form of money, before being converted to commodities again.

This is a point that monetarism in all its forms, whether the old monetarism of Ricardo or the monetarism of Walras or the monetarism of Milton Friedman and his successors, does not understand. Underlying monetarism is the implicit assumption that money is a mere medium of circulation but not a form of wealth-holding, for if wealth was held in the form of money, then, as Keynes demonstrated, Say's Law that "supply creates its own demand" would break down and the problem of deficiency of aggregate demand, which undermines monetarism, would arise. But money cannot constitute a medium of circulation (which monetarism assumes) without simultaneously being a form of wealth-holding (which monetarism implicitly denies); and if money is assumed to be a form of wealth-holding, then monetarism becomes invalid. (All attempts to build a monetarist argument even while giving money the role of a wealth-form, such as by invoking the "Pigou Effect" or the "Real Balance Effect," can be shown to be logically inconsistent.[8])

But the role of money as a form of wealth-holding, which in real life it is, gets threatened if its value is expected to fall vis-à-vis commodities, i.e., if wealth-holders expect inflation to occur in commodity prices. In such a case they would be tempted to shift from holding money to holding commodities. The first question that arises in this context therefore is: What does their expected rate of inflation depend upon? And the immediate answer that would strike one would be: the current rate of inflation.

This, however, is not necessarily true. Even when the current rate of inflation is positive, if the money wage rate remains fixed and the output can expand without any increase in current input coefficients, then wealth-holders will expect prices, no matter how high they may currently be, to come down in the future to some "normal" level, or at the very least to stabilize at their current level. The expected inflation rate in such a case would be negative or zero, no matter how high and positive the current inflation rate. *The expected inflation rate in this case would certainly not be positively related to the current rate of inflation.*

But if the money wage rate moves up (with a lag) when prices move up, then even if output can expand at given input coefficients, the expected inflation rate will become a positive function of the current inflation rate. And, likewise, if output cannot expand at all (or can do so only with a rise in input coefficients, though this is a case we consider only later), then too the expected inflation rate becomes a positive function of the current inflation rate. This is because, even with a given money wage rate (per efficiency unit of labour), the price in such a case depends not on the unit prime cost any longer but upon demand. There is nothing to "tether" price to any particular level, and if demand is high enough to cause a positive rate of current inflation, then everyone would expect it to be higher still in the future to cause a positive rate of inflation between the current period and the next. In other words,

$$\{(p_{t+1}-p_t)/p_t\}^e = f\{(p_t-p_{t-1})/p_{t-1}\}, \text{ with } f' > 0;$$
$$\text{and } f(0)=0 \ldots \ldots \ldots \ldots (A)$$

But then a second question arises: Does any current inflation rate, which in the case of vertically increasing supply price also influences the expected rate of inflation for reasons just discussed, dislodge money from its role as a form of wealth-holding? The immediate answer is likely to be "no" for the following reason. Since commodities have a "carrying cost," which includes the cost of storage and the cost of decay or damage during the period of storage, while money has zero carrying cost, commodities can never possibly become a substitute for money as a form of wealth, unless the rate of inflation expected to obtain *exceeds* the carrying cost. More precisely, if we ignore risks, and denote the carrying cost of a commodity (in terms of itself) by c per unit, then the commodity would be held in lieu of money only if its expected rate of price inflation exceeds c—i.e., $\{(p_{t+1}-p_t)/p_t\}^e > c$.

If, for instance, a commodity costs $100 and its price is expected to rise to $110 by the end of the time horizon, then it would be worth holding the commodity in lieu of money only if its carrying cost in terms of itself is less than 10 percent. If, say, decaying is assumed to be the only form of carrying cost, then a commodity with an expected appreciation of 10 percent in its money price would be held in lieu of money only if less than 10 percent of it decays over the period. But since commodities usually have large carrying costs, it is not *any* rate of expected inflation but only *a high enough* rate of expected inflation that would induce a shift from money to commodities. And since, in the case of increasing supply price, the expected rate of inflation is linked, as we have seen, to the current rate of inflation, it is only a sufficiently high rate of *current* inflation that would induce a shift from money to commodities. In other words, it would be argued that *inflation per se does not constitute a threat to the role of money as a wealth-form; it constitutes a threat only when it exceeds a certain "threshold" rate.*

This argument, however, is invalid, because it takes all wealth-holders and all commodities as being identical, which is not the case. Different wealth-holders have different expectations about inflation, even when they all experience the same current inflation rate, i.e., they have different f-functions. If, whatever the current inflation rate, *some wealth-holders* expect the inflation rate in future to exceed the carrying cost, then they would shift from money to commodities. Since there is no offsetting symmetrical movement from commodities to money by anybody else, as nobody was holding commodities as a wealth-form to start with, this would cause an excess demand for commodities, raising their prices further and hence the current rate of inflation further. This in turn will increase the expected inflation rate for *all*, since f' > o for all, despite the f-function being different for each, which will persuade some more wealth-holders to move from money to commodities, and so on. With the very onset of inflation, in other words, *even when its rate is less than c*, there will be no equilibrium with money being a form in which wealth is held.

Exactly the same result arises, and even more powerfully (which is why we shall concentrate upon it here), when we take into account the fact that all commodities are not identical and have different carrying costs. In particular, there is one commodity, gold, which has a very low carrying cost but about which people are generally confident that its value in the long run will never fall vis-à-vis commodities in general. In a period of inflation therefore there would be a shift, *if not from money to commodities in general, then at least from money to gold as a hedge against inflation.* If money consists of currency with gold backing and bank deposits, then in a period of inflation, wealth-holders would shift from money to gold, which would make it impossible to sustain the gold backing for the currency. Even if money does not have gold backing, the flight from money to gold will destabilize the value of money.

This is precisely how the Bretton Woods system broke down. Under that system the U.S. dollar was a reserve currency convertible into gold at the rate of $35 per ounce of gold. By taking advantage of this role of the dollar, the United States ran large current account deficits for maintaining its string of military bases all around the world. (This role also enabled American companies to buy up European firms with dollars printed in the United States but sanctified by the system to be "as good as gold.") As the Vietnam War escalated, the U.S. current account deficit widened, and a torrent of dollars poured out of the United States, even as excess demand pressures appeared in the world economy and increased the rate of inflation to levels that could no longer be ignored (Kaldor 1976). There was therefore a rush to gold, in which President De Gaulle of France took the lead, the gold-dollar link could no longer be sustained, and the Bretton Woods system collapsed.

Of course in the uncertainty that followed this collapse there was an actual rush to hold commodities, which pushed up commodity prices for a while until the recession in the world economy brought down these prices, but with one notable exception, namely, the price of oil, which the OPEC cartel even jacked up to create the first "oil shock." But the collapse of the Bretton Woods system, which has been usually put down to President De Gaulle's "bloody-mindedness," was in reality a result of the fact that money with gold backing cannot function as money in the face of inflation. This is exactly what we are arguing.

On the other hand, if money has no gold backing whatsoever, then that does not help matters either. If gold price is expected to increase in terms of money because of inflation, then since gold too has very little carrying cost, gold would still become a favoured form of wealth-holding. And there is no "equilibrium" value of gold in terms of money at which the wealth-holders would be prepared to hold both. In other words the preference for gold would persist no matter what its value, which would in effect render money worthless compared to gold.

It may be thought that if over any one period commodity prices are expected to rise by say 10 percent and if gold prices are supposed to move in tandem with commodity prices, then all that this would do is push up the spot price of gold by 10 percent, and once that has happened there would be no further reason for the spot price of gold to rise, since the expected rise in its price *from that position* would simply become zero, the same as with money in terms of itself. In other words, the relationship captured in equation (A) above for commodities in general need not hold for a single commodity, gold, so that our claim that there is no finite upper limit to the price of gold, if its price is expected to increase at all in terms of money, is invalid.

But this is not the case. While this counter-argument against our claim could be valid if the rise in commodity prices was episodic, it does not hold if commodity prices are expected to rise in the next period, *and in the period after that, and in the period after that, ad infinitum*, because of the phenomenon of vertically increasing supply price, and the same expectation holds for gold prices as well.

There is no reason in this case why, even after spot price of gold has increased by 10 percent, wealth-holders should still not go on wanting to buy gold. Suppose for instance that commodity and gold prices are expected to rise by 10 percent over a period T. If inflation is not episodic but persistent, then over a period of 2T, the expected increase in commodity, and gold, prices would be 20 percent, in which case, since gold, like money, has negligible carrying cost (so that holding it for 2T periods costs no more than holding it for a period of T), its spot price should increase by 20 percent, and not 10 percent. It follows therefore that with persistent expected inflation, there is no equilibrium spot price of gold at which wealth-holders would be indifferent between holding money and holding gold, which means that gold would displace money from its role as a medium of wealth-holding, and hence as a medium of circulation.

Put differently, if inflation is expected to occur in every "period" in the future, then the notion of "period" itself loses any boundedness. With inflation, commodity prices *over a long enough time horizon* cease to have any specific upper limit, and the same holds for gold as well. Hence, with zero carrying cost of gold, even spot gold price would cease to have any upper limit.

It follows then that if inflation occurs in commodity prices and is expected to continue, then the value of money in the metropolis gets destabilized.[9] This destabilization would happen more rapidly if the money wage rate in the metropolis is either linked to a cost of living index or rises almost immediately at any given level of economic activity (or unemployment rate), because of trade union bargaining in response to a rise in the cost of living index. For in such a case wealth-holders would be even more anxious to shift to gold without any further delay. But even if it does not rise immediately, so that real wages in the metropolis do get eroded, even then after some time when there has been considerable erosion, the workers would demand to be compensated for this erosion, and this would add to inflation and compound the destabilization of the value money.

But let us take the following extreme case. Suppose these tropical commodities do not enter as current inputs into the products of the metropolis but are required only as wage-goods. And suppose the money wage rate in the metropolis does not rise at all, i.e., there is a long run secular decline in real wages (with labour productivity assumed, for the sake of simplicity, to be given). In such a case even if there is a rise in the prices of tropical products over time owing to the increase in their supply price, there is no rise in the prices of metropolitan goods. Would there still be any threat to the value of money in the metropolis?

The simple answer to this question (which is examined in a later chapter) is "yes." Even if within the metropolis there is no tendency for wealth-holders to shift from money either to the tropical commodities whose price is expected to rise owing to increasing supply price or to gold as a surrogate for such commodities—i.e., even if there is no immediate change in the asset-preference within the metropolis—*there would certainly be such a change within the tropical region itself.*

Faced with a rise in the price of local products, wealth-holders in the tropical region would like to hedge against inflation by moving to gold. They would, it may be argued, move to the metropolitan *currency* from their own currency, since the price of the metropolitan currency vis-à-vis gold should have no reason to change (except possibly through their own action). But in either case, there will be no equilibrium with a positive value of the currency of the tropical region vis-à-vis gold or the metropolitan currency, which itself would be an untenable situation. A system in which the product of the periphery has the form of a commodity with a positive exchange value becomes impossible if the value of the currency of the periphery falls to zero.

Besides, if wealth-holders in the tropical region associate some risk with holding metropolitan currency (whose price vis-à-vis gold could conceivably change), but none with holding gold, and if they therefore shift from the tropical currency to gold as their first preference, when faced with a persistent rise in the prices of tropical goods, then there would be a further problem. At the base relative prices of the three assets—viz., gold, tropical currency, and metropolitan currency—there would be an excess demand for gold, which would raise the gold price in terms not only of the tropical currency but also of the metropolitan currency. This would also make metropolitan wealth-holders shift from money (of the metropolis) to gold and thereby destabilize the value of money there. Hence, the point is not whether there is inflation in the prices of products of the metropolis; the point is the shift away from money as a form of wealth. And this would happen even when there is no actual inflation in the prices of goods produced by the metropolis itself.

If we postulate that there is no long-run secular decline in the real wage rate relative to labour productivity in the metropolis, our argument of course is strengthened; but even if there is such a secular decline, this fact *per se* does not invalidate the argument that increasing supply price of commodities undermines the role of money as a form of wealth-holding. In other words, how rapidly the workers in the metropolis are compensated for the rise in commodity prices is not germane to the *validity* of this argument.

It follows from this that the argument about the weight of tropical products in the wage-basket of the metropolitan workers or (if we are talking of raw materials) in the gross value of output in the metropolis being too small to matter is really beside the point. That argument is concerned with how much inflation a rise in the price of tropical products may cause within the metropolis; but the real issue relates to asset preference, taking wealth-holders *both in the metropolis and in the periphery*.

Our argument against the objection to a theory of imperialism on account of the small weight of third world products in the gross value of metropolitan output is different from that of Harry Magdoff (1969). He had rightly emphasized that these products, no matter how small their share in the gross value of output of the metropolis, were *material inputs without which metropolitan production simply could not occur at all*. The weight of, say, raw materials in the value of manufactured output may be small, but there can be no manufacturing at all without raw materials. While accepting this point, our argument brings in an additional point—namely, the question of the value of money in the metropolis.

Of course if it was only an episode of inflation, then it might not be of much consequence, no matter where it occurred. But any persistent inflation, such as would occur in the case of increasing supply price, must necessarily affect the choice of wealth-form; and because of this fact, no matter where such inflation occurred, it would undermine the value of money *both in the metropolis and in the periphery*.

IV

An Alternative Statement of the Argument

We have so far been assuming that the increase in supply price of tropical commodities takes the shape of a vertical curve. Let us continue with that assumption, which means that the magnitude of output of the tropical product is given in absolute terms. As the *ex ante* demand for it increases on account of capital accumulation, there has to be forced reduction of consumption on the part of some groups: i.e., the peasants themselves, or other petty producers and workers in the tropical region who are buyers of these commodities, or even the workers in the metropolitan core.

This forced reduction can occur in two different ways, through a change in prices at given money incomes, which is what we have considered until now, or through a squeeze on money incomes with no change in prices. Or, expressing this idea more elaborately, we can say that the reduction in absorption can occur either through a rise in price relative to the money wage rate per efficiency unit of labour in the periphery or in the metropolis or in both; or it can occur through a decline in the money wage rate (or money income of petty producers) per efficiency unit of labour in the periphery or in the metropolis or in both. The threat to the value of money in the metropolis arises, we argued earlier, when there is a rise in the nominal price that keeps occurring in every successive period, no matter where it occurs—i.e., when there is a rise in the nominal price of the commodities in the metropolis or in the periphery or in both. The threat in short arises when the first route is followed.

What the threat-to-the-value-of-money argument states is that *if the forced reduction in consumption that occurs within the tropical region through a squeeze on money incomes and the forced reduction in consumption in the metropolis that occurs through a decline in the money wage rate per efficiency unit of labour in the metropolis, are together insufficient in successive periods to eliminate excess demand for the tropical commodity whose output cannot be augmented because of the fixity of the tropical landmass, then the stability of the value of money in the metropolis gets undermined*. It follows therefore that metropolitan capitalism must necessarily make every possible effort to ensure that these other ways of reducing consumption of the tropical product, which obviate the necessity for an increase in the nominal price of the commodity in the metropolis and also in the periphery, are adopted to a sufficient extent to eliminate the excess demand for the commodity.

V

The Specificity of "Increasing Supply Price"–Based Inflation

The foregoing argument may appear odd because, after all, increase in the absolute nominal price of tropical commodities has been occurring in the metropolis for a long time now. Nobody can possibly claim that the absolute prices of tropical goods in the metropolis today are what they were at the time of the Napoleonic Wars. So, why has there been no threat to the value of money in the metropolis in the sense discussed above, namely, a collapse in this value relative to gold, which undermines the entire monetary system?

The answer to this question lies in the specificity of increasing supply price–based inflation, which is what we have been discussing until now. Increasing supply price–based inflation entails that in every successive period the price keeps increasing (assuming that the other ways of forced reduction of consumption are insufficient to prevent this). And it is this, as we saw earlier, which makes the shift to gold from money worthwhile for wealth-holders. But suppose we have a sudden cost-push inflation or even an excess demand-caused inflation (as during a war), *which is episodic in nature*. In such a case there is no reason to expect the price to keep increasing over time, and hence no reason to shift from money to commodities or to gold.

It may be thought that since such episodes keep appearing from time to time, expectations of a continuous increase in prices would still be generated, and there would be no difference between this case and the previous case of increasing supply price–based inflation. The two cases however are different. To see this let us first assume that every episode of inflation is one in which gold price moves up in tandem with commodity prices. Even then, however, since there would be no predictability about when the next episode of commodity price inflation will occur, wealth-holders will not move from money to gold (let alone to commodities). Gold, strictly speaking, does entail some slight inconvenience compared to money as a medium of wealth-holding. Our assumption that gold is as good as money and has zero carrying cost is only approximately but not exactly true. In reality gold, though it can easily replace money as a form of wealth, is not a perfect substitute for money, especially as far as convenience of use as a medium of circulation is concerned, in which case inflationary *episodes* will not encourage a shift to gold and cause a destabilization in the value of money, as long as they remain episodes whose time of emergence remains unpredictable. In other words, increasing supply price–based inflation that occurs continuously is certain to raise commodity prices between now and *any* future date, but episodic inflation is completely different: we do not know when the next episode will arise.

In addition, however, gold and commodity prices do not always move in perfect synchrony. Even if gold price in the long run moves in tandem with commodity prices, in the short run there is considerable fluctuation in their relative prices. If in the current period there is an inflationary episode that is expected to come to an end, and if commodity prices are expected to stabilize at a higher absolute level thereafter, at least for a certain period, then there would be little point in shifting from money to commodities or even to gold. True, in some future period, such an episode may again be repeated, but holding gold in lieu of money from now until that period would be pointless, since when that period would come is not known in advance, and it is quite possible that at the beginning of that period the gold price may be lower than at the end of the current period.

Put differently, since the money price of gold can fluctuate in the short run, there is a risk associated with holding gold compared to money, which is why money continues to be held, despite both money and gold having zero (or in the latter case near-zero) carrying costs. But with increasing supply price–based inflation, this risk disappears, since there is an expected steady upward trend in the money prices of gold as well as commodities. We become absolutely certain over any arbitrarily chosen time period that these prices will rise, which is not the case with episodic inflation.

As a matter of fact, the main periods of inflationary increase in prices in the twentieth century have occurred during the two World Wars (and their immediate aftermath), when the inflation, though very pronounced, would have been considered episodic, and hence not warranting a shift from money to commodities or gold, except during the period of the inflationary episode itself; and the freedom of asset choice would have been curbed anyway during those periods by the conditions of war. We shall come back to this issue in a later chapter.

VI

A More General Case

We have so far talked about a vertical supply curve where increasing supply price takes the form of a vertical straight line. Given the fixed supply of the tropical landmass, in the absence of any "land-augmenting" technological change, this indeed would be the shape of the supply curve. (Textbook economics of course defines the supply curve by precluding technological progress, and the supply curve is supposed to shift owing to technological progress. For our purpose here, however, we need not distinguish the shift of the curve and a movement along the curve, as long as the output at which the curve is vertical is unaffected by any technological progress, i.e., as long as technological change is not land augmenting.)

But the argument developed till now is equally applicable if instead of a vertical straight line, we have a supply curve that merely slopes upwards. In such a case an increase in demand will call forth an output increase, but at a supply price that increases with such output increase for any given level of money wage rate per efficientcy unit of labour in the tropical region (again this description also covers the case in which technological progress occurs through historical time). Even in this case, however, the threat to the value of money in the metropolis under the conditions specified earlier remains. These conditions can be restated to cover this case as follows.

If an *ex ante* excess demand for the tropical product arises at the old level of output and price, and if this excess demand is not eliminated through a forced reduction in the consumption in the tropical region itself and in the metropolis through a reduction in the money wage rate per efficiency unit of labour (or money income per labour applied, measured in efficiency units, which actually accrues to producers), then there will have to be an increase in output, a necessary condition for which is an increase in supply price. This increase in supply price would threaten the value of money in the metropolis because, once again, it makes the expected rate of inflation a function of the current rate, even at given money wages.

To sum up, the fixity in the size of the tropical landmass, which, in the absence of land-augmenting technological change, entails that higher output can be produced only with an increase in supply price for a given level of the money wage rate per efficiency unit of labour in the tropical region, constitutes a threat to the value of money in the metropolis. This threat can be warded off if the *ex ante* increase in the demand for tropical products is negated through forced reductions in consumption in both regions, brought about by income adjustments per unit of labour measured in efficiency units. How are such adjustments undertaken? Or, put differently, how is the threat to the value of money in the metropolis warded off? Let us turn to this issue next.

CHAPTER THREE

Coping with the Threat

THERE CAN BE FOUR possible ways of coping with the threat
to the value of money in the metropolis. More specifically, given the
fact that the tropical landmass is fixed in size and fully utilized, there
are four possible ways in which the growing demand for tropical products, arising from capital accumulation in the metropolis (and in the
tropical region itself), can be met, so as not to entail a shift from the
money of the metropolis (and of the periphery) to other forms of
holding wealth, which a continuous rise in prices of such products
would ordinarily cause. Let us discuss these seriatim.

I

Land Augmentation

The first way is through land augmentation. The essence of land augmentation is an increase in output per natural unit of land. This can
occur through multiple cropping, which typically requires irrigation,

and also through an increase in the productivity of *gross sown area*, which requires appropriate water availability, better farm practices, high-yielding varieties of seeds, heavier dosages of fertilizer use, and other such measures. What is striking about these measures is that they typically require state action in the form of investment in public irrigation works; investment in research and development; a public extension service network to make the results of research available to peasants; and assured profits to peasants so that they can embark on the adoption of these new land-augmenting farm practices, through the provision of cheap subsidized inputs and assured procurement of crops at remunerative prices. In addition, they also require land reforms that break the hold of landlordism and the "rent barrier" to which it gives rise (on this more later) and which reduces the incentives *on the part of both the landlords and the tenants* to introduce better farm practices; and of course cooperative and collective forms of agricultural organization, which create opportunities for yield-raising.

The centrality of public irrigation to agricultural growth in the tropics has been long recognized. Even private irrigation, for instance through tube wells, becomes profitable when public irrigation in the form of canals comes to an area. Karl Marx recognized both the importance of irrigation and of the state for providing it in his famous remarks on India: "There have been in Asia, generally, from immemorial times, but three departments of Government: that of Finance, or the plunder of the interior; that of war, or the plunder of the exterior; and finally, the department of Public Works. Climate and territorial conditions . . . constituted artificial irrigation by canals and water works the basis of Oriental agriculture. . . . This prime necessity of an economical and common use of water . . . necessitated, in the Orient, . . . the interference of the centralizing power of Government."[1] These remarks of Marx have given rise to some fanciful theories, such as that of Karl Wittfogel (1957) concerning "oriental despotism."[2] But on the basic issues of the need for irrigation and for the state to take a leading role in providing it, Marx was certainly right.

On the question of research and development and of provision of subsidies and remunerative prices to peasants, the need for state intervention is too obvious to need restating. All these, like irrigation, require expenditure by the state. The epoch of capitalism, however, has meant that in third world societies, including in countries located on the limited tropical landmass, the state is constrained in the matter of expenditure. In the colonial period, when tax revenue was used as a means of siphoning off the surplus from the colonies to the metropolis (to be discussed in a later chapter), and when the dictates of "sound finance" under the gold standard meant that the colonial governments had to balance their budgets, hardly any resources were left for the state to undertake any investment in irrigation, let alone in research and development for improving agricultural practices. In addition the colonial government, in India for instance, insisted on public investment earning a minimum rate of return to justify it, which ruled out any significant investment. It is noteworthy that in the entire history of the British Empire, the "canal colonies" of Punjab were the only significant irrigation investment undertaken; they were never replicated anywhere else.

Since the whole colonial regime needed the support of landlords and local feudal elements, there was no question of carrying out any land reforms to improve the conditions of the peasants or increase their incentives. At the same time, the displacement of traditional craftsmen by the import of manufactured goods from the metropolis, a process referred to by Indian nationalist writers as "deindustrialization," increased the pressure of population on land, which, in turn, raised land rents and lowered rural wages (Chandra 1968). Tenants typically bore all costs of cultivation and provided not only labour but the required livestock and equipment; so rent was an income for landlords obtained gratis by virtue of their property right alone, not as return on any investment. ("Rent" here refers to Adam Smith's and Marx's concept of rent as arising from monopoly of landed property ownership and not to Ricardo's concept, which is not germane to the present discussion.) High rents under these conditions constituted a barrier to yield-raising investment on land. While the tenants had neither the means nor the incentive for undertaking such investments, a substantial part of the returns from which would have "leaked" into the hands of the landlords, the landlords themselves were also hamstrung by this "rent barrier," which can be understood as follows.

Any yield-raising investment on land would typically require the resumption of the land from petty tenants for direct cultivation by hired labour so that the landlords could be sure of actually getting the benefits of such investment. But in such a case, the investment that the landlord now had to make, had to earn not only the going average rate of return on capital (in its alternative uses), *but an additional amount to cover the rent foregone.* The higher the rent per unit area the greater of course was this additional amount that had to be earned, which meant that the high rents that actually prevailed as a consequence of colonial deindustrialization erected a formidable barrier against land-augmenting technological change (U. Patnaik 1976),[3] over and above the factor of state apathy mentioned earlier.

While the colonial period saw little land augmentation, there was a change in this respect after decolonization. The dirigiste regimes that came to power as legatees of the anticolonial struggles were committed in a sense to providing some relief to the peasantry. While they by and large eschewed any radical land redistribution (except in East Asia under American occupation as a means of breaking the power of Japanese landlords, or where Communist regimes came to power), they did carry out land reforms up to a point, usually to facilitate a transition to capitalist farming, which would typically be an admixture of both peasant capitalism and landlord capitalism. Such measures included giving ownership rights to rich tenants who could then take to capitalist agriculture.

Additionally, the dirigiste regimes did undertake several important measures, such as protecting agriculture against world market price fluctuations, providing subsidized credit and other inputs, carrying out some research and development, setting up a wide extension network, investing in irrigation, and providing assured remunerative prices. No doubt the bulk of the benefits of these measures accrued to the emerging capitalist class in the countryside, but some also went to other sections of the peasantry.

At any rate, owing to the sharp rise in yield permitted by "green revolution" technology, the rent barrier was overcome, and land augmentation did occur. As a result, there was a considerable increase in agricultural output under the dirigiste regimes, even in countries with fixed and fully utilized tropical landmasses, compared to the colonial period (U. Patnaik 1986).

However, like the Keynesian demand-management regimes in advanced capitalist countries, the dirigiste regimes represented an unusual interlude. They had come into being in a very specific and extraordinary conjuncture when world capitalism was fighting for its survival against the growing strength of the working-class movements in the metropolis and the growing strength of the anticolonial movement in the periphery, all against the backdrop of the "Communist threat." The concessions made for its survival, through decolonization and through the adoption of Keynesian demand management (which, though it might have taken the form of larger military expenditure in the United States, did entail significant welfare expenditure in Europe), did not represent the "spontaneous" working of the system. Such "spontaneous" working in a sense got restored under latter-day "globalization," which sapped domestic trade union strength and "rolled back" both Keynesian demand management and third world dirigisme.

Not surprisingly, under "globalization" once again we find "land augmentation" receding to the background. With globalization of capital, especially in the form of finance, occurring in a world of *nation-states*, each such state, once it gets into the vortex of "globalization," has willy-nilly got to bow before the demands of globalized capital, for fear that otherwise capital would leave its shores, precipitating a financial crisis. In other words, whereas during the dirigiste period, the bourgeois state, even while promoting the development of capitalism, appeared to be standing above classes and "looking after" the interests of all (and hence making concessions to other classes as well, and controlling to an extent the operations of the bourgeoisie), now the state becomes far more tied to promoting the exclusive interests of the corporate-financial elite, which is integrated with international finance capital.[4]

Once again, therefore, since finance capital prefers "sound finance," there is "fiscal responsibility" legislation limiting the size of the fiscal deficit relative to the gross domestic product (usually to 3 percent or less nowadays as opposed to zero in colonial times); and since this happens together with substantial tax concessions to the corporate financial elite, the neoliberal state curtails "land-augmenting" expenditure and investment, just as it curtails welfare expenditures and transfer payments to the poor. At the same time, subsidies to the peasants are cut, cheap credit is no longer made available, input prices are raised, public extension services dwindle, protection against world market price fluctuations is removed, and even procurement operation at assured remunerative prices is wound up (since it also falls foul of World Trade Organization rules). "Land augmentation" therefore, as had been the case in colonial times, takes a back seat.

Not surprisingly, per capita agricultural output in the third world, which had stagnated or even declined in the colonial period, but had made considerable progress during the dirigiste period, once again moves into stagnation and decline.[5] It is also not surprising that large numbers of peasants find even "simple reproduction" impossible to carry on. In countries like India they are leaving agriculture in considerable numbers and are also resorting to large-scale suicides (over 240,000 peasant suicides have occurred in India over the first decade and half of the present century).

The point being made, in other words, is that capitalism in its "spontaneity" does not bring about "land augmentation." Since such land augmentation requires state effort, and since the requisite state effort is not forthcoming under capitalism in its spontaneity, land augmentation suffers. The colonial state worked directly and exclusively in the interests of metropolitan capital, while the neoliberal state works directly and exclusively in the interests of international finance capital, which is the lead actor in the current epoch. *The state acting directly and exclusively in the interests of the lead actor of the world capitalism of the time is what capitalism in its "spontaneity" demands.* This precludes "land augmentation" as a means of coping with the threat of increasing supply price of products of the tropical landmass to the value of money in the metropolis.

II

Income Deflation in the Periphery

The commonest means of coping with the threat historically has been through a reduction in the absorption of the products of the tropical landmass within the periphery itself by the population of the countries located on this very tropical landmass. And the primary instrument of this has been the imposition of an "income deflation" upon them, through a curtailment of their purchasing power so that, out of a relatively unchanging output of the fixed tropical landmass, they are obliged to release more and more goods for use in the metropolis. This happens either directly, in that the same goods that are released from local mass absorption are then absorbed in the metropolis; or it happens indirectly in that land that was previously devoted to the production of goods for which mass demand declined because of income deflation is now diverted to the production of other types of goods demanded by the metropolis. In either case, any threat to the value of money in the metropolis is warded off, and supplies are obtained from the tropical landmass to meet metropolitan demand without the problem of increasing supply price coming into play at all. Within income deflation in the periphery, however, we have to distinguish between two elements: income deflation imposed by the state and "spontaneous" income deflation. In the colonial period the chief instrument of the former was the colonial system of taxation, which, for much of the period, fell heavily upon the peasantry, i.e., upon the producing class itself. The crux of the matter is readily apparent from the early period of colonial rule in India when the East India Company had a monopoly of trade and had obtained the sovereign right of tax collection starting from 1765. The peasant producers directly, or the landlords to whom they paid rent, were taxed in cash as were artisans; a large part of total taxes—on average one-third, was used by the Company to "purchase" goods for export, from these very same producers. The producers appeared to be paid, but were not actually paid since their economic surplus extracted as tax payment merely changed its form, from money to goods. The producers did not smell a rat however, because the agent of the Company who collected the tax from them was different from the agent of the Company who bought their goods by using the very same tax monies, a fact they did not know. These goods obtained completely *gratis* were shipped abroad as export surplus without entailing any external payment liability for the metropolis, any *quid pro quo*, thereby effecting the "drain" of surplus, or transfer referred to earlier. As the requirement of such goods, or of substitute goods that were produced on the same landmass, increased, if the output from the landmass remained unchanged, then the tax burden simply had to increase to restrict local mass consumption even more, to balance supplies of such goods with the metropolitan demand for them. These goods were imported as a matter of policy, far in excess of the absorptive capacity of the metropolis itself, because tropical goods were in much greater demand in other temperate lands that, like the metropolis, could never produce them, than were the goods produced domestically in the metropolis. The excess of tropical imports by the Company into Britain, was re-exported to the emerging capitalist countries in continental Europe and to the temperate regions of new European settlement, in exchange for those temperate land goods Britain could not produce in adequate volumes. Re-exports boosted the purchasing power of Britain's domestic exports on average by

54 percent during 1765 to 1804 (U. Patnaik 2006, 35). In the Netherlands which ruled over Java, re-exported goods were more than its export of domestically produced goods in the eighteenth century (Maddison 2006, 83). A cold temperate country which acquired political control over a tropical region, in effect sat on a gold mine: it not only got goods it could never produce, completely free for its own use, it also got such goods free to exchange against imports from sovereign temperate lands, all as the commodity-equivalent of taxes raised from the colonized population.

Visualizing taxation and transfer in the situation when the Company's monopoly of trade ended by 1833 and colonial goods went directly to many countries makes no analytical difference to this simple picture. The linking of the fiscal and trade systems (using taxes to obtain export goods) continued, but now using bills of exchange as explained below. The "drain of surplus," or transfer, was never shown as such; it was camouflaged under certain heads of administered expenditure that occurred only because the colonised periphery was ruled by the metropolis, which showed its administered expenditures both in the government budget and also in the balance of payments. Say Rs1,000 of taxes (or £100 at the current exchange rate) was set aside in the colony's budget for "expenditure abroad" on the various drain items. The metropolis simply siphoned off £100 of the merchandise export surplus earned by the colony from the rest of the world, by showing on the debit side of the colony's external account £100 of administered invisible liabilities. These consisted of the same drain items as in the budget, leaving both the budget and the current account balanced.

The producers of the £100 merchandise export surplus in the colony got no claim on the gold, sterling, and other currencies they had earned. Exporting agents in India were sent bills of exchange by foreign importers (issued by the Secretary of State for India in London to these importers against deposit of the £100 worth of import proceeds in his account). These bills on submission to local exchange banks got the agents and through them the producers, "payment" of Rs1,000 in local currency out of the budget—that is, out of the producers' own tax contributions. The producers' entire earnings from merchandise export surplus to the world, were intercepted and appropriated in London. Thus, export surplus of goods continued to be the commodity form of taxes, and thereby continued to accrue in a costless manner to the metropolis. The exporting agents took a substantial cut from the sum that came to the producers, so that effecting a "drain" of £100 entailed a correspondingly greater squeeze on the latter.

While both the budget as well as the current account of the balance of payments would appear balanced, there would actually be a budgetary surplus of Rs1,000 equivalent to £100 and a current account surplus of £100 if we leave aside the "drain"-constituting invisible payments. As the demand for tropical goods rises, then, without involving any rise in output and hence without bringing increasing supply price into play, the taxes would be raised, together with the amount of the "drain," so that even though the budget and the balance of payments continue to remain apparently balanced, in effect more would be taken out of the given output through a heavier dose of income deflation. One important element of the drain items in the budget, the Home Charges rose from 18 percent in the early 1860s to 26 percent of public expenditure by the late 1920s (Bhattacharya 2005, Kumar 1984).

The "spontaneous" income deflation in the colonial period, by contrast, arose from the fact of "deindustrialization" mentioned earlier. If imports from the metropolis of manufactured goods worth £100 replace local artisan products of the same magnitude, then the artisans thrown out of work suffer an income deflation; what they were absorbing earlier (or their substitutes produced on the same landmass) can now be exported to pay for the manufactured goods imports, involving no increase in output, and hence no problem of increasing supply price. As long as the peripheral economy is kept open to trade (and hence to deindustrialization), there is a "spontaneous" income deflation imposed upon its population, which makes supplies of tropical goods available to the metropolis without any threat to the value of money there. (The "second-order effects" of the artisans' suffering income deflation in the form of a possible shrinking of demand for metropolitan manufactured goods within the periphery are not being considered here since they do not affect the logic of the present argument.)

Income deflation of the colonial period had a directness. A similar process occurs in a more indirect manner under neoliberalism. Public finance in a neoliberal regime takes the form of keeping the fiscal deficit controlled while giving tax concessions to the domestic and foreign corporate-financial elements. This necessarily entails either a rise in taxation upon other classes or a reduction in government expenditure that would have otherwise put purchasing power in their hands. What fiscal policy achieves, therefore, is a redistribution of purchasing power from the other classes to the domestic and foreign corporate-financial elements in the country. Since the "propensity" to absorb tropical goods per unit of income in the hands of these corporate-financial elements is lower than the corresponding propensity of the other classes, such redistribution has the effect *ceteris paribus* of reducing the domestic absorption of tropical products within the periphery. (This argument incidentally remains valid in principle even when the economy of the periphery where such redistribution occurs is not itself a producer of tropical goods.)

Indeed any redistribution of purchasing power, not just through fiscal policy, but by any other means as well, has the same effect of releasing tropical products from absorption within the periphery to meet the demand of the metropolis without increasing output and hence without bringing increasing supply price into play. And we know that in a neoliberal regime, such redistribution occurs in a pronounced manner—an obvious example being the entry of agribusiness in the form of seed, fertilizer, and marketing multinational corporations, which, at any given international price of the product, take a larger proportion of the value of output for themselves, leaving a smaller proportion for the peasantry than before. The entry of agribusiness entails in short a redistribution of the value of output in favour of agribusiness and against the peasant producers, which has the effect of reducing the absorption of tropical goods within the domestic economy.

There is of course a basic difference between the colonial income deflation and the neoliberal income deflation, which is that in the former a part of the reduction in income was simply taken as "drain" without any *quid pro quo*, while in the latter this is not always the case. But that makes little difference to the present argument, which is concerned with showing how a larger amount of tropical products can be made available to the metropolis without an increase in their output, and *not* with how this amount made available is financed by the metropolis (whether entirely gratis, or through borrowing, or some other means).

Some of the mechanisms mentioned above in the context of neoliberalism can also be categorized as "spontaneous" deflation, but we have something more specific in mind when using that term. Growth under neoliberalism is essentially stimulated by "bubbles" whose collapses plunge the economy into crises; but let us for a moment assume away the problem of deficiency of aggregate demand and visualize an economy in the periphery experiencing growth. The existence of substantial labour reserves, to start with, keeps real wages tied to some "subsistence" level. Along with growth, however, there is an increase in labour productivity, which means that the share of "surplus" in total output increases. At the same time, though, expenditure out of the surplus is typically on goods that have a lower employment-intensity than the goods upon which wage incomes, or more generally the working people's incomes, are spent. We therefore have a vicious circle: rise in surplus leading to a rise in labour productivity, which in turn keeps the relative size of the reserve army of labour intact or even enlarged, and hence keeps wages at the subsistence level, which, in the context of labour productivity increases and raises the share of the surplus still further.

The rise in the share of surplus therefore follows *ipso facto* from an increase in labour productivity through structural change. But this rise in the share of the surplus also in turn contributes to an increase in labour productivity. We thus have a self-sustaining mechanism that brings about a spontaneous income deflation over time.

Two additional factors also operate in the same direction. The first is that the rich tend to demand newer and newer goods; that is, the commodity composition of the demand of the rich involves a faster rate of product innovation than the commodity composition of the demand of the working people. And since product innovation typically occurs in the metropolis before being transferred to the periphery, it tends to be labour-economizing, which means that as the share of surplus rises, the rate of growth of labour productivity also increases over time because of this very rise in the share of surplus.

On the basis of econometric work done by P. Johannes Verdoorn, Nicholas Kaldor propounded the Kaldor-Verdoorn law, which postulated the rate of growth of labour productivity to be an increasing function of the rate of growth of output (Kaldor 1968). However, the Kaldor-Verdoorn law implicitly presumes income distribution to be constant; if it is shifting in favour of surplus earners, then this function itself would not be stable, but would keep rising over time for any given growth rate.

The second factor is the demand of surplus earners not just for commodities produced by labour and by produced means of production (where we have so far been examining how employment intensity moves over time), but for land itself, in the form of real estate—for country houses, golf courses, and such like—which generate very little employment but displace much labour on agricultural land, though not necessarily only on agricultural land.

When we put all these factors together, we find that the capacity of the growth process under neoliberalism to generate employment is very limited; and this fact itself ensures that labour reserves persist, wages remain tied to a subsistence level, and the share of surplus in output keeps rising, thus causing a vicious circle. This vicious circle, however, also means that there is a *spontaneous* restriction on the growth of demand for the goods produced by the tropical landmass. True, as the last example shows, the restriction on the demand for goods produced by the tropical landmass may also be accompanied by a reduction of cultivated area and hence of output (which would also hold in the case of income deflation on the peasants); but this is a matter we shall discuss later. The point here is simply that there is a spontaneous restriction of demand for goods produced by the tropical landmass as capital accumulation occurs within the periphery.

The curtailment of local absorption within the periphery of goods produced on the tropical landmass is one way of ensuring that the problem of increasing supply price does not come into play and there is no threat to the value of the currency in the metropolis as capital accumulation occurs there.

III

Profit Inflation Within the Periphery

The third possible way is the following. Supplies of tropical products can be squeezed out from the periphery for use in the metropolis through what Keynes (1930) called a "profit inflation" in the periphery itself; and if such profit inflation is accompanied by an equivalent depreciation in the currency of the periphery vis-à-vis that of the metropolis, then there appears to be no threat to the value of money in the metropolis.

Let us examine this a little more closely. Profit inflation entails a rise in the price of commodities vis-à-vis the money wage rate of the workers, or more generally vis-à-vis the money incomes of the working people, including the self-employed. It entails in other words a shift from wages to profits (whence the term "profit inflation"), or more generally from the working people to the surplus earners (including the traders in agricultural goods who are the beneficiaries of the price rise of such goods). Since surplus earners have a lower ratio of consumption to income than working people, such a shift of income distribution has the effect of bringing about a net reduction in the absorption of commodities out of a given output.

The increased "saving" in output thus squeezed out of the working people is referred to as "forced saving." They get no reward for it, since the reduced consumption enforced upon them accrues as increased "savings," and hence as increased wealth, to the surplus earners. In fact, the reduced consumption enforced upon them is usually a multiple of the increased wealth of the surplus earners, *since the latter's consumption also increases at the expense of the former.*

A simple illustration will clarify the point. Consider a universe with only two classes: workers (who are the sole element in the set of working people) and capitalists (who are the sole element in the set of surplus earners). Suppose the workers consume their entire income while the capitalists consume only half of their income. Then, for "savings" to increase by 100 (for running an export surplus to the metropolis for meeting its increased demand), the consumption of the workers must be squeezed by 200 through a rise in the price vis-à-vis the money wage: of these 200 units that would accrue as additional profits to the capitalists, 100 would be consumed by them (since they consume half of their income), and 100 would be "saved" by them, which, in turn, would augment their wealth while enabling an export surplus to be run. The actual "sacrifice" (to use a Marshallian term) for meeting the increased demand from the metropolis is made by the workers; but the capitalists get to *both* consume more *and* increase their wealth without having made an iota of "sacrifice." Keynes (1940) had referred to this 200 accruing to the capitalists as a "booty" that would land on their laps through profit inflation at the expense of the workers.

Even if output is not given, but increases in part to meet the increased demand from the metropolis, so that the phenomenon of "increasing supply price" at given money wages in the periphery does literally come into play, even then "profit inflation" would manifest itself. With given money wages, prices would rise to exactly that extent, where the additional output produced, *plus* the reduced consumption of workers (compared to the base situation) *minus* the additional consumption by the capitalists (because of their higher profits) equals the export surplus to the metropolis for meeting its increased requirement. In short, increasing supply price entails that higher demand causes both an increase in output and also "forced saving" by the workers. And the sum of these two must equal the increased consumption of the capitalists and the export surplus to the metropolis.

Such profit inflation can pose a threat to the value of money in the metropolis in two possible ways: one, to the extent that the rise in prices of tropical products gets "passed on" as higher inflation in the metropolis, itself, via a rise in raw material or wage goods costs in the metropolis; and two, even if there is no inflation in the metropolis as a result of the higher tropical goods prices, if wealth-holders in the periphery shift to gold, which raises gold prices in general and thereby jeopardizes the value of money in the metropolis. *Neither of these avenues, however, would be effective if the exchange rate of the currency of the periphery vis-à- vis that of the metropolis depreciated exactly to the same extent as the rise in tropical goods prices.*

To see this, let us suppose that with given money wages the price of tropical goods rises by 10 percent in local currency, which creates an export surplus for the metropolis. If there is a 10 percent depreciation of the local currency vis-à-vis the currency of the metropolis, then there is no rise in the tropical good's price in terms of metropolitan currency, and hence no question of any cost-push inflation in the metropolis. At the same time a 10 percent depreciation of the periphery's currency vis-à-vis that of the metropolis, exactly matching the 10 percent rise in the price of its good, presupposes that there is no change in the price of gold in terms of the currency of the metropolis; i.e., the decline in the price of the periphery's currency is with respect to *both gold and the metropolitan currency, with no change in the relative price of the latter two.* In such a case there is no reason for any shift by wealth-holders from metropolitan currency to gold, and hence no threat to the value of money in the metropolis.

Let us assume that this happens, and that there is no threat to the value of the currency of the metropolis because of profit inflation in the periphery. Even so the question arises: Is such a scenario sustainable?

What the above discussion has ignored till now is the threat to the value of money *in the periphery itself.* We have already seen in chapter 2 that there is a distinction between episodic inflation and the sustained inflation that increasing supply price gives rise to: in the latter case there cannot be any positive equilibrium level at which the value of the currency in terms of which inflation is occurring can settle vis-à-vis gold (or any currency that has a fixed value in terms of gold). In the present context, it follows that if increasing supply price were to generate a *process* of profit inflation in the periphery, in terms of the periphery's currency, then the monetary system in the periphery will collapse, even if *ex hypothesi* there is no direct threat to the value of the metropolitan currency. A process of profit inflation in the periphery cannot therefore be the means through which the metropolis can, in a sustainable manner, cope with the threat of increasing supply price of goods produced in the tropical and subtropical regions.

Profit inflation in the periphery also entails a second problem. It implies that locating the production of any footloose industry in the periphery becomes more profitable than locating its production in the metropolis, because the wage rate in the periphery in terms of the local currency has remained unchanged (the assumption behind profit inflation), while its exchange rate has actually depreciated in terms of the metropolitan currency.

In the pre–World War II world of colonialism, where capital, though juridically freely mobile across countries, was in fact not mobile but went into the tropical periphery only in sectors like plantations and mines (i.e., only as a complement to the colonial division of labour), such wage differences did not matter for the location of activities. Profit inflation in the periphery accompanied by an exchange rate depreciation therefore would not have aroused any opposition from the workers in the metropolis. In other words, this mechanism had some potential in the colonial period. *But precisely in the colonial period the need for this mechanism did not really arise because the combined effects of colonial taxation and of "deindustrialization" perpetrated in the colonies were quite sufficient to ensure adequate supplies of tropical products to the metropolis without causing any profit inflation in the periphery and endangering the value of its money.*

In the current era of globalization, when colonial-style surplus appropriation from the periphery is no longer possible (a manifestation of which is that the largest and the most powerful metropolitan economy at present is also the most indebted)—when, in other words, the need for this mechanism of profit inflation, among others, *does* arise for extracting tropical products to meet metropolitan demands—the world has ceased to be segmented. The use of this mechanism in the current era will lead to a shift of capital from the metropolis to the periphery for locating production units in the latter for sales to the world market, which would arouse opposition from the workers in the metropolis and hence some pressure on metropolitan states to explore alternative mechanisms. In fact it is significant that successive U.S. administrations have been systematically pressurizing Asian economies, which have provided favourable sites to metropolitan capital (including especially American capital), for locating production units in them for meeting global demand, to *appreciate* their currencies vis-à-vis the U.S. dollar.

True, as we have argued earlier, the nation-states' policy stances in the current era are driven by the demands of international capital, because of which the interest of domestic workers scarcely matters for policy. But the United States, whose currency is still believed by the world's wealth-holders to be almost "as good as gold," does have a degree of autonomy vis-à-vis the caprices of globalized capital, and hence can afford to take steps to prevent an avoidable alienation of domestic workers, which is why profit-inflation-cum-exchange-rate-depreciation can scarcely constitute a major instrument for extracting supplies from the periphery.

It follows that, for the reasons just mentioned, money income deflation in the periphery takes precedence over profit inflation as a means of coping with the threat of increasing supply price. This is not to say that profit inflation never occurs. It certainly does in exceptional circumstances like wars, when income deflation alone may not suffice and when wealth-holders' freedom to move their wealth across assets is in any case constrained. The most glaring example of a profit inflation being unleashed on an economy of the periphery to make it provide larger supplies for metropolitan (war) needs was during the Second World War, when such a profit inflation caused a massive famine in Bengal, which resulted in the deaths of 3.1 million people.[6]

IV

Income Deflation Within the Metropolis

Here again, as in the case of the periphery, we have to distinguish between spontaneous income deflation and state-imposed income deflation. In the metropolis, the mechanism of spontaneous income deflation is exactly similar to what has already been discussed in the case of the periphery. Spontaneous income deflation comes into its own only when real wages are kept down at some particular level, even as labour productivity increases, because of the effect of large labour reserves; and this typically happens only under the present globalization regime, when metropolitan workers are exposed to competition from the low-wage workers of the periphery and hence indirectly to the baneful consequences of the massive labour reserves of the periphery.

Even with free movement of goods across national boundaries, a squeeze on the wages of workers in the metropolis would happen if there were no barriers in the way of the periphery producing the same goods that the metropolis produces; in such a case, too, metropolitan workers would be competing against lower-wage periphery workers, a situation that would constrain their own upward wage movement. But with free capital mobility, the barriers to the periphery's producing the same goods as are produced in the metropolis are certainly lowered, since metropolitan capital itself takes advantage of lower periphery wages to locate plants there.

As real wages in the metropolis do not increase, even as labour productivity increases, the share of surplus increases in metropolitan output. Even assuming no problems of realization—i.e., of deficient aggregate demand, since the surplus is spent on less employment-intensive goods and also on goods that entail a higher rate of product innovation, where each new innovation typically means higher labour productivity—a steady increase in the share of surplus is associated with a lower and lower rate of employment growth for any given rate of output growth. This means that, even when there is no crisis of over-production (or of inadequate demand), a spontaneous check will occur on the rise in the size of the total wage bill, and hence on the rise in demand for tropical products, which are likely to be figuring more prominently in what the workers demand than what the capitalists demand (including investment goods). There is therefore some spontaneous check on the rise in demand for such products.

But clearly spontaneous check is not enough. Even if we accept that per unit income, the workers demand more tropical products than the capitalists (including through the inputs required for investment goods), *the demand of the latter for tropical products per unit income is certainly positive.* With growth of output, unless there is an actual spontaneous shrinking of the incomes of the workers in absolute terms, there would certainly then be *some* positive increase in the demand for such products. Spontaneous income deflation in the metropolis cannot then provide an escape route from the problem of increasing supply price, and hence from the problem of maintaining the value of money in the metropolis.

That leaves state-imposed income deflation within the metropolis itself to keep down the demand for imported tropical products. But clearly, metropolitan states would impose an income deflation on their own populations, if at all, only after income deflation has been imposed on the population in the periphery. It follows then that metropolitan capitalism would be constrained to ensure at all times that the international arrangements are such as to squeeze out supplies from the periphery at the expense of the local population to meet the demands of the metropolis, without giving rise to a situation where the value of money in the latter is jeopardized. *In other words, it cannot do without the phenomenon of imperialism, an integral part of which is the imposition of income deflation on the working population of the periphery.*

V

A Restatement of the Argument

The argument presented until now can be restated as follows. Capitalism cannot do without a whole range of goods produced by peasants located in the tropical and subtropical areas that have a fixed landmass— goods that either cannot ever be produced in temperate lands or cannot ever be produced in adequate volumes. As the *ex ante* demand for such goods increases with capital accumulation, it cannot be met by increased output from this fixed landmass without threatening the value of money in the metropolis because of the increasing supply price of such output at any given money wage rate. If land-augmenting investment and land-augmenting technological change could occur in the tropical periphery for raising this output, then increasing supply price could be kept in abeyance. But that requires a relationship between the capitalist state (which has to play a crucial role for such change) and the peasantry, which, other than a brief period of dirigisme in the postcolonial era, simply cannot exist: the tendency under capitalism is to pursue *inter alia* a fiscal policy characterized by "sound finance" that precludes state activism in this regard.

As a result, this *ex ante* excess demand for tropical and subtropical goods is met by the imposition of income deflation upon the periphery itself, in order to squeeze out larger supplies from a given output at the expense of local absorption. The alternative route of a profit inflation combined with exchange rate depreciation in the periphery threatens the value of money within the periphery and is unsustainable; besides, it does not remove the threat to the value of money in the metropolis, apart from arousing political opposition from the metropolitan working class. An income deflation upon the workers in the metropolis itself is unlikely ever to be imposed, if it is imposed at all, to an extent that does away with the need for income deflation on the working people in the periphery. In short, squeezing local absorption in the periphery to meet the demands of capital accumulation in the metropolis is an essential feature of capitalism, and this, far from being obviated by capital accumulation (and the development of capitalism) within the periphery, only makes the problem even more serious. Reducing such local absorption by poor populations through income deflation is the essence of imperialism.

CHAPTER FOUR

The Reserve Army of Labour in the Periphery

THE THREAT to the value of money in the metropolis does not arise only because of excess demand pressures for commodities produced on the fixed tropical landmass. It could in principle also arise from excess demand for commodities produced in the capitalist sector proper, but this, as a moment's reflection would suggest, is not a serious threat. Since the supplies of commodities produced within the capitalist sector are augmentable over time—i.e., since there is no long-run fixity of inputs for the production of such commodities (other than those produced on the fixed tropical landmass)—even in the event of an increase in their prices in the short term, the expectation would be that these prices would come back, for a given level of the money wage rate, to a constant level (which would be equal to the long-run supply price at the given money wage). They would not therefore constitute a threat to the value of money, since there would be no tendency to move either to such commodities or to gold (as a hedge against inflation) from money as a form of holding wealth.

Besides, as Kalecki (1971:168) pointed out, capitalist economies in any case scarcely ever reached full capacity output, even at the peak of a boom. Hence, a rise in the demand for commodities produced in the metropolis does not raise their prices *even in the short run* (as long as sufficient inventories of current inputs produced on the fixed tropical landmass are available). Hence, the value of money in the metropolis is not threatened by the emergence of any excess demand for goods produced within it, the way it is threatened by the excess demand for goods produced by a host of petty producers on the fixed tropical landmass.

There is, however, a possible threat to the value of money that can arise from cost-push factors, whether because of an autonomous rise in the money wage rate within the metropolis itself or because of a rise in the price of primary commodities produced in the periphery, *not on account of any excess demand for them but because of an autonomous rise in the money wages/producers' incomes in the periphery.* Any such autonomous cost-push is kept in check by the existence of the reserve army of labour. But given the fact that the autonomous wage push can arise either in the metropolis or in the periphery itself, the capitalist system needs a reserve army in the periphery in addition to the reserve army that it has within the metropolis. This reserve army in the periphery is in fact generated by the encroachment of capitalism itself into the economy of the periphery (via the processes of "drain of surplus" from colonies and the "deindustrialization" of the colonial economies, mentioned earlier).

I

Two Reserve Armies of Labour

The standard discussion of the reserve army of labour in the literature on Marxian economics has two obvious limitations. First, the role of the reserve army is seen entirely in terms of keeping the *real* wages in check, with very little cognizance of its role in keeping *money* wages in check, and hence keeping the value of money intact. The concern, in other words, has been with explaining why the capitalist system always has a positive rate of surplus value. And here, while economists like Schumpeter (1952) claim that the process of accumulation of capital, by stepping up the demand for labour power, would exhaust the reserve army and lead to a rise of real wages to a point where surplus value would disappear, the Marxist argument against this claim has been that accumulation itself would dry up if the rate of profit fell below a threshold level. In other words, the Marxist argument has been that the reserve army can never get exhausted by the process of accumulation (Goodwin 1967). Since demonstrating this has been the focus of attention, it is the role of the reserve army in keeping down *real* wages that has been in the forefront. The question of the role of the reserve army in keeping down *money* wages has scarcely been discussed at all.

This distinction did not matter for Marx. Since he was talking about a commodity-money world, real and money wages moved together; hence there was no separate discussion of the role of the reserve army for maintaining the value of money. But when we move from a commodity-money world into a credit-money world, and retain the assumption that the wage bargain is always in money terms (which is an assumption in keeping with reality), maintaining the value of money by preventing autonomous increases in money wages assumes importance; and the role of the reserve army of labour in doing so becomes crucial.

This fact has been recognized more recently outside of the Marxist tradition, albeit in a somewhat refracted form. Joan Robinson (1956) was among the first to see that a certain minimum level of unemployment had to be maintained in a capitalist economy if it was not to come up against an "inflationary barrier." Subsequently this idea reappeared in the literature on the Non-Accelerating Inflation Rate of Unemployment (NAIRU), though this has to be distinguished from the Natural Rate of Unemployment (NRU) of the monetarists, which, though having a family resemblance to the NAIRU, constitutes *de facto* full employment.[1]

The NAIRU literature misses a central point, however. The issue is not one of *accelerating* inflation; the issue is of inflation itself, even if such inflation occurs at a steady rate. *No noncommodity money can fulfill its role of being a form in which wealth continues to be held if there is persistent inflation in the economy, even if such inflation occurs at a steady rate.* If such money has gold backing, i.e., if it is *de jure* commodity money even if having the physical form of paper money, then there would be a rush from such money to gold even in the event of a steady inflation, making its convertibility into gold impossible to sustain. And if it has no gold backing, i.e., it is not convertible at all, then its value in terms of gold, as we have seen, would plunge downwards in the event of even a steady inflation, as wealth-holders flee to gold from such money, making it ultimately worthless. What prevents such a denouement in a capitalist economy is *inter alia* the perennial existence of a reserve army of labour. Such a reserve army therefore is necessary not just for the existence of a positive rate of surplus value (and hence a positive rate of profit), as Marxian literature has traditionally emphasized; it is necessary for the very preservation of the value of money in the metropolis.

The second way in which the reserve army discussion in Marxian literature has been limited is that it takes no cognizance of the products produced in the periphery but used in the metropolis. The discussion of the modus operandi of the system is invariably placed within the setting of a capitalist economy that consists of workers and capitalists and produces all the commodities it needs; and the reserve army exists on the fringes of this universe to keep the workers in check in various ways, by imposing work discipline among them, by ensuring that wage demands are restricted, and so on.

Once we reckon, however, with the obvious fact that capitalism located in the metropolis cannot do without products that are produced in the periphery by precapitalist petty producers, who supplement their own labour with that of hired workers in particular seasons, then the role of an additional reserve army of labour located within the periphery becomes clear. It keeps down the money wage rate/money incomes within the periphery and hence prevents any possibility of an autonomous cost-push in the case of such commodities.

Capitalism in short has always used two reserve armies of labour and not one: one of these located within the metropolis, which, as Marx discussed, has served to "discipline" the workers who are directly employed by capital;[2] the other one located within the periphery, which has served to keep down the money wages/incomes of those engaged in producing goods for the capitalist sector, and also to keep them "disciplined."

The latter, not recognized in traditional Marxist literature, is far more important in a sense than the former, since it can be relied upon even to provide a source of recruitment for the capitalist sector's direct employment whenever the need arises. Indeed, it did so in the post–Second World War period when immigrants from the former colonies and dependencies were allowed to throng to the metropolis to join the workforce. Since the reserve army of labour located in the metropolis cannot be expected to "discipline" the primary commodity producers in the periphery, while the reserve army located in the periphery can be used, via greater immigration into the metropolis, to "discipline," or at least to "tame," the workers directly employed by capital in the metropolis, the latter has an even greater importance in the functioning of capitalism.

It also has the "advantage" that most would not even recognize it as a reserve army of labour *for* capitalism. The fact that its very existence has been caused by capitalist penetration into the periphery via the processes of "drain" and "deindustrialization" mentioned earlier, and the fact that it is also useful for capitalism in its current phase would not be appreciated by many.

On the contrary, this distant reserve army would appear to be a feature of the peripheral economy, arising from the infirmities that "naturally" characterize such economies. And since it is seen as an internal, specific, and preexisting feature of the periphery, the impact of capitalism upon it is seen entirely as a beneficial one. The capitalist sector is seen as occasionally relieving the travails of the periphery by taking away a part of these unemployed labourers for its own use. This supposedly beneficial role of capitalism, however, is as untrue as the view that the reserve army in the periphery is a legacy of its own past, unrelated to the encroachment by capitalism.[3]

Why, it may be asked, should capitalism need an internal reserve army *in addition to the one* located in the periphery? In other words, even if we accept the argument mentioned above that the internal reserve army cannot substitute the external one, surely the latter can substitute the former; why then should there be two distinct reserve armies of labour?

The answer lies in the fact that there is a qualitative difference between the two reserve armies. The one located within the metropolis can strictly be called a reserve army while the one located in the periphery is not so much a reserve *army* as simply a massive labour reserve whose disciplining role for the workers directly employed by capital in the metropolis can at best be an imperfect one. This is because such labour reserves are devoid of the skills that even the "unskilled" workers in the metropolis possess. Besides, the large geographical distance that separates the active army of labour employed by metropolitan capitalism from *these labour reserves* makes them inadequate for "disciplining" this active army.

II

The Need for "Price-Takers"

The labour reserves in the periphery play an additional role in the functioning of capitalism, which is insufficiently recognized. And this consists in the fact that they make the primary commodity producers of the periphery, catering to the demands of the capitalist metropolis, "price takers" in the sense that such producers become incapable of raising their money prices *even when they are faced with a rise in prices in other sectors.* And this in turn helps eventually to damp down the rise in prices elsewhere, though at the end of this damping down, these producers are worse off in real terms than they were at the beginning.

The necessity of having a group of "price-takers" for the stability of the capitalist system was underscored by Keynes himself who saw the workers as constituting such a group. Keynes pooh-poohed the neoclassical idea that while real wage flexibility always ensured full employment under capitalism, the level of money wage depended upon the magnitude of money supply, which meant that real wages were more stable than money wages (since the latter varied with every variation in monetary policy, according to this argument), and said: "That money wages should be more stable than real wages is a condition of the system possessing inherent stability" (1949:239). If money wages were not stable while real wages were (in the sense of being tied to the "marginal productivity of labour" at the full employment level that was always maintained), then every change in the "marginal propensity to consume" or in the "marginal efficiency of capital," he had argued, would make money wages tumble to zero or zoom up to infinity. The capitalist system, it followed, needed the stability of money wages, or more generally, the existence of a group of price-takers.

Keynes's own explanation of *how* such stability of money wages came about in a capitalist system, however, was not very convincing. He attributed it to "money illusion" on the part of the workers, i.e., to the fact that they were generally so focused on the *level* of their money wages that as long as this level was not going down, they did not notice reductions in real wages caused by increases in the price level. But this psychological explanation is less than persuasive. A far more plausible explanation can be found in the fact that the level of unemployment within which they are ensconced is so high that they lack the sheer bargaining strength even to defend their real wages in the face of rising prices. The most they can hope for is that the level of money wages is not cut; in fact, the maintenance of money wages has a certain social sanction which helps them even in the midst of mass unemployment.

This incapacity, owing to being surrounded by massive labour reserves, of a group of producers who sell to the capitalist sector, however, is more likely to afflict the petty producers in the periphery than the workers in the capitalist sector proper. The real "price-takers," upon whose incapacity to defend real incomes in the face of a rise in prices the stability of capitalism rests, are to be found not within the metropolis, not among the metropolitan workers, but in the periphery, among the petty producers and the workers they employ to supplement their own labour (P. Patnaik 1997).

The need for a group of "price-takers" arises not just for the reasons that Keynes had mentioned—namely, a sudden increase in the propensity to consume or a sudden fillip to the inducement to invest. Keynes had seen these as problematical because a rise in aggregate demand for these reasons would increase output *and hence prices*, because of increasing short-run supply price of the output produced in the metropolis for a given money wage. This would cause a reduction in real wages, which had somehow to be made to stick if output was in fact to be flexible.

But in addition to these factors, and even in the case emphasized by Kalecki (1954)—which is more realistic in conditions of monopoly and oligopoly, where the supply price remains constant for a given money wage in the neighbourhood of "equilibrium"—the absence of a group of "price-takers" would destabilize the value of the currency in the event either of a rise in the profit-mark-up margin (or what Kalecki called the "degree of monopoly") or of an autonomous money wage-push. The existence of large labour reserves, in other words, acts not only to prevent an autonomous money wage-push by the working people whom it surrounds, but to make out of them a group of "price-takers," who, in the event of such a push by *some other segment* of the working population, serve to stabilize the value of money.

Galbraith (1963), in his analysis of postwar American capitalism, emphasized this: that is, he actually distinguished between the organized and the unorganized sectors of the economy and argued that money wage increases by the workers in the organized sector (for any given level of labour productivity) raise unit labour costs, and hence unit variable costs, and get "passed on" in the form of higher administered prices by the capitalists. The system nonetheless has an "equilibrium" because there exists a group of "price-takers" who cannot change their money earnings in response to such price increases because they lack the capacity to "administer" the prices *they* charge for their own products.

Late nineteenth- and early twentieth-century capitalism was characterized by the emergence of monopolies in the form of cartels and trusts. Even in the subsequent period when there was no explicit collusion to fix prices, there was always implicit collusion (in the form for instance of "price-leadership") to charge administered prices (Baran and Sweezy 1966). Likewise, there was a growth of the trade union movement that extracted significant concessions from the capitalists in the form of wage increases (until the recent weakening of this movement in the era of globalization, on which more later). Such parametric increases in the bargaining strength of the workers and in the mark-up margins of the capitalists (which is what collusion ensures) would have destabilized the system, exactly in the way Keynes had visualized as arising from the side of demand, in the absence of such a group of "price-takers."

These labour reserves were located not within the metropolis itself, but in the periphery, making the producers of the periphery's goods that are required in the metropolis into a group of "price-takers." Kalecki (1954) argued that the share of wages between roughly the end of the third quarter of the nineteenth century and the beginning of the Second World War remained constant in the advanced capitalist economies, because the rise in the "degree of monopoly" (causing a rise in the mark-up margin) was counterbalanced by a decline in the ratio of raw material prices to the unit wage costs. The former on its own would have lowered the share of wages; it did not do so because of the squeeze on raw material prices, of which the adverse terms of trade movement for primary commodities vis-à-vis manufactured goods in the world economy (emphasized by Prebisch [1950], Singer [1950], and Lewis [1966]) was a symptom.

These, however, were not two independent fortuitous movements that happened to cancel one another in their impact on the share of wages, leaving this share unchanged in the aggregate. This unchanged wage share was the expression of a dynamics wherein the parametric increase in the *ex ante* profit share (owing to the rise in the "degree of monopoly" from collusive price-fixing) was offset by a squeeze on the group of "price-takers," whose location in the midst of vast labour reserves incapacitated them in the matter of defending their real incomes (P. Patnaik 1997).

III

Migration Streams and Labour Reserves

With the reduction in the weight of primary commodities in the gross value of output in the metropolis—and, for that matter, in the gross value of output of the capitalist sector of the world as a whole, located both in the metropolis and in the periphery itself—this stabilizing role of the labour reserves has obviously become attenuated. The question may then arise: Has capitalism in recent times lost this prop of stability?

Even as the stabilizing role played by the existence of a group of "price-taking" petty producers in the periphery has been attenuated, capital, not just in the form of finance but even productive capital, has become globalized to a degree unprecedented in the history of capitalism. This has also linked the position of the workers in the metropolis to the labour reserves located in the periphery to an extent unparalleled till now. One implication of this, already mentioned earlier, has been the stagnation, or even decline, in the real wage rate in the most powerful capitalist economy, the United States, over the last four decades. But the other implication is that the "price-taking" role that was earlier played by the petty producers in the periphery has begun to devolve on the workers in the capitalist segment itself, including in the metropolis. In other words, what Keynes had conceptualized, namely that workers engaged within the capitalist sector act as "price-takers" and thereby lend stability to the system, is becoming more relevant today than it was in Keynes's own time.

But the real point is not so much *who* constitutes the group of "price-takers" but *what* compels "price-taking" behaviour. And this compulsion, whether in the earlier period or under the current phase of globalization, undoubtedly comes from the vast labour reserves that exist in the periphery. To be sure, if labour reserves were located in the metropolis itself rather than being located in the periphery, they would have played the same role of stabilizing the system by making the metropolitan workers into "price-takers." But their location in the periphery, which of course was not *planned* in any way (since capitalism is not a planned system) but arose out of the interaction between the capitalist and the precapitalist sectors, confers several advantages upon the system, even while imparting stability to it.

The first advantage is social stability within the metropolis itself. The existence of vast labour reserves within the metropolis would have entailed an extent of social and political turmoil that would have threatened the capitalist system, much the way that Marx had argued and imperialists like Cecil Rhodes (quoted in Lenin [1977]) had explicitly admitted.

The fact that the petty producers displaced within the metropolitan area itself did not linger on as a vast unemployed and underemployed mass was not because they were largely absorbed into the domestic capitalist sector, as is commonly believed. Early machines, although simple, displaced labour on too massive a scale for its full reabsorption into the growing factories. (A single "spinning Jenny" with 80 spindles displaced 78 traditional spinners; jennies with up to 800 spindles each were known in England by the end of the eighteenth century [Mantoux 1928]). The labour reserves built up within the metropolitan countries by the process of expropriation of the local petty producers, and owing to technical change in the leading factory industries, were reduced to a significant extent through large-scale emigration to the much vaster temperate regions of white settlement in the New World. Those who migrated from Europe had already decimated and displaced indigenous inhabitants in these regions while occupying their lands. Capital from Europe—mainly from Britain and France—migrated to these lands in the wake of population migration, effecting an immense diffusion of capitalism from its West European home base to the temperate regions of white settlement, such as Canada, the United States, Australia, and New Zealand (Bagchi 1972). In turn, capital exports on such a large scale depended substantially on colonial transfers, whose mechanism we discuss in chapter 8.

The scale of this emigration can be gauged from one simple figure. Between 1821 and 1915, over 16 million persons migrated permanently out of Britain (Kenwood and Lougheed 1971:40), a number larger than Britain's 1821 population. British emigration alone made up 36 percent of all emigration from Europe during this period. The average number of persons migrating every year from Britain over this period works out to nearly half the annual increase in population (U. Patnaik 2012).

In the case of the periphery, however, although there was substantial displacement of petty producers owing to the mechanisms of "drain" and "deindustrialization," there was neither any scope for emigration on this scale, nor was there even any domestic development of capitalist production (except in mines and plantations) that could absorb some of the persons displaced. No doubt there was emigration: between 1831 and 1915, 17 million Indian, Chinese, and other Asian labourers emigrated (a more accurate description would have been "were made to emigrate by metropolitan capital") to other tropical regions for working on mines and plantations there (Northrup 1995:155–157, quoted in Bhattacharya 2006:198), while 45 million people emigrated from Europe to the temperate regions of white settlement. Both in absolute terms, as well as relative to their own populations and relative to the numbers displaced from their traditional occupations because of the encroachment of capitalism, permanent emigration from Asia was far smaller than that from Europe.

The Asian emigration was, besides, "low-wage emigration." The migrants did not occupy land in the places to which they went; they did not set up as independent farmers; and their emigration did not have the effect of raising the "reservation price" and hence the real wages of those left behind. They went as indentured labour at the behest of capital, not on their own independent initiative, from lands that had seen the emergence of modern mass poverty owing to the expropriation of petty producers (Raychaudhuri 1985). Moreover, *they were not allowed to move to the temperate regions through official restrictions on migration from tropical to temperate regions.*

The nineteenth century marked a break from the earlier forced removal of enslaved people from West Africa to work not only tropical plantations but also temperate lands in North America. An estimated 9.8 million enslaved humans had been transported to the Americas and the Atlantic basin between 1480 and 1867 (Bhattacharya 2006:197). Slavery was not abolished until the mid-nineteenth century, but the major waves of new arrivals of enslaved humans had ceased by the beginning of that century (Drescher and Engerman 1998), and indentured labour replaced slavery.

Thus, there were two quite "distinct streams of migration" in the nineteenth century as W. A. Lewis (1979) had stressed: a low-wage Asian migration at the behest of capital from tropical/subtropical lands to other tropical/subtropical lands; and a high-wage European migration from temperate regions to other temperate regions. *These two streams of migration were kept separate, with restrictions being placed on Asian migration to the temperate regions, and such restrictions continue to this day.* The net result of all this was the continuation, after the initial displacement of petty producers, of vast labour reserves within the periphery, contrasted with relatively smaller labour reserves in the metropolis, which had the advantage that the metropolis could use the labour reserves located in the periphery for its systemic *economic* stability, even while achieving a degree of *social* stability within its own frontiers.

The second advantage of the location of vast labour reserves in the periphery from which metropolitan capitalism benefited but for which it was not held responsible (except in "nationalist" writings, which scarcely entered, even in their heyday, the political economy discourse that was always centred on the metropolis, and which do so even less now, not only in the metropolis but even within the periphery itself), was clearly ideological. It became possible for political economy to dissociate the mass poverty in the periphery from the capitalism in the metropolis, and therefore even to argue that the solution to this mass poverty lay in permitting unrestricted encroachment by capitalism, i.e., in giving free rein to the very factor that had given rise to the problem in the first place. In any case, a prettified and sanitized picture of capitalism could be presented, as the unemployment and mass poverty it generated and continues to take advantage of are located at a safe distance.

The maintenance of these labour reserves is essential for the systemic economic stability of capitalism. To say this is not to suggest that the entire amount of labour reserves that exist in the periphery, down to the last unemployed person, is somehow functionally necessary for the system; but any serious depletion in it would undermine the economic stability of the system. In other words, capitalism, not just earlier but even to this day, rests upon an asymmetric structural relationship, whereby the periphery continues to be saddled with mass unemployment, underemployment, and poverty. Such mass unemployment and poverty in the periphery cripple the bargaining strength of the workers in the metropolis (in the current era of globalization of capital) so that the latter too become "price-takers."

IV

Concluding Observations

Let us draw together the threads of the argument. The relation of metropolitan capitalism that emerged in Europe to the temperate regions of the world was vastly different from its relation to the tropical regions. The commodities it required from the temperate regions were produced within the context of a massive diffusion of capitalism from Europe to these temperate regions. Underlying this diffusion was emigration from Europe, which, apart from bringing fresh land into use, snatched land resources away from the original inhabitants who were decimated through war and disease, while their remnants were confined to a few "reservations."

In the case of the tropical regions, however, land was already quite intensively cultivated long before capitalism came into being by populations densely concentrated on these lands. And whatever land augmentation was possible could be undertaken only by the state, but *in the era of capitalism it was loath to do so.* This reluctance on the part of the colonial state to undertake land augmentation arose *inter alia* from its class orientation, which predisposed it towards "sound finance" approved by metropolitan capital rather than expenditure that would have raised peasant incomes. Even if such increased incomes could have been taxed away by the state (and no doubt the colonial state did tax the peasantry heavily), it saw little reason for raising their incomes in the first place. There was in any case continuous expansion of tax collections over time through territorial conquests, starting from 1757 in Bengal to 1885 in Burma.

At the same time, wholesale appropriation of peasant lands for the development of capitalism in the tropics, would have caused no land augmentation *per se* and hence brought about the same result, viz., mass income deflation in the periphery, which occurred anyway. But it would have brought about this result in a far more violent form for capitalism, in a far more socially and politically unsustainable form, than the actual forms of income deflation that were resorted to. No doubt, if capitalism had supplanted peasant agriculture in the tropical lands, then the reluctance on the part of the colonial (or semicolonial) state to undertake land-augmenting expenditure might have been less, since the beneficiaries of such expenditure would have been not tropical peasants but (realistically at the time) a group of capitalists largely drawn from the metropolis itself. But, if there had been capitalism in tropical agriculture, then the massive income deflation it would have meant in the form of dispossession of the peasantry would have made it unnecessary for the state to undertake any large-scale expenditure on land augmentation anyway. This is because supplies from the tropics for the requirements of metropolitan capitalism would have been available aplenty by this very fact of dispossession and hence the extraordinarily massive income and demand deflation that such dispossession would have entailed.

The capitalist sector's demand for tropical products therefore was met historically, and continues to be met today, through an income deflation imposed on the periphery, *even while retaining broadly the framework of a peasant agriculture (notwithstanding the more recent development of capitalism, both landlord capitalism and peasant capitalism, at the margin, from within such agriculture).*

Such income deflation imposed on the periphery, which has been a necessary accompaniment of the accumulation of capital within the capitalist system (not just in the metropolis but even in the periphery itself) except in the brief period of dirigisme, also has the "advantage" from the point of view of capitalism that it sustains, and strengthens the prevalence of, "price-taking" behaviour. Indeed in the era of "globalization," which entails above all the "globalization" of capital, such behaviour extends even to the workers in the metropolis. This structural relationship, which entails the imposition by capitalism of income deflation upon the working people in the periphery and the related maintenance of large-scale labour reserves, *informs imperialism in all its phases.* But it has not received the attention it deserves. Let us therefore turn in the next chapter to a closer examination of it.

CHAPTER FIVE

Capitalism, Poverty, and Inequality

I

Marx and "Immiseration"

Karl Marx famously said in *Capital*: "The accumulation of wealth at one pole is, therefore, at the same time accumulation of misery, agony of toil, slavery, ignorance, brutality, mental degradation, at the opposite pole, i.e. on the side of the class that produces its own product in the form of capital" (1978:604). This passage has always been taken to mean *less* than it should have for at least three reasons, and one cannot absolve Marx entirely from the responsibility for understating the tendency towards "immiseration" under capitalism.

First, the term "misery" in this passage has been generally interpreted not necessarily as referring to the *material* deprivation of the total army of labourers available to capital; rather it has been seen in a broader, more inclusive sense, as incorporating, in the language of the passage itself, "agony of toil, slavery, ignorance, brutality," and "mental degradation." These latter afflictions no doubt are piled on the working masses by capitalism, but the suggestion has been read into the passage that capitalism does not necessarily inflict *material* deprivation upon them.

Indeed, Marx's own remark a few lines earlier, "that in proportion as capital accumulates, the lot of the labourer, *be his payment high or low*, must grow worse" (emphasis added), strengthens this perception that what capitalism causes is not necessarily growing immiseration in any material sense—i.e., in the sense of exposing the working population, taking both the active and the reserve armies of labour together, to growing material deprivation, on average, as wealth increases through accumulation; rather, capitalism causes an increase in misery only in a more general sense.

In the wake of the significant rise in real wages in the post–Second World War period in the metropolitan centres of capitalism, prolonged discussions in Marxist circles, which sought to distance Marx from any theory of "absolute immiseration," strengthened this rather broad and general interpretation of the passage. This "distancing" of Marx from any suggestion of "absolute immiseration" in the material sense may well have been a valid one, in the sense that Marx perhaps did not have any such "absolute immiseration" in mind while analyzing capitalism in his *opus, Capital*. But without doubt it arose also from a concern among Marxists, *focused almost entirely on the metropolis,* that no stigma of being "out of date" must come Marx's way, on account of the big postwar gains of the metropolitan working class. In the process, however, a deeper Marxist analysis of capitalism, going beyond the "model" of Volume I of *Capital*, which is a model of a "closed capitalism" without any colonial possessions or imperialist domination, was avoided.

This brings us to the second problem with the passage above, which consists in the fact that the industrial reserve army that Marx talks about in the part of the text from which the passage is taken refers exclusively to the reserve army located in the metropolis, in the vicinity of the capitalist sector itself. The reserve army located in the periphery does not figure in it. There is no awareness in that passage, or in Marx's entire discussion in that chapter, that the labour reserves created in the periphery through the processes of "drain" and "deindustrialization," *even when they are never drawn upon for direct use by capital* (which occurs only in the post–Second World War years, long after Marx's time), nonetheless play an essential role in the functioning of capitalism in that they serve as a source of stability for it. Marx must have been aware of these labour reserves since he wrote at length about colonialism. His plans for *Capital*, however, for reasons we need not go into here, precluded any discussion of colonialism. But for later Marxism to continue with the Volume I "model" of a "closed capitalism" meant a missed opportunity both to set things right and to deepen scientific understanding by taking a more comprehensive view of the capitalist system. At any rate the labour reserves *created* in the colonies and semi-colonies are not recognized in the passage cited.

The third problem with the passage is that the *modus operandi* of the system through which "misery" is supposed to be getting generated refers exclusively to the processes whereby capital, on the one hand, "releases" labour through technological change accompanying capital accumulation, and, on the other hand, absorbs labour on account of this same accumulation, leaving on balance a perennial reserve army of unused labour. Even if the displacement of petty producers and craftsmen in the colonies and semi-colonies owing to the encroachment of capitalist products is taken note of, the production of "misery" at one pole accompanying that of wealth at another is still seen entirely through these processes of labour displacement via competition and of labour absorption via accumulation. The question of tropical raw materials, of primary commodities extracted in increasing quantities from a given tropical landmass owing to capital accumulation, does not enter the discussion at all.

This also means that the *specificity* of the *spatial* configuration of capitalism in relation to a whole group of precapitalist producers located in a particular region does not enter the picture either. But once this aspect is taken into account, and our perception of the area of operation of capitalism is widened beyond the "closed capitalist universe" of the metropolis that Marx was concerned with in his *opus*, we get a very different picture of the relationship between capitalism and the production of mass poverty, compared to what even that remarkable passage of Marx quoted above suggests.

II

Substitution of Tropical by Temperate Foodgrains

In the absence of land-augmenting technological progress, the total output of the tropical landmass, assuming for simplicity a given level of land productivity, may be taken proximately as a given amount of foodgrains. The non-grain crops like sugar, raw cotton, and so on can be expressed in terms of foodgrain-equivalents as regard the land resources they require. As the demands from the metropolis for the products grown on this tropical landmass increase (say in terms of grain plus grain-equivalents), the availability per capita of tropical foodgrains for the noncapitalist or peasant sector decreases, *even assuming a given, nonincreasing population.* If the purchasing power of the consumers of such foodgrains in the noncapitalist sector could increase to prevent the diversion of land use towards the products demanded by the capitalist sector, then, even though there might be unrestrained inflation, these consumers would not be any worse off. (Their not being worse off is precisely what would make the inflation unrestrained.) This, however, does not happen (if anything, purchasing power in their hands declines as we know on account of income deflation). *These consumers, it follows, must be worse off as a consequence.*

The question may be asked: As long as in the temperate regions of the world, the "frontier" has not been reached (i.e., as long as there are still "empty spaces" that can be used by ousting local inhabitants), cannot the reduction in per capita foodgrain availability in the tropics (owing to the diversion of tropical land towards other commodities demanded by the metropolis), be made up by greater imports of foodgrains from the temperate regions through an increase in the latter's output? Is the imposition of income deflation on the population of the tropical lands necessary, as long as output can be expanded on temperate lands? Or, to put it in terms of the argument we have been developing, if there is a *constant* supply price for foodgrains in the temperate regions, which can be imported into the tropical countries, then even if the latter experience *increasing* supply price, why should there be any threat to the value of money?

There are at least three reasons why such a threat would still exist. First, and most obviously, the presumption underlying this argument, namely that the foodgrains produced and consumed in the tropical lands are the same as those produced in the temperate regions, has dubious validity. While rice is the predominant food crop in the tropics, it is wheat that is the main staple in the temperate regions. Secondly, there is a theoretical reason why income deflation in the tropics still remains necessary even if tropical and temperate foodgrains were identical. To see this let us in fact assume that tropical and temperate food crops are identical (but tropical food crop output must shrink to make room for the needed export crop to the metropolis). Let us also assume away transport costs since they are not germane to the present argument.

Suppose in the absence of food imports that the domestic price would have increased (because of the export of the tropical crop to the metropolis) from a base level of 100 to 120 and that at the base exchange rate, any increase in food price above 100 induces imports. The exchange rate, however, does not remain constant when the domestic food price rises. If wealth-holders expect the exchange rate to depreciate because of inflation—which, in an economy with a large weight of the agricultural sector, will be influenced significantly by movements in the foodgrain price—then they would shift from the domestic currency to gold or to the metropolitan currency. The exchange rate of the tropical currency vis-à-vis the metropolitan currency, in other words, will depreciate.

But such depreciation increases the import price of foodgrains into the tropical lands. Hence as long as there is *any* depreciation of the exchange rate in response to an initial rise in foodgrain price in the tropical country, *there will necessarily be some inflation owing to the diversion of tropical land for meeting metropolitan demands.* And since this would be a persistent inflation over time owing to the phenomenon of increasing supply price, and not a mere sporadic episode of inflation, the monetary system in the tropical country will become unsustainable for reasons we have already discussed. Income deflation to prevent persistent inflation therefore becomes necessary. This necessity, to recapitulate, arises because imports never increase instantaneously to nip inflation in the bud; rather, some price increase must first occur to induce increased imports at all; and this price increase has an effect on the exchange rate and hence the cost of imports.

If the state in the tropical country played a proactive role to nip inflation in the bud, then matters would be different. But neither the colonial state nor the neoliberal state plays such a proactive role. On the other hand, the local distribution of grains in the tropical country, including even of the imported grains, is typically controlled by a few large grain traders, who are also the prime beneficiaries of the profit inflation. They can hardly be expected to wipe out this profit inflation entirely.

Under the textbook assumption of perfect competition, they may be visualized as doing so, but this assumption itself is an utterly unreal one: typically, a limited number of traders control the business, and even though they compete against one another, this competition does not entail an absence of collusion on their part, at the very least to prevent a slide back of prices in terms of the wage unit to the initial level that had prevailed. And this fact itself keeps down imports, which means that the traders are not even saddled with any excess unwanted stocks while preventing a slide back in price to the initial level.

This situation itself can get repeated in every period, with a decline in real wages and the real incomes of producers, a decline in the per capita foodgrain absorption as a consequence of exports of tropical products to the metropolis, and a decline in the nominal exchange rate of the tropical country occurring together. But, as argued earlier, if tropical wealth-holders anticipate that such inflation is going to happen in every period, then the currency value will collapse.[1] The sheer fact of the availability of imports from the temperate regions, in other words, would not make the imposition of income deflation on the tropical population unnecessary.[2]

Thirdly, *in a regime where income deflation is already in operation*, the attempt to nip in the bud any tendency for a price rise of foodgrains owing to the diversion of land for producing the crops demanded in the metropolis is made not through larger imports, but precisely through a further intensification of income deflation. In other words, between the two alternative ways of combating inflation—namely, importing more to maintain the living standards of the working population or imposing income deflation on the working population—a regime in which income deflation is already in vogue would typically choose a continuance of the latter option.

And when such income deflation occurs, it causes absolute material deprivation among the working people in the periphery. There must, in short, be an absolute worsening of their nutritional standards, or, as some would put it, in their "nutritional poverty."

III

The Tendency Towards Absolute "Immiseration"

But what is the connection between "nutritional poverty" and general "poverty"? Some would see no necessary link between a worsening of nutritional standards and the growth of "poverty." They would accept the fact of a worsening of nutritional standards on account of the diversion of tropical land to crops needed in the metropolis, *but would stop at that*. It can, however, be argued that "nutrition" for which foodgrains are an input, directly or indirectly (the latter via processed foods and animal products, into which foodgrains enter as feedgrains), constitutes a priority for any consumer. A consumer typically wishes, as far as possible, to maintain his or her nutritional standards by diverting spending from other avenues if necessary. This is all the more true in a country where a large proportion of consumers have initial nutritional levels that are already below or just at the levels consistent with working health. A reduction in (direct and indirect) foodgrain intake therefore must necessarily be accompanied by a reduction in other expenditures in real terms, in a situation of free choice in the market. This means that if we actually observe a reduction in foodgrain intake then we can infer from it a worsening in the overall material living standard of the consumer.

Besides, even if, for argument's sake, we do not take this *strong* position that a reduction in foodgrain intake is invariably accompanied in real terms by a *reduction* in the intake of other items, but instead take a *weaker* position that a reduction in foodgrain intake is *never* accompanied by an *increase* in real terms in expenditure on any other item, even then we can conclude from an actual reduction in food intake that there must have been a vector-wise reduction in *all commodity intakes*. (In other words, if there is an observed decline in total foodgrain intake, then it must be that $a \leq b$ but $a \neq b$ where a and b are vectors denoting commodity intakes in the initial and subsequent situations.) On the basis of a decline in foodgrain availability we can argue, therefore, that there is an increase in absolute poverty in the case of a *household* (a typical decision-making unit in this realm).

It thus follows that if we find a decline in per capita food availability for a *region* or *a group* as a whole, then we can legitimately conclude on the basis of this that at least significant sections of *the working people*, i.e., leaving aside those to whom the economic surplus accrues, have become worse off.

There is strong empirical support for the proposition that increased food absorption and improved real income are monotonically related. It has been shown from household data that whenever there is an increase in command over the bundle of goods purchased in the base year, i.e., whenever the household's "real" income, calculated by deflating money income by a base-weighted (Laspeyre) price index, increases, the magnitude of foodgrains absorbed by it, *taking both direct and indirect absorption into account,* the latter through processed foods and animal products, also increases. In other words, as households become better off in terms of their command over the bundle of goods and services they were purchasing, they absorb, directly and indirectly, more foodgrains.

Quite remarkably, when taking pooled cross section and time series data for a number of *countries* over a number of years, we even find that when per capita real income (per capita money income deflated by a base-weighted price index) increases for a *country*, its per capita total (i.e., direct plus indirect) absorption of foodgrains also increases (Krishna 2013). This occurs until a very high level of per capita real income is achieved (well beyond what has ever prevailed in the periphery or prevails today), after which such absorption flattens out.

It would follow from this that a decline in foodgrain absorption cannot, unless certain peculiar parametric changes are invoked, go hand in hand with a rise in command over the base-year bundle of goods purchased. In the absence of such changes, a reduction in per capita foodgrain absorption in the periphery cannot be said to have occurred if there is a rise in per capita real income. Hence, if it *has occurred*, then, unless one can plausibly adduce such parametric changes, it must have been thrust upon the people and must have been associated with a reduction in per capita real income.

In short, a decline in per capita foodgrain absorption, if we rule out certain peculiar parametric changes, must be associated with a rise in poverty, in the sense of a reduction in per capita command over the base-year bundle of goods and services. We shall refer to this measure of poverty as "basket commanded."

The usual parametric change invoked by those who seek to dissociate the two phenomena, viz., a reduction in foodgrain absorption and an increase in poverty, is a change in tastes and preferences. They argue that a change in tastes and preferences, involving greater demand for education or healthcare, would bring about a voluntary reduction in food intake, so that every such reduction need not indicate a process of immiseration. But two points about this argument must be noted.

First, even if this argument is accepted in principle, its practical bearing, at least during the colonial period, upon the present discussion is limited, since there was very little increase in education and healthcare facilities available to the people during that period. Secondly, and more importantly, this argument is without any relevance in the present context since *ex hypothesi* the decline in per capita foodgrain output on the tropical landmass that we are talking about occurs *not in response to reduced demand from within the countries located on such landmass, but in response to increased demand for other products, producible on the same land mass, from the metropolis.* When the latter occurs, the "basket-commanded" measure of poverty *must* show an increase.

The second parametric change that can be invoked relates to product innovation. Take, for instance, the introduction of new medical drugs that are life-saving but expensive: the consumers' *choosing* to spend on such drugs *at the expense of buying foodgrains* would express itself as a spurious reduction in real income (since the price index would be spuriously inflated because of not taking cognizance of the change in the *quality* of the product, in this case drugs), and also of course as a reduction in foodgrain consumption. The reduction in foodgrain consumption would then *appear* forced, associated with an increase in the "basket-commanded" measure of poverty, while in fact it is based on consumer choice, and does not entail any decline in living standard because of the improvement in the quality of the product.

But, here again if the decline in foodgrain absorption was on account of more being spent by consumers on new drugs, which, though expensive, raise their living standards, the fall in foodgrain output for local use would have been the result of reduced demand from within rather than increased demand for products of the tropical landmass from outside. This was neither the case historically nor relevant in the context of our argument. Hence within the context of our argument, whose relevance has to be judged on its own merit, a decline in per capita foodgrain availability is *invariably* associated with a rise in the "basket-commanded" measure of poverty.

Put differently, there are two quite distinct issues here: First, does an increase in the supply of products from the fixed tropical land mass for the capitalist market entail increased immiseration of the population outside of the capitalist sector? *The answer here is unambiguously "yes."* The second issue, which is of general theoretical interest but not germane to our discussion in this book is: If a decline in foodgrain absorption is occurring in a situation of product innovation, can we say that poverty, as measured by the "basket-commanded" measure, is increasing?

To answer this second question, we have to distinguish between two different kinds of product innovation. One is what was discussed above, where a new product such as a life-saving drug, despite being more expensive, is *voluntarily chosen* by (almost) everyone over the old product. The second is where there is no such scope for voluntary choice, even as product innovation occurs, such as for instance a shift from a bazaar, consisting of petty shopkeepers, to a shopping mall, which is forced upon consumers either by state action favouring big capital (under some pretext, like the enforcement of standards of hygiene, which petty shopkeepers allegedly violate) or by the preference of a small segment of middle-class consumers having a decisive voice in the matter.

In the first case of product innovation, since the apparent rise in the price of drugs relates to two different drugs of which everyone prefers the latter, the apparent price-rise does not constitute an actual rise in price, in which case there is no decline in the size of the "basket-commanded": the two "baskets," in the initial and the subsequent situations, are not vector-wise comparable as being "more" or "less," since in one there is more food while in the other there is less food and better drugs. In other words, it is not just that the original basket of goods and services has ceased to be very meaningful, and with it the "basket-commanded" measure itself, but that the measure itself cannot give a comparison in terms of "more" or "less." From the observed decline in foodgrain absorption we cannot say that there has been a reduction in the size of the "basket-commanded." But in the second case of product innovation, where there is no expressed preference for the shopping mall over the bazaar, and people go to the former because they simply have to, as it has replaced the bazaar, the increase in price they have to pay for the "service" of retail sale amounts in effect to inflation (the quality difference between the two kinds of services not being pertinent from their point of view). In this case, we *can say* that the reduction in foodgrain absorption entails an increase in the magnitude of poverty, by the "basket-commanded" measure. In short, whether reduced foodgrain absorption in the context of product innovation constitutes an increase in the "basket-commanded" measure of poverty depends *in principle* upon whether the product innovation is imposed on consumers or conforms to their preference.

This to be sure is not easy to determine in practice. What is more, even in the case of, say, a life-saving drug becoming available, the actual price charged has a large element of monopoly rent, and the concept of people's preference itself becomes largely irrelevant because there are not enough varieties of the new drugs that they can choose from. Indeed, in recent years what may appear as an increase in drug price owing to product innovation turns out on closer examination to have been an increase caused by the removal of price controls enforced in the dirigiste period by the state upon drug firms. In other words, the increase has been a fallout of neoliberal policies, including those arising from the acceptance of the Trade-Related Intellectual Property Rights regime rather than being the result of any genuine product innovation. *And to the extent this is true, associating a decline in foodgrain absorption with an increase in the "basket-commanded" measure of poverty acquires greater generality.*

But in any case, as already mentioned, this entire discussion is not germane to our present argument when the decline in foodgrain absorption in the periphery is forced upon the people from the supply side. Even when their demand for foodgrains is also curtailed, it is because of income deflation rather than any voluntary preference for some other commodity at the latter's supply price, i.e., at a price excluding monopoly rent. (Indeed charging them a price inclusive of monopoly rent is nothing else but a means of enforcing income deflation.)

We have so far argued that the growing demand for tropical products from the capitalist sector owing to capital accumulation necessarily entails reduced per capita foodgrain absorption and growing poverty by the "basket-commanded" measure for *segments* of the working people in the periphery. It is logically conceivable however that *some* sections of the *working people* may be getting better off even while others are being squeezed. For instance, the peasants who grow the cash crops required in the metropolis, at the expense of foodgrains on the tropical landmass, could witness an improvement in their living standards (including an increase in food intake, which, however, has the effect of only making the condition of the others even worse.)

But in a situation of massive labour reserves, *unless the peasants happen to own their land*, they are unlikely to witness any improvement in their living standard. The landlords can always lease out their land to those waiting in the wings (i.e., to those who are part of the labour reserves), especially in a situation where the latter are becoming worse off owing to reduced food availability, to prevent peasants who happen to be their current lessees from becoming better off as a result of the switch to cash crops. *In other words, just as the labour reserves keep down the wage rate in the periphery, they also keep down peasant-tenants' incomes.* It follows from this that the working people *as a whole* would become worse off by the "basket-commanded" measure in a vector-wise sense (with nobody among them becoming better off while some become worse off), as a consequence of the growing demand of the metropolis for the commodities produced by the tropical landmass.

To say this is not to suggest that there has been no improvement in all these years in the living standards of the people in the periphery, when capital accumulation has occurred in the metropolis. *The increase in poverty we are arguing to be a consequence of capital accumulation is in terms of nutritional poverty, and also in terms of the basket-commanded measure.* It is in other words an increase in poverty in a very specific sense. At the same time, however, there has been an improvement in people's living standards owing to the sheer availability of new life-saving drugs, such as penicillin and antibiotics: such drugs, and greater awareness of hygiene and health matters, have brought down infant and maternal mortality rates and increased life-expectancy, so that we cannot say that the people in the periphery today are in the same abysmal state of living as they were half a century ago. But our point is that there has been, as we shall show in detail later, a reduction in per capita foodgrain availability, and hence in the "basket-commanded" measure of poverty, which is not due to such innovations, but which has been a necessary fallout of the process of capital accumulation within the capitalist sector of the world.

IV

Poverty and Inequality

To sum up, in addition to Marx's point in the passage cited earlier relating to capitalism's production of wealth at one pole and misery at another, which concerned the active and reserve armies of labour *within* the capitalist sector, there is a further and far more serious process of production of poverty under this system. This poverty[3] is produced in the periphery; it afflicts the working people in the periphery; *and the "spontaneous" tendency of capitalism is to keep aggravating it in abso-lute terms over time as a consequence of capital accumulation.* The proposition about absolute immiseration, repudiated by Marxist theo-rists because of its obvious unrealism in the context of capitalism in the advanced countries, is quite apposite (as a "spontaneous" tendency of capitalism that was briefly arrested and even reversed under postwar dirigisme) in the context of the periphery, where the working people are consumers of the products of the tropical landmass.

We have, to be sure, assumed above that the output from the trop-ical landmass is given and derived our conclusion about increasing im-miseration from that assumption. In fact, there could be some increase in tropical output occurring over time, even without entailing in any significant sense the problem of increasing supply price. We have in like manner, however, also assumed a constant population among whom the tropical output, minus what is sent out to the capitalist sector, is distributed. This, too, has to be relaxed for a realistic understanding of the effects of capitalism in the periphery. But the crux of the immis-eration argument, though ensconced in empirical complexities, is as stated above.

This immiseration, to recapitulate, arises because of the decline in the output of foodgrains that can be accessed by the people in the periphery. If income deflation is strong, i.e., if the compression in their demand is strong, then the availability of foodgrains to the people in the periphery may fall even below what the per capita output could sustain, but that only means a worse poverty scenario than warranted by the decline in per capita output. Nonetheless, immiseration *per se* follows from the decline in per capita output.

If there is such a decline, then *there must be an increase in income inequality as well.* With a tendency towards absolute immiseration among the working people as a whole, the real wages of the workers proper within the periphery can hardly be expected to increase; at the most, they would remain fixed at some bare subsistence level. If we di-vide the entire universe of the periphery between the working people, consisting of the petty producers and of the rural and urban workers on the one side, and the "others" on the opposite side, then quite ob-viously the per capita real income difference between these two groups must increase over time.

But while this is undeniable, there are two possible scenarios here that are of interest. In the first scenario the real wages of the advanced country workers are dissociated from those of the periphery, which is what happened over much of the history of capitalism. This is because capital *does not* move freely from the metropolis to the periphery (except to "enclaves" like plantations and mines), while labour *cannot* move freely from the periphery to the metropolis. Labour can move within the periphery, or, in geographical terms, within the tropical region, at the behest of capital; but it is not free to move from the tropical region to the temperate region that constitutes the geographical heart of capitalism (Lewis 1979). In addition to these two types of immobility, however, there is a further immobility, namely, of manufactured goods produced by newly emerging capitalists within the periphery with the help of cheap local labour, which could potentially out-compete the production within the metropolis using the same technology but more expensive labour. The production of such goods is either discouraged by colonial governments and the general ethos of the colonial economy (Bagchi 1970); or such goods are simply not allowed into the metropolis except at very high rates of tariff (Dutt 1963; Lewis 1978).

In conditions of such immobility, where the world economy is segmented and workers in the metropolis are insulated against the restraining effect on their real wages by the massive labour reserves of the periphery, the growing inequality takes the form of an increasing distance between the metropolis and the periphery. This, as already mentioned, is what happened over much of actual history; and traditional theories of development-underdevelopment are concerned with this. (The surplus earners of the periphery can be put along with those of the metropolis for the purpose of this discussion.)

Contemporary globalization however breaks down such immobilities. Capital is more freely mobile across the "north-south" divide now than ever before, even if labour still is not. But along with the mobility of capital, we also have greater access in the metropolitan markets for manufactured goods and services produced in the periphery (which is an important reason for the mobility of capital in any case, since it locates production in low-wage economies for exporting to the metropolitan countries). The metropolitan workers' wages in this scenario get closely tied to those of the workers in the periphery, at least in the sense that despite being different, they no longer tend to diverge secularly. The growing inequality in this case is no longer between two geographical segments of the world economy but between surplus earners in both the metropolis and the periphery on the one side, and the workers in both the metropolis and the periphery on the other. We have in short not a spatial division but one between the capitalists and the "workers" (including the working people in the periphery) within the world economy.

But no matter whether the division is between regions or classes, the growing gap between them is because of the existence of massive labour reserves in the periphery, which, in turn, are linked to the process of getting tropical products for metropolitan requirements without undermining the value of money in the metropolis. It is ironic therefore that the phenomenon of imperialism is denied on the grounds of an obliteration of the spatial distinction and its replacement by class categories, *when underlying these class categories themselves is the reality of imperialism.*

V

Ex Ante Underconsumption in the World Economy

There is, however, an important difference between the one case, where the growing inequality refers to regions, i.e., is between the capitalist metropolis and the periphery, and the other, where it relates to the inequality between the working people the world over on the one side and the surplus earners the world over on the other.

In the former case the share of wages of the workers in the value added in the metropolis remains more or less constant, as many argue was the case between the late nineteenth century and the Second World War and even into the postwar period. The product wages of the workers in the metropolis, in other words, increase more or less in tandem with labour productivity. This acts to keep up the level of aggregate demand in the metropolis and to keep any tendency towards underconsumption at bay.

An *ex ante* tendency towards underconsumption arises, however, if the share of profits in value added has an upward trend. Since the "propensity to consume" (to resort to a much-used Keynesian term) out of wages is higher than out of profit, such an upward trend implies that there is an *ex ante* tendency for the weighted average of the two propensities to consume, from wages and profits, to come down, i.e., for the *ex ante* share of consumption in total income to come down. Unless there is an increase in the magnitude of investment expenditure as a proportion of output to offset this *ex ante* tendency, for which there is no reason whatsoever, such a reduction in the weighted average propensity to consume entails a secular tendency for the level of actual income to reduce relative to the potential income, i.e., a secular tendency towards growing unutilized capacity and unemployment. Growing unutilized capacity in turn would bring down investment expenditures further, and growing unemployment would reduce the share of wages further, compounding the problem and pushing capitalism into deeper crisis. This no doubt is an *ex ante* tendency whose realization may be prevented by other factors, such as military expenditure by the metropolitan states or by the leading metropolitan State (as postwar U.S. military expenditure had done according to Baran and Sweezy [1966]). Nonetheless a tendency towards underconsumption poses a serious threat to the system under these circumstances.

But of course if the share of wages in the metropolis remains more or less unchanged, there is no reason for such a tendency to develop (though there may still be problems of inadequate aggregate demand arising from time to time for other reasons, such as the collapse of particular exogenous stimuli that might have sustained investment earlier). Indeed, Joan Robinson (1963) argues that one of the factors keeping the tendency towards underconsumption at bay in metropolitan capitalism over a long period, against the prognostications of Rosa Luxemburg, was the rise in (product) wages in tandem with labour productivity.

But we are in a situation, within the regime of globalization, in which the mobility of capital links the metropolitan wage rates to those prevailing in the periphery and the vector of world real or product wages (let us not worry about the distinction for the moment) does not show any upward trend because of the existence of the vast labour reserves in the periphery. Hence, the rise in world labour productivity raises the share of surplus in world output and thereby unleashes a tendency towards underconsumption. This tendency encompasses the world economy as a whole including the metropolitan capitalist economies (P. Patnaik 2011a).

Again, within the regime of globalization, where the hegemony of international finance capital that characterizes such a regime typically entails a restriction on government expenditure, the chief instrument that remains available for keeping such a tendency at bay is *credit-financed* private expenditure. And since there are limits to which such credit-finance would be forthcoming except against assets, what really counts for boosting expenditure is the credit-finance available against assets.

But here a peculiar problem arises. If the prices of assets remain unchanged, then with a reduction in the share of wages, the credit-finance relative to the base value of assets must *increase* to prevent the realization of the *ex ante* tendency towards underconsumption. For instance, let the base value of assets be K, the output-capital ratio be β (at some "normal" level of capacity utilization), the share of wages be α to start with, and investment be b.K; and let the entire β.K output be realized in the base period. And let us assume that all wages are consumed but only a part c of surplus is consumed as a matter of course.

Now, suppose the share of wages falls to α'. If the tendency towards deficient demand on account of this fall is to be prevented, i.e., if demand has to be kept up so as to realize output β.K as before, then noninvestment expenditure must rise by β.K (α-α')(1-c), i.e., by a proportion β.(α-α') (1-c) of the base value of the capital stock, which has to be financed by credit expansion. As α' falls, the net credit expansion (apart from repayment) needs to rise as a proportion of the base value of capital stock to keep up aggregate demand.

In capitalist conditions such an increase in net credit-finance relative to the value of assets cannot be expected to occur (we are not considering here the various layers of intermediation). Credit-financed expenditure for boosting aggregate demand therefore requires an increase in the value of assets, i.e., the formation of "bubbles" on the asset markets. *Thwarting the tendency towards underconsumption under a regime of globalization therefore necessarily requires the formation of "bubbles."* But with the bursting of such "bubbles," the capitalist sector plunges into a severe crisis when the implications of rising global inequalities stand clearly exposed. The sector may emerge out of such a crisis through the formation of a new "bubble," but even when that happens, it constitutes only the prelude to a further severe crisis that must follow. The rising global inequality, in short, is bringing capitalism to a denouement the like of which it has never encountered in its entire history.

CHAPTER SIX

Further Elaborations
and Clarifications

THE ARGUMENT of the foregoing chapters has been that increasing supplies of tropical products for use within the capitalist sector can be obtained only at an increasing supply price, which poses a threat to the value of money within this sector. This threat is met by diverting the already produced output of such goods from existing users outside of the capitalist sector to those within the sector. The means for such diversion, which obviates any need for larger production and hence any prospects of increasing supply price, constitute the essence of imperialism. Additionally, imperialism also generates and maintains a pool of unemployed labour within the periphery, which serves to thwart any autonomous cost-push in the case of tropical commodities required by the capitalist sector, and serves in general to stabilize the system.

I

The Low Weight of Tropical Commodities

The most obvious criticism that will be leveled against this argument is that within the capitalist sector, the weight of tropical goods in the total gross value of output, or even in the total value of consumption, is so small that the belief that a rise in the prices of such goods because of increasing supply price (at a given money wage rate) would pose a threat to the value of money in the capitalist sector is extremely far-fetched. The rise in the prices of final goods produced in the metropolis would hardly be much affected by the rise in prices of tropical goods; and even the money wage demand from the workers in the metropolis is hardly likely to be much influenced by the prices of such goods, given their low weight in consumption. Hence the inflationary consequences for metropolitan goods of a rise in prices of tropical goods are quite negligible.

As regards the rise in prices of the tropical goods themselves, rather than of metropolitan goods into whose production they enter either as current inputs or as "labour-feeding inputs" (to use Francis Seton's [1957] expressive phrase), making them a favoured form of wealth-holding compared to money or money-denominated assets in the metropolis, the following counter-argument can be easily made.

Since these goods, like all goods, have high carrying costs, one cannot plausibly conceive their taking the place of money or money-denominated assets except in cases of extreme inflation, which we have no reason to postulate, especially in view of the large unemployment in the periphery (which would prevent money wages in the periphery from adjusting to these prices). And if it is argued, as we argued earlier, that wealth-holders would switch not to commodities directly but to gold, since gold has a low carrying cost and gold prices are generally expected to move in tandem with commodity prices, then the riposte can be easily made: "Yes, gold prices do move in tandem with commodity prices, *but not necessarily these commodity prices.*"

Hence, unless the rise in *these* commodity prices generates a general inflation in all commodity prices, there is no reason why metropolitan wealth-holders would move to gold from money or money-denominated assets. And since we have just seen that the low weight of these commodities ensures that a rise in their prices would not cause, or even be expected to cause, a general inflation, metropolitan wealth-holders will not actually move to gold. The entire argument presented above then seems to have been built upon foundations that, even if they had substance earlier when the weight of these commodities in the gross value of metropolitan output was larger, are flimsy at present.

A distinction needs to be drawn here between the importance of tropical commodities as *use values* in the metropolis and their importance in terms of *exchange value*. Harry Magdoff's (1966) argument that even though the weight of raw materials in the gross value of manufacturing output in the metropolis is small, there simply can be no manufacturing without raw materials, draws precisely this distinction: raw materials as use values are indispensable to the metropolis, no matter how small their weight in terms of exchange value. Exactly the same can be said of all tropical products. The metropolis simply cannot do without them, no matter how small their weight in the gross value of output or the value of consumption in the metropolis (on this more later).

This low weight is reflective of *social relations.* In fact, the reason for the negligible weight of tropical products in the gross value of output in the metropolis lies in imperialism itself, which shifts terms of trade against the primary producers located on the tropical landmass and engaged in producing these commodities (P. Patnaik 1997). But while this point may be conceded, it would still be argued that *given the fact of low weight of tropical products in gross value of output in the metropolis,* imperialism ceases to have any *contemporary* relevance. In the *past,* when imperialism took the form of colonialism, it might have been responsible for reducing the weight of the value of tropical commodities, whether as current inputs or as "labour-feeding inputs" in the gross value of output in the metropolis. But this very low weight robs it of its relevance in today's context, at least in terms of the argument presented in this book.

This counterargument against our position, however, is invalid for two reasons, one obvious and the other not so obvious. The obvious point is that since the low weight of the value of tropical products, used as current and "labour-feeding" inputs, in the gross value of output in the metropolis is a reflection of a social relation, *maintaining this low weight requires a perpetuation of this social relation, i.e., a perpetuation of the dominance that characterizes imperialism.* The low weight in short, instead of being an argument against the existence of imperialism, must be seen as something that reflects imperialism as a perennial phenomenon. If the entire network of imperialist relationships, including a vast reserve army of labour in the periphery, did not exist, then it *could have been possible* for the tropical producers to charge higher prices for their products and increase the relative weight of these products in value terms in the gross value of metropolitan output; or, if this was resisted, then to cause accelerating inflation without any upper bound, arising from the autonomous tropical-product-price-push. This latter would have undermined the value of money in the metropolis.

The less obvious answer is the following. Even if we assume that because of the low weight of tropical products, a rise in their prices will not have much impact on those of metropolitan goods, and also that metropolitan wealth-holders will not shift to other forms of wealth-holding in lieu of the money of the metropolis, a rise in these products' prices, owing to their being subject to the phenomenon of increasing supply price, still poses a problem. A rise in such products' prices, even when they do not cause much inflation in the metropolis, certainly causes high inflation within the periphery itself, where their total weight among commodities is high. *The wealth-holders in the periphery therefore would shift to other forms of holding wealth in lieu of money of the periphery*; indeed, as we have already seen, the monetary system of the periphery would become untenable in such a case.

Even if the metropolitan currency does not collapse, the universe within which metropolitan capitalism operates will become untenable *owing to the collapse of the periphery's currency.* Trade between the metropolis and the periphery, for instance, will not be viable if the latter's currency—and hence the latter's labour-power, which is paid in terms of this currency—has zero value in terms of the former. To prevent such a denouement, such a collapse in the periphery's currency, income deflation will have to be imposed on the working population of the periphery itself. This, as we have been arguing, is an important constitutive element of imperialism.

It follows therefore that if the system within which metropolitan capitalism operates, which includes obtaining tropical products that are not producible within the core itself, is to be tenable, then the value of the currency of the periphery cannot fall to zero relative to the currency of the metropolis. But if it cannot be allowed to fall to zero—i.e., some lower bound to its relative value vis-à-vis the currency of the metropolis must be enforced—then a rise in tropical product prices would pose a threat to the value of the metropolitan currency as well.

In either case, it therefore becomes necessary to avoid a rise in tropical product prices, and thus it becomes necessary that the phenomenon of increasing supply price must not be allowed to manifest itself. In short, an income deflation becomes necessary; and the weight of value of tropical products entering as current and "labour-feeding" inputs into the gross value of metropolitan output is irrelevant to this argument.

II

Some General Theoretical Propositions

The basic theoretical point underlying our argument is simple, though, strangely enough, it has not been made in economics. This point can be stated in the form of two propositions. The first of these propositions is: *if there is a commodity that is in fixed supply in an economy that is otherwise nonstationary, then no other commodity except this commodity itself, if it has negligible carrying cost (or another commodity that has negligible carrying cost and whose relative price vis-à-vis this commodity, is generally believed, for whatever reason, rightly or wrongly, to remain invariant), can possibly function as money under the usual rules of market exchange, i.e., in the absence of constrained choices (or rationing equilibria).*

The fact that such an economy is doomed to reach a stationary state has been known since the days of David Ricardo, who of course postulated "diminishing returns" rather than the more stringent assumption of a fixed supply (but the difference is immaterial for the present purpose). And the Von Neumann rate of maximal balanced growth in such an economy is zero. But the point is that even while making a traverse to the stationary state, no other commodity can possibly act as a store of value, which is the primary function of money even when it is being used as a mere medium of circulation.

The obvious conclusion that follows from this and has been discussed at length earlier is that under the usual rules of market exchange, a modern credit money economy is incompatible with the existence of any commodity that has negligible carrying cost and is fixed in supply, or subject to increasing supply price at given money wages (for the Ricardian reasons of "diminishing returns").

But something far more important also follows from this, namely, that even an economy with commodity money, including gold-money, is incompatible, under the usual rules of market exchange, with the existence of such a commodity (which, to repeat, is fixed in supply and has negligible carrying cost). This is because while both gold as well as the commodity in fixed supply *ex hypothesi* have negligible carrying costs, the latter will drive gold, which itself is not in fixed supply in the same way, from becoming a form of wealth-holding, in the sense that under the usual rules of market exchange, there will be no stable equilibrium in such an economy where wealth will be held in the form of gold.

But this is not all. If gold itself happens to be the commodity subject either to fixity of supply or to Ricardian "diminishing returns," then it would restrict the scope for other commodities, such as factories, houses, and the like, to become forms of wealth-holding. And the same would be true if it is not gold but some other commodity that happens to be in fixed supply and has negligible carrying cost: the expected rate of increase in the price of such a commodity would put a floor to the "own rate of interest" (i.e., the rate of return less the risk premium less the carrying cost, all measured in terms of the asset itself) that an asset must earn for it to be a form of wealth-holding.

It may be thought that if gold as a commodity is in fixed supply or subject to diminishing returns, then paper money that is convertible to gold can always be used to augment the supply of money consisting of gold and the gold-substitute paper. But in such a case it would be difficult to maintain the convertibility of paper money to gold, especially if there is also some other commodity, apart from gold, that has both fixity of supply and low carrying cost.

This brings us to the second proposition, namely that not only is it impossible for an economy where there is fixity in supply of some commodity that also has low carrying cost, to have any other commodity acting as money, but that *this commodity itself, while making it impossible for any other commodity to act as money, would put a constraint on wealth-holders also holding "non-money assets."*[1]

And what is more, even when non-money assets are held, the equilibrium, with wealth-holders holding their wealth both in the form of this commodity and also a range of produced goods with nonincreasing supply price, will be an unstable one. Any deviation in favour of this commodity, i.e., what would constitute an increase in "liquidity preference" in such a world, would cause a cumulative deviation that would drive out other forms of wealth-holding, because it would push up, and keep pushing up, the relative price of this commodity vis-à-vis the other "non-money" commodities in terms of which wealth is also held.

We have so far been talking about a commodity that is subject to increasing supply price and also has low carrying cost. But the argument of the previous paragraph suggests a stronger conclusion. Suppose the commodity that is subject to increasing supply price *has some positive carrying cost*. And suppose there is a rise in its price. *Some* wealth-holders would estimate its expected price appreciation to exceed its carrying cost and hence to move to this commodity. This fact would raise its current price further and induce *some more* wealth-holders move to this commodity, and so on. It follows, therefore, that *even* if the commodity that is fixed in supply, or subject to increasing supply price, *has positive carrying cost*, it would still make a monetary economy, in which some other commodity acts as money and constitutes a form of wealth-holding, impossible; and it cannot itself act as money without making the holding of wealth in other assets untenable. In short, a capitalist economy in which the normal rules of market exchange prevail becomes untenable if there is any commodity subject to increasing supply price. This is what we have been arguing.

Put differently, a capitalist economy with fixity of supply (or increasing supply price) of some commodity not only grinds towards a stationary state, as economic theory has held all these years, but is fundamentally unviable under the usual rules of market exchange. Capitalism is preeminently a money-using economy, and if no viable money can function in such an economy, then the system itself becomes unviable. And this would necessarily happen because the fixed-supply commodity can neither permit any other commodity to function as money nor itself function fruitfully as money, i.e., without putting constraints on the holding of other assets.

Since we know that capitalist economies have functioned for a long time despite having commodities that are in fixed supply or are subject to increasing supply price (of which minerals, including above all oil, are one obvious example, and the mass of products from the fixed tropical landmass are another), the question naturally arises: How has this been possible? And the answer lies simply in the fact that the usual rules of market exchange have not been followed. But they have been by-passed not in the sense that rationing equilibria and constraints on asset choices have been the norm under capitalism, but in a very different sense: namely, through the exercise of coercion in the form of imperialism, whose economic content, in the form of income deflation, etc., has been explored in earlier chapters. Capitalism is supposed to be based on the rules of market exchange; but if capitalism were based merely on the rules of market exchange, indeed any set of rules of market exchange, it would be an impossibility. Capitalism without imperialism is an impossibility.

III

Lenin, Luxemburg, and Imperialism

Much discussion has taken place in economics on the exact rules of market exchange. A contrast for instance has been drawn between the classical notion of "free competition," which entails an equalization of the rate of profit and the wage rate (for homogeneous labour) across sectors through the free mobility of capital and labour respectively, and the subsequently developed concept of "perfect competition," which entails not only equal wages and rates of profit across sectors, but *zero profits*. Perfect competition with zero profits can obtain only if in addition to the free mobility of labour and capital across sectors, there is also free entry into the ranks of the capitalists in case they earn positive profits; and such entry can only be from the ranks of the workers. Perfect competition, therefore, is based on the assumption of perfect social mobility, and hence the nonexistence of any class distinctions in society—a proposition that classical political economy had rejected.

These distinctions are important, as is Sraffa's (1960) revival of the classical notion of the natural price, if only to underscore the point that the distribution of output between the workers and the capitalists is determined socially by the balance of class forces, which is outside of the sphere of demand and supply, rather than through the full employment marginal products as neoclassical economics suggests.

But all these strands of theory still look upon capitalism as a self-contained, isolated system, rather than as a system set in the midst of precapitalist petty producers with whom it interacts and from whom it must obtain supplies of goods that it needs, and in growing quantities as it accumulates capital, at nonincreasing prices. Because economics does not look at capitalism as it has really existed, it has also not come to terms with the fact that obtaining goods at nonincreasing prices from petty producers located on the tropical landmass, *whose products are not producible within the capitalist sector that has grown up in the temperate region of the world*, is simply not possible under the normal rules of market exchange. It has therefore not accepted the fact that capitalism is unsustainable under the normal rules of exchange. It requires coercion to be exerted on this outside world, a coercion that we call "imperialism."

Imperialism, in short, is a coercive relationship exercised by the capitalist sector on the "outside" world to ensure, first, that it obtains the products that it needs from this "outside" world and second, that it does so at nonincreasing prices. This conception of imperialism, it should be noted, does not refer to the mere fact of imposition of the usual rules of exchange upon precapitalist producers. As Rosa Luxemburg (1963) emphasized, dragging these producers into an exchange relationship with capitalism itself involves breaking down their natural economy, which cannot occur without coercion. But even after they have been drawn into commerce with capitalism, such commerce under the usual rules of market exchange—no matter how we define these rules, in classical or neoclassical manner—is not enough for the viability of the system. A further continuous exercise of coercion is needed to ensure that the goods of such petty producers are obtained at nonincreasing prices.

The fact that imperialism is thus absolutely essential for capitalism, because, without it, capitalism would face increasing prices for these "outside" products, which would make the system unviable by undermining the value of money, has not been recognized until now by any strand of economics. Strands outside of the Marxist tradition generally ignore imperialism; and strands within the Marxist tradition, while accepting imperialism as a phenomenon linked to capitalism, provide other explanations for it, because Marx himself did not place much credence either on diminishing returns à la Ricardo or on fixity of supply of tropical or any other products. His concern was more with technological progress raising the capital-output ratio *in general* over time, from which he derived his falling tendency of the rate of profit for a given distribution of income between wages and profits; but he did not take seriously any tendency for a rise in the capital-output ratio over time, and hence for a fall in the rate of profit, *because of Ricardian diminishing returns.*

While a few economists outside of the Marxist tradition have recognized the phenomenon of imperialism, they have not seen it as having anything to do with capitalism. Schumpeter (1951) is a prime example. He saw imperialism not as being essential for capitalism but as the product of a precapitalist "superstructure" that persists into capitalism. He did not see any logical flaws in the analysis of capitalism advanced by Walras, even as he superimposed his own theory of innovations upon Walras's analysis; consequently, he did not see any necessity under capitalism, for the viability of its economy, to take recourse to imperialism.

Within the Marxist tradition imperialism has been seen as being organically linked to capitalism. Rosa Luxemburg (1963) saw accumulation as being impossible without capitalism's interaction with the surrounding precapitalist sector, but except in stray passages suggesting otherwise, she saw such interaction as a destruction and assimilation of the precapitalist sector by capitalism, which of course reaches a limit when the entire world is under the exclusive domination of capitalism and hence accumulation becomes impossible. While Luxemburg has been hailed as a precursor of the theory of aggregate demand that came into the forefront with the "Keynesian Revolution," and consequently also of the theory of the necessity of exogenous stimuli, outside of "multiplier-accelerator" type mechanisms, for sustaining growth under the capitalist system (both of these ideas were later developed by Michal Kalecki [1954]), her theory, notwithstanding its tremendous insights, provides a shaky basis for a theory of imperialism as an *abiding relationship under capitalism.*

For a start, it detaches imperialism from any spatial location. The destruction and assimilation of the precapitalist sector is a universal phenomenon, relating, as she said, to sociology rather than to geography. Besides, because of her emphasis on the "realization" question (even though in discussing accumulation she talks about capitalism's need for raw materials, wage goods, and labour power from the precapitalist sector), the fact that the capitalist state can take on the role of providing demand (as Keynes later suggested), making imperialism as she saw it unnecessary, weakens her theory of imperialism.[2]

There is no doubt that encroaching on precapitalist markets kills several birds with one stone for capitalism: it provides a source of demand and keeps accumulation going (the very fact of such accumulation however entails *ex post* that this source of demand is not *actually* much tapped [P. Patnaik 1972], but let us leave that aside), even while by the same act of encroachment it also ensures supplies of raw materials, wage goods, and labour power for itself. The provision of demand by the state by contrast does not simultaneously release any raw materials, wage goods, and labour power. Encroaching on precapitalist markets is therefore more favourable for capitalism than having the state undertake "demand management." But her *theoretical* emphasis on the demand issue alone pushes this aspect to the background.

Lenin's (1977) theory of imperialism on the other hand was meant to explain the conjuncture of the First World War and the immediate postwar years and to provide the theoretical background to his call for a world revolution. Even though he recognized the *spatial* nature of imperialism by referring to it as a "world system of colonial oppression and financial strangulation of the overwhelming majority of the population of the world by *a handful of 'advanced countries'*" (Lenin [1977], 637; emphasis added), his confining the use of the term "imperialism" only to the monopoly phase of capitalism meant that this system of *spatial* exploitation in its historical entirety remained untheorized by him, and consequently by the communist movement as a whole. Colonialism of course was very much a part of the communist discourse but there was no communist theory of colonialism, let alone a communist theory of imperialism *inclusive of the colonial phase.*

A second feature of Lenin's theory of imperialism, which is not often recognized, is that it was not a functional theory. Imperialism was not "explained" in any way as being functionally necessary for capitalism, as in the case of Rosa Luxemburg. It was simply the expression of rivalry among monopoly combines in an era when capitalism had become characterized by monopoly combines and when competition among capitals had taken the form, consequently, of global rivalry for "economic territory." Hence imperialism was just the outgrowth of capitalism; *it was monopoly capitalism*—a proposition that his contemporaries like Karl Kautsky found so difficult to understand. They were looking for a functional theory of imperialism, a theory that would explain it as being in some sense "necessary" for capitalism, fulfilling some specific role without which capitalism would be in the doldrums.

But such a perception, of imperialism being the outgrowth of capitalism, though it was pertinent for the monopoly phase when there was close *personal union* among big financiers, large industrialists, and the state, could not be used for explaining colonialism, for that, as Lenin's own discussion suggested, corresponded to the period of free competition. Hence the entire phenomenon of colonialism did not get properly theoretically comprehended in the communist tradition that took off from Lenin. Correspondingly there was also no theory that covered both the "colonial" and "imperial" periods and could explain why capitalism *universally* engaged in this *spatial* exploitation. As the nation-based finance capitals became transformed into international finance capital, the absence of such a theory created scope for the question: Does imperialism as a *spatial category* remain relevant in the era of globalization?

The answer to this question requires in our view a theory of imperialism as a system of *spatial exploitation*. Such a theoretical perception cannot of course constitute the totality of the theory of imperialism; but it needs to be embedded within any overarching discussion of imperialism. This is what we have attempted to provide in this book. It is not an alternative to the ideas of Lenin or Luxemburg or the many other authors who have discussed imperialism, but something that remains valid in every phase of capitalism, whether free competition or monopoly, *no matter what else can also be said about colonialism or imperialism.*

IV

The Contrast Between Colonialism and Contemporary Globalization

There are nonetheless important differences between the colonial regime and what prevails now over much of the periphery. The two situations we are contrasting should be clearly distinguished. They do not correspond to the distinction between free competition and monopoly, since our argument has been that notwithstanding the other important differences between these two phases that Lenin highlighted, *in the matter of obtaining tropical primary products from the periphery at the expense of local absorption of such products, they scarcely differ.*

Likewise the distinction we are making cannot be reduced to one between colonialism and imperialism, since we use the term "imperialism" in an inclusive sense such that the colonial period is part of imperialism; we can scarcely therefore treat colonialism and imperialism as separate categories.

Our distinction is between two periods during each of which capital was juridically free to move all over the globe (even though in actual fact it may not have moved around freely). And the distinction between these two periods, which had this common feature that the periphery was open to capital inflows (and hence outflows as well), consists in the fact that during the first, the metropolis directly controlled the periphery through a colonial or semi-colonial state, while during the second the periphery had been formally politically decolonized but was in thralldom to global capital. By focusing upon these two periods, *which are not contiguous*, we leave out of account the period of the immediate post-decolonization dirigisme, which was altogether *sui generis* and which meant a release of sorts from the stranglehold of imperialism. *We are thus in effect comparing two periods of imperialist dominance over the periphery, one before decolonization, and the other after the overthrow of third world dirigisme.*

Now, one important difference has already been discussed, namely, the breakdown of the segmentation of the world economy because of which advanced-country wages get restrained by the existence of the massive third world labour reserves. This breakdown of segmentation in turn arises from the fact that although capital was juridically free to move to the periphery even earlier, it hardly did so except to sectors like mines and plantations (Nurkse 1954); it did not move to sectors where it could have used the low-wage workers of the periphery to produce for the world market the same goods that it was producing in the metropolis.

One consequence of this breakdown of segmentation, which has also been noted, is the tendency towards global underconsumption, which manifests itself in a secular tendency towards crisis and stagnation in the world economy, especially in the metropolitan economies. A second consequence, which has also been noted earlier, is that insofar as "spontaneous" income deflation arises from the fact that the purchasing power in the hands of the working people does not grow rapidly enough because growing income inequalities create demand for goods that are not particularly employment-intensive, such "spontaneous" income deflation now affects the workers both in the metropolis and the periphery. It ceases to be a specific burden imposed on the workers and peasants in the periphery and instead comes to be generalized to the working people of the world as a whole.

A second difference between the two periods is even more important. In the colonial period, not only did income deflation imposed on the working people in the periphery keep down the local absorption of tropical commodities, but the mode of imposing such income deflation was to a large extent through the colonial tax system, which also meant that *such commodities were obtained gratis by the metropolis.* In the recent period of globalization, while income deflation is imposed likewise through taxation and "austerity" measures of the state, since the state is not a colonial one, the metropolis does not get such commodities *gratis.*

This has an important implication. A hallmark of the capitalist world economy has always been the following: the "leader" of the capitalist world "permits" a current account deficit against itself by its rivals, including the newly emerging capitalist economies of the time, so that their ambitions are accommodated within the system, which is thereby kept going (P. Patnaik 2006). If the leading capitalist economy resorted to protectionist measures in order to insulate its own market against the goods emanating from its rivals and from newly emerging economies, both for domestic employment and for balance of payments reasons, then the international monetary system would become unviable, pushing the world capitalist economy into a crisis marked by generalized protectionism. Not surprisingly, Britain, the former leader of the capitalist world, maintained a current account deficit vis-à-vis continental Europe and the United States in the late nineteenth and early twentieth centuries when these economies were industrializing rapidly (Saul 1970); and the United States, the present leader of the capitalist world, is doing the same today vis-à-vis Germany and East Asia.

Of course, the reason for such a current account deficit lies in the fact that the newly emerging economies have lower unit costs of production than the leading economy. This, in the case of Britain, used to be attributed to lower productivity for more or less similar wages, owing the so-called "penalty of the early start" (which saddled Britain with a large body of relatively old equipment), and in the case of the United States today is attributed to higher wages for more or less similar productivity. The point, however, is not the reason for the current deficit of the leading economy vis-à-vis its rivals and emerging economies; the point is that given these reasons, and hence the current deficit, within a regime of more or less "free trade" and free capital movements, overcoming this deficit through protectionism by the leader destroys this regime with deleterious consequences for world capitalism as a whole.

But then how can the leader meet such a deficit? In the colonial period, Britain met this deficit by taking away the export surplus earnings of the colonies *gratis*. In fact, the surplus it took away was larger than what was required to meet its total current deficit vis-à-vis its rivals and emerging economies of the time, because of which Britain actually made substantial capital exports to these economies. What is more, *not only was this the case in general, but even in individual years the surplus extracted appears to have been calibrated.*

In the case of colonial India, for instance, there was always a merchandise and current account surplus vis-à-vis the rest of the world (mainly with Britain's rivals, the late industrializing countries and the "newly emerging economies"), a surplus that came to be the second largest globally after that of the United States. There was always a current account deficit vis-à-vis Britain owing *inter alia* to explicit invisible items of drain of wealth like the so-called "Home Charges" and earnings from the monopoly that Britain instituted in shipping and insuring Indian goods, in addition to the deindustrializing British net exports to India. These two—the export surplus earnings of the colony and the mainly administered invisible liabilities it had vis-à-vis the colonizing economy—miraculously always balanced themselves over any stretch of time! India's merchandise export surplus *to the world as a whole* always appeared to match or marginally fall short of India's net invisible imports vis-à-vis Britain (including explicit government administered "drain" items like the "Home Charges"), so that on the eve of the Second World War, there was only a small amount of net debt against India.

It appears therefore that whatever India's export surplus happened to be with Britain's rivals and "emerging economies," it simply magically disappeared into thin air without benefiting India. And even variations in this surplus from one period to the next left no palpable mark (except in years of a very sharp drop, when a small debt was contracted by India).

This matter is discussed at greater length in a later chapter, but the basic point here is that Britain could maintain its leadership role, which called for running a current account deficit with rivals and "emerging economies," because it used for the purpose what it earned through its "deindustrializing exports" to the colonies and what it appropriated *gratis* from the colonies' export surplus to the world.

Today, in the case of the United States, matters are different. The United States also has to run a current account deficit vis-à-vis its rivals and "emerging economies" as part of its leadership role. Its not doing so, and going protectionist instead, would plunge the capitalist world into trade rivalry and damage the interests of international finance capital (which wants unrestricted trade and capital flows). This, in turn, would shake the so-called "confidence of investors," and, *within the current regime of fiscal "responsibility,"* precipitate a further crisis. Since it cannot extract any tributes from the colonies as Britain had done, the United States perforce fulfils its leadership role by running up its own net external debt, which is why we have this remarkable spectacle of the world's most powerful capitalist economy also being the most indebted.

But the need for continuous borrowing by the leading metropolitan capitalist economy also requires that the value of its currency, the U.S. dollar, and of assets denoted in terms of it, must not be undermined by inflation, so that they continue to be attractive forms of holding wealth (whence the current obsession with "inflation-targeting"). The necessity for imposing income deflation therefore becomes particularly acute. The "spontaneous deflation" referred to above is not enough. It is supplemented by several measures typical of neoliberalism, such as fiscal "austerity."

V

Inflation and the Dollar

Of course, notwithstanding all measures of income deflation, a rise in the prices of tropical products may still occur. Indeed, we do know that during the first decade of this century, there has been a rise in prices of primary commodities generally. In the case of food grains, this rise has occurred owing to the decline in per capita global grain output as lands in developing countries were diverted to export crops, without any compensating rise of grain output in advanced countries; and it has been aggravated by the increasing diversion of grains for biofuels during the last decade. The period from 2004 to 2006 saw an *absolute decline* in global cereal output by 56 million tons, even as world use of cereal for ethanol conversion *rose* by 27 million tons. The single year 2007 alone saw grain diversion to ethanol at an all-time high of 28 million tons, and although output improved, there was still a net decline in per capita grain availability.[3]

Notwithstanding income deflation, this diversion of grain for biofuel was bound to and did eventually cause a situation of excess demand. Grain prices rose from 2007 onwards, spiking the next year. Commodity speculation thrives on such experiences and expectations of supply constraints and becomes pervasive in the era of neoliberalism through *inter alia* the removal of restrictions on forward-trading. The fact that this rise has not undermined the confidence of wealth-holders in the U.S. dollar, in contrast to the commodity price upsurge in the early 1970s and its effects, would be held against the argument of the present book. This is an issue, therefore, that needs clarification.

Before looking at this argument, however, a brief examination of *what had happened in the early 1970s* may be in order. The increase in commodity prices during that time is often interpreted as a temporary panic reaction following the collapse of the Bretton Woods system (Kaldor 1976). The story, as we have already seen in an earlier chapter, is usually narrated as follows: the persistent U.S. current account deficit, owing *inter alia* to its maintaining a string of military bases all around the globe, meant that under the Bretton Woods system, in which the U.S. dollar was ordained to be "as good as gold," other countries were forced to hold on to the dollars pouring out of the United States. When this outpouring became a torrent during the Vietnam War, France under President De Gaulle became unwilling to hold dollars anymore. It demanded gold instead, which forced the suspension of the dollar-gold link and the subsequent collapse of the Breton Woods system. This collapse created panic among speculators, who, on finding themselves suddenly denied a secure monetary form of holding wealth, moved to commodities, thereby causing the worldwide commodity price explosion.

A more plausible explanation, however, as already pointed out earlier, is as follows. In the context of the *generally* high levels of aggregate demand maintained through state intervention in metropolitan capitalist economies, including above all through high U.S. military spending, escalating expenditure on the Vietnam War gave rise to a state of excess demand, especially for primary commodities; since the scope for imposing income deflation on the "outlying regions" did not exist as in colonial times, this pushed up their prices, which the speculative factors, underscored by the first interpretation described above, further aggravated. The commodity price explosion in short was the inevitable denouement that capitalism, enfeebled by decolonization, which robbed it of its traditional weapon of income deflation against third world producers, faced in the postwar period.

Postwar capitalism, though it kept up its level of aggregate demand through Keynesian demand management, did not have any means of keeping down raw material prices in the face of growing demands for such raw materials arising from accumulation, and hence warding off threats to the value of money. This fact was exposed in the early 1970s.

France's moving to gold instead of U.S. dollars thus becomes explicable not as an act of intransigence on the part of President De Gaulle, but simply as an expression of the "debauching of the currency" that Keynes (1919), quoting Lenin, had talked about. And the weakness of the Bretton Woods system, in comparison with the gold standard, is then seen to consist in the fact that the latter was based on a colonial system that made possible the imposition of income deflation on the "outlying regions," while the former was crippled by the fact of decolonization, and hence a loosening of the bonds of imperialism.[4]

To be sure, nothing comparable has happened in recent years to commodity prices. But a rise in such prices, caused by excess demand aggravated by speculation, becomes a threat to the value of money in the periphery, which itself needs to be avoided; and it can even become a threat to the value of money in the metropolis if it induces a shift from such money to gold. Controlling inflation therefore becomes an overriding objective.

Indeed, we can reiterate in this context a point made earlier in response to the question: If, as argued in this book, there is such a threat to the viability of the capitalist system associated with the rise in prices of goods, then how is it that the price level of commodities has increased so much over the years *within the metropolis itself* and yet nothing has happened to the system? The answer lies partly in the fact that the most pronounced increases in the price level have occurred during war years, when in any case there are severe restrictions on asset preference. In addition, however, it is also the case, as we have seen, that inflation poses a threat by inducing a shift from money to gold. Not all inflation need cause such a shift; indeed, as we have also seen, episodes of inflation, perceived as episodes and not as a continuous phenomenon, may not cause such a shift. But even the danger of some episode of inflation causing such a shift is ever present, which is why capitalism seeks at all costs to avoid inflation, including resorting to income deflation, though it does not always succeed in doing so.

CHAPTER SEVEN

Metropolitan Demand on Tropical Landmass

The Empirical Picture

WE HAVE PUT FORWARD three propositions in the preceding chapters. First, the stability of the value of money under capitalism, and hence of the entire financial system founded upon money, requires that as capital accumulates, there should be no persistent tendency for a rise in the price of any commodity that is essential for the metropolis and is considered significant by wealth-holders, whether located in the metropolis or in the periphery. Second, given the limited size of the tropical landmass and the fact that capitalism can neither do without nor replicate elsewhere the products of this landmass, the *ex ante* tendency towards persistent inflation in such products therefore becomes a threat to capitalism. And third, this threat is countered *inter alia* by imposing an income deflation on the users of these products in the periphery, so that capitalism's growing requirement for them is met by squeezing the absorption by these users, without the problem of increasing supply price coming into play at all. Such income deflation, imposed on the users of the tropical products located in the periphery, constitutes an essential feature of imperialism.

If these propositions are right, then we should observe two phenomena: first, there should be a certain inverse relationship (to be defined more precisely) between exports from the periphery to the metropolis and food availability in the periphery; and second, accompanying such an inverse relationship, we should find not any significant profit inflation, but rather a state of relative stability in tropical commodity prices (and an adverse movement in their terms of trade vis-à-vis manufacturing, which contradicts Ricardo[1]), as is to be expected with income deflation.

It may be thought that a precise testing of such an inverse relationship[2] requires the specification of an alternative scenario that *would have obtained* in the absence of capitalist encroachment in the periphery. This, however, is not needed for our purpose. An *observed* inverse relationship between the movement of exports of tropical products to the metropolis and the movement of per capita foodgrain availability within the periphery is *sufficient* to show the existence of a metropolis-induced squeeze on the population on the tropical landmass. This is so for the following reason.

If, in the absence of capitalist encroachment, per capita foodgrain availability would have *increased or remained constant*, then an observed *decline* can be taken as being indicative of a metropolis-induced squeeze; and if, in the absence of such an encroachment, the per capita foodgrain availability would have *declined* anyway, then an observed decline can be taken as being indicative of a metropolis-induced squeeze that only worsened matters. From an observed decline in per capita foodgrain availability *in a situation of rising crop exports to the metropolis*, we can therefore safely infer the existence of a metropolis-induced squeeze. It becomes difficult to infer such a squeeze only when there is an observed *increase* in per capita foodgrain availability within the periphery accompanying an increase in its exports to the metropolis.

In fact one can go further. Even if there is no increase in the periphery's exports to the metropolis but merely a decline over time in per capita foodgrain availability in the periphery *in a situation of substantial (but not necessarily growing) tropical exports to the metropolis*, then that too is sufficient to show such a metropolitan squeeze. This is because in the absence of such a squeeze in the form of an income deflation, even the maintenance of these substantial exports in the face of a decline in per capita foodgrain availability would not have been possible without jeopardizing the value of money in the metropolis.

What is remarkable, however, is that *a decline in per capita foodgrain availability in the periphery, accompanying an increase in exports of tropical products to the metropolis, is exactly what has happened in history.* The present chapter establishes this point on the basis of historical data for several countries and also examines trends in absolute poverty. The next chapter discusses the phenomenon of income deflation in the colonial period and how it underpinned the entire international monetary system. In short, the chapters that follow provide historical material to support the theoretical argument of the book.

I

Trends in Foodgrain Availability in the Indian Economy

The tropical landmass has the remarkable property that it can sustain production all year round, producing under favourable conditions as many as three crops per year. The constraint here can arise from the absence of water, which irrigation facilities seek to overcome, but not from climatic conditions such as a harsh winter when the ground is frozen. A number of crops that are grown in the cold temperate northern regions in summer but cannot be grown there in winter, are produced in tropical and subtropical lands in winter.[3] In addition, a whole range of products, from tea and coffee to cane sugar and raw cotton, which have become a routine part of the northern consumption basket, can be produced only on tropical and subtropical lands.

The demand of the capitalist core upon the tropical landmass therefore is of two kinds: to produce a whole range of goods that it consumes but simply cannot produce; and to produce a whole range of goods that it can produce only in certain months but whose fresh supplies it needs all year around. Meeting these requirements in the absence of land-augmentation necessarily involves restricting the use of this land for meeting domestic demands within the periphery, which in turn is achieved by curtailing these demands through income deflation. And the most important demand that is curtailed is for foodgrains.

The fundamental asymmetry, which consists in the fact that the capitalist core requires tropical products but not vice versa (in the sense that whatever the tropical countries import from the core is in principle producible by them) and is as important today as in the past, is captured by table 7.1, which shows that import dependence was far greater for advanced countries.[4]

A supermarket in West Europe or North America carries on average today about 12,000 items of food in raw or processed forms. At least two-thirds of these items have a partial or total import content from tropical areas (Friedman 1990). Supplying these items from tropical lands has entailed historically, and even today, a decline in per capita foodgrains output and availability in countries located there.

Table 7.2 gives figures for per capita foodgrain output and availability for British India for the half century before independence as five-year averages.[5] Even ignoring the last year, 1945–46, which saw a precipitous decline in both, there was nonetheless a decline of around 27 percent in output and over 25 percent in availability over the half-century. Since a common tendency is to attribute declines in per capita magnitudes in the periphery to excessive population increase, it is worth recalling that India's population growth became noticeable for the first time only when the 1931 census figures were compared with the 1921 census figures. And yet per capita foodgrain output and availability had already declined markedly by the 1920s. This decline therefore had to do not so much with population increase as with the shift of acreage towards the production of export crops.

The argument of this book remains unaffected if metropolitan demand for tropical products remains *unchanged* despite capital accumulation, while growing population in the periphery increases the demand for such products, or if the increase in (*ex ante*) demand arises for both these reasons. In all these cases the pressure on the tropical landmass makes the satisfaction of metropolitan requirements of tropical products impossible without the metropolis resorting to income deflation to preserve the value of its money. And such income deflation constitutes, in our argument, the essence of imperialism.

The shift away from foodgrains is evident from the fact that between the five years ending in 1901 and the five years ending in 1941 the trend growth rate of foodgrain output was a meagre 0.11 percent per annum (that for per capita output was -1.14 percent); but over exactly the same period the annual trend growth rate of non-foodgrain output was over ten times higher, at 1.31 percent (Blyn 1966). The colonial period, in short, constitutes the classic example of the use of the tropical landmass for meeting the requirements of the metropolis at the expense of local foodgrain production and absorption.

TABLE 7.I
Imports As a Percentage of Domestic Production by Major Food Groups for Selected Countries (1992–1994)

Food Group	Developed Countries				
	UK	USA	Germany	France	Japan
1. Vegetables and Fruits	151.4	39	156	34.4	26.4
2. Sugar and Sweeteners	77.9	12.9	16.9	13.8	90.1
3. Vegetable Oils	151.1	19.7	83.3	93.4	35.9
4. Stimulants	572.1	434.5	→∞	584.4	261.4
5. Meat, Milk, and Eggs	20.1	5.7	21	13.2	28.2
6. Fish and Seafood	233	51.7	760.4	218.9	62.1
7. Spices	→∞	978.6	→∞	→∞	→∞
8. Cereals and Roots	20.1	2.2	18.6	7.3	197.1

Food Group	Developing Countries							
	China	India	Indonesia	Bangladesh	Pakistan	Thailand	Vietnam	Philippines
1. Vegetables and Fruits	0.1	0.1	1.6	4.4	1.1	0.7	0	1.5
2. Sugar and Sweeteners	12.9	3	10.5	5.6	2.7	0.2	20.2	28
3. Vegetable Oils	30.8	5.5	0.1	196.2	234.6	10.2	25.5	3.6
4. Stimulants	13.5	0.3	1.3	8.2	271.1	10.5	0	13.5
5. Meat, Milk, and Eggs	0.6	0.1	18.3	11	0.5	41.7	9	63.6
6. Fish and Seafood	18.7	0	11.7	0	0	30.8	0	24.6
7. Spices	2.5	0.7	4.2	15.7	8.9	7.3	0	4.5
8. Cereals and Roots	2	0.3	6.7	5.1	10	2.5	1.6	14.9

SOURCE: Food Balance Sheets/Supply Utilization Accounts (FBS/SUA), United Nations Food and Agriculture Organization.
NOTE: Original data are volumes in thousand kilograms. Three-year annual average (1992 to 1994) of output and imports used to derive percentage of imports to output. Where imports are positive and domestic output is zero, the latter is treated as tending to zero and the ratio as tending to infinity, using the symbols →∞.

TABLE 7.2

British India, 1897–1946: Net Output, Imports, and Availability of
Foodgrains (five-year averages except last year)

Period	Net Foodgrain Output (000 ton)	Net Foodgrain Import (000 ton)	Net Foodgrain Availablity (000 ton)	Population (million)	Output per Head (kg)	Availability per Head (kg)
	1	2	3	4	5	6
1897–1902	44196.84	−475	43721.84	219.74	201.1	199
1903–1908	41135.94	−1105.83	40030.11	225.79	182.2	177.3
1909–1914	47292.59	−1662.83	45629.76	231.3	204.5	197.3
1915–1920	45298.31	−336	44962.31	232.81	194.6	193.1
1921–1926	44607.21	−203.67	44403.54	239.18	186.5	185.6
1927–1932	43338.46	858.83	44197.29	253.26	171.1	174.5
1933–1938	41786.79	1374.67	43161.46	270.98	154.2	159.3
1939–1944	42702.91	521.83	43224.74	291.03	146.7	148.5
Single Year						
1945–1946	41397.13	596	41993.13	307	134.8	136.8

SOURCE: Primary source is G. Blyn (1966); this table is from U. Patnaik (2008).
NOTE: Net foodgrains output is obtained by deducting one-eighth for seed, feed, and wastage from gross output data in source, in conformity with current official practice. Therefore, columns 5 and 6 are comparable with present-day official figures of output and availability per capita.

Let us now consider the post-independence period. With much strenuous effort, starting with the "Grow More Food" campaign of the early 1950s, the dirigiste regime in India, reviled ceaselessly these days by the proponents of neoliberalism, pushed up the figure for per capita net domestic foodgrain availability, which had shrunk to below 137 kg in 1945–46 for British India, to an annual average of 177 kg for the country as a whole for the triennium ending 1991–92 (comparable to the pre–First World War level during 1903–1908, before the decline had begun). This substantial per capita gain of 40 kg meant a rise for the population in average daily energy intake per head by nearly 400 calories, as well as a rise in daily protein intake of about 6 grams.

The gain of forty years of effort was lost after the introduction of neoliberal reforms starting in 1991, which entailed income deflation, and particularly after trade liberalisation in the mid-1990s, which initiated diversion of land to export crops. There has been a fall, gentle at first but sharp thereafter, in per capita average annual availability for three-year periods ending in the year specified: 174.3 kg for 1994–95, to 174.2 kg for 1997–98, and to 155.7 kg for 2002–03, which was lower than the average figure (159.3 kg) for the prewar period 1933–38. The figure for the triennium ending 2006–07 was in fact 159.88 kg, almost the same as for 1933–38, and for the triennium ending 2011–12, 163 kg. *The conclusion is inescapable therefore that the net per capita food grain availability by the first five-year period of the current century has been lowered below that prevailing before reforms and below that of British India on the eve of the Second World War.*

The decline in per capita availability after the dirigiste period was not solely the result of decline in per capita food grain output, though the latter did see a decline with area diversion: the annual growth rate of food grain output over the period of neoliberal policies, 1990–91 and 2011–12, which were both good crop years, was 1.80 percent. By contrast the annual growth rate of population between 1991 and 2011, both census years, was higher, at 1.85 percent. What is remarkable, however, is that the decline in per capita availability was much greater than the decline in per capita output. The difference between grain output and availability showed itself in a combination of rising public grain stocks and rising grain exports.

There has been a noticeable increase in foodgrain output in the very recent period after 2010, though it does not negate our general point about the overall decline in per capita foodgrain output during the reforms. *There has been no such increase in availability, however.* Between the triennium ending 2006–07 and the triennium ending 2011–12, the annual foodgrain output in the country increased by 17.4 percent. But the food grain availability over exactly the same period increased only from 159.9 kg to 163 kg, which, at less than 2 percent, was hardly any increase at all. In other words, *the squeeze on people's absorption of foodgrains owing to income deflation has been even sharper than the output trend would warrant, resulting in the holding of substantial stocks with the government and substantial exports, even as there has been some increase in food grain prices in recent years.*

II

The Shift in Government Policy: The Indian Case

Government policy in the neoliberal era differs from the policy under dirigisme in at least two crucial ways. One, while the dirigiste regime, formed as a sequel to the anticolonial struggle, had supported, protected, and promoted peasant agriculture in keeping with the promise of that struggle, the neoliberal regime withdraws such measures of support and promotion. Under the dirigiste regime, for instance, peasant agriculture was protected against world market price fluctuations; it enjoyed significant input subsidies; it enjoyed subsidized credit, with banks, after their nationalization in 1969, being obliged to meet "priority sector" lending targets; there was a system of guaranteed remunerative prices for producers in twenty-two crops, with a mechanism of public procurement to make it effective; there was a network of government extension services, together with a substantial research and development effort under government auspices; and there was a significant step-up in public investment in irrigation and other heads of rural development. True, the benefit of this state support did not accrue to *all* producers, but was garnered predominantly by the landlords and rich peasants who constituted the core of the emerging capitalist tendency in the agrarian economy. Nonetheless, it did help to break the retrogression in Indian agriculture that the last half century of colonial rule had brought about. With the progressive withdrawal of these measures under neoliberalism, we are witnessing a retrogression in agriculture again.

The progressive withdrawal of these measures of support and promotion for peasant agriculture amounts *de facto* to an income deflation imposed upon the peasantry. The shift of bank credit towards other sectors (even though "priority-sector" lending targets continue to remain nominally in force) increases peasants' dependence upon private money lenders and raises the cost of credit. The withdrawal of input subsidies; the enforced reliance of peasants on multinational corporations providing seeds and marketing facilities, owing to the withdrawal of the government from R&D, and also extension, activities; the exposure to the price fluctuations in the world market owing to trade liberalization—all of these have the same effect of reducing peasant incomes. And even when there is no direct reduction in peasant incomes following from any of these steps, there is invariably an indirect reduction following from the increase in peasants' vulnerability as a consequence of these steps.

Not surprisingly, the period of liberalization has seen mass suicides of peasants—more than 240,000 peasants have taken their lives in the decade and a half since 1997, substantially in excess of the rate of suicide in the general population; and it has also seen a reduction in the profitability of agriculture, leading to hundreds of thousands of peasants abandoning agriculture and migrating to cities in search of non-existent jobs. The per capita foodgrain output decline, reestablishing the trend of the colonial period and negating the reversal of this trend that had been achieved during the dirigiste period, is an outcome of this income deflation imposed on the peasantry.

Secondly, however, *this* income deflation has been embedded within a larger income deflation affecting broader sections of the working people, because of which the demand for foodgrains has shrunk so much that, notwithstanding the decline in per capita foodgrain output, large stocks have been held by the government even in the midst of growing hunger (on which more later). In fact in the entire period between 1991–92 and 2012–13, there have only been six years when the magnitude of government stocks has fallen below what is considered the "norm"; in every other year the government has held abnormally large grain stocks, culminating in over 82 million tonnes by mid-2012.

The government could easily get rid of these excess stocks and reduce the extent of hunger by distributing them through the public distribution system. But here the argument has been that any such distribution, which would have to be at a price lower than the one at which the crop was procured from the producers (plus transport and storage costs), would raise the subsidy bill of the government and hence enlarge the fiscal deficit; *and that this would exacerbate inflation!* In practice food grains have been exported to the massive extent of 50 million tonnes between 2012 and 2014, even while average nutritional intake has been falling (see section iv below).

The argument about inflation is completely wrong: the level of aggregate demand is not altered one iota whether commodities are locked up as additions to stocks or consumed. What is still more remarkable is that even from a monetarist point of view, such sale of foodgrain stocks through the public distribution system should be disinflationary rather than inflationary: since the government has already financed its purchase of foodgrain stocks through bank credit and has added to the money supply, the dishoarding of such stocks should bring down money supply and hence the inflationary threat. What the argument about inflation shows is the thralldom of government policy to the fallacious doctrine of "sound finance."

Indeed, the income deflation unleashed upon the peasantry, which itself is embedded within a process of income deflation unleashed upon larger segments of the working population, is justified in the name of achieving "fiscal responsibility," a euphemism for adhering to "sound finance," which in turn is what finance capital generally (and *international* finance capital in the current context) demands. This predilection of finance is what underlies Joan Robinson's (1966) epithet for the theory that fiscal deficits should always be eschewed: "the humbug of finance."

The phenomena noted above, namely the withdrawal of the state from its role of supporting, protecting, and promoting peasant agriculture (and petty production in general), its apotheosizing "sound finance" as demanded by international finance capital, and its reversion on this pretext to a policy of imposing income deflation on the working people are all indicative of a change in the class orientation of the state. Instead of being an entity apparently standing above classes and mediating between them (even as it promoted a relatively autonomous capitalist development, as the dirigiste regime did), the state in the period of globalization becomes associated almost exclusively with promoting the interests of international finance capital and the domestic corporate-financial elite that becomes integrated with it. The undermining of petty production that occurs is just the other side of this coin.

But this undermining of petty production has also been accompanied by an opening up of crop production to the demands of the metropolitan (and now also domestic) capitalist sector, and hence a shift to cash crops for exports (and even to exports of foodgrains as feedgrains, and of meat into which feedgrains go as inputs). Between 1990–91 and 2011–12, for instance, the gross area under foodgrains declined from 127.8 to 125 million hectares. Over exactly the same period, if we take just two major cash crops, sugarcane and cotton, the gross area under them increased from 11.1 million hectares to 17.3 million hectares. The demand of the metropolis and the domestic capitalist sector (where an affluent middle class has grown during this period) for goods produced on the fixed tropical landmass has meant a decline in per capita foodgrain production and availability. This decline in actual availability would be even sharper if we were to take into account the fact that a part of the foodgrain produced, which is not simply added to government stock or exported, is used as feedgrain for the increasing part of meat production that is exported.

The end of the period of dirigisme—a period that, we have argued, was marked by some loosening of the bonds of imperialism—has thus meant a re-strengthening of these bonds. Saying this must not be construed as subscribing to a "conspiracy theory" of some kind. Capitalism, especially when it is unfettered by dirigisme, is a "spontaneous" as opposed to a planned system. What happens under it is not a consciously contrived denouement. But even in its restored "spontaneity" in the neoliberal period, it recreates, though with important differences, many of the features of the colonial period.

The question may be asked: If "imperialism" is essential for capitalism, then why did the period of dirigisme, when the bonds of imperialism were loosened somewhat, not produce a crisis for capitalism? We have seen that it did in the early 1970s when the Bretton Woods system collapsed. But how did the so-called "Golden Age of Capitalism" manage to sustain itself for so long even when the traditional means of income deflation were not operating under the dirigiste regimes in the periphery? Many authors, including W. A. Lewis (quoted in Kaldor [1976]), had in fact predicted that in the postwar years there would be a significant increase in raw material prices. But after the Korean War boom there was a remarkable period of relative price stability in the metropolis until the "wage explosion" in 1968; and the rise in primary commodity prices came only afterwards.

While this question needs to be carefully examined, one possible answer could be that in their eagerness to industrialize, for which foreign exchange was needed for importing machinery and other capital goods, each of the newly decolonized economies of the periphery competed with the others to push out as much of its traditional primary commodity exports as it could. The suppression of nominal prices of tropical commodities (and the adverse movement in the terms of trade), which had been brought about through income deflation under colonialism, continued even after decolonization for this reason, despite the absence of colonial-style income deflation. This process, however, came to an end in the early 1970s.

III

Trends in Foodgrain Absorption in Some Other Countries

Let us now consider the historical experience of some other countries.[6] In Java under Dutch rule, per capita paddy output fell by nearly 20 percent over a period of fifty-five years between 1885 and 1940: the

TABLE 7.3
Java, 1885–1938: Output of Paddy Rice and Export Crops

Year	Population million	Paddy Rice million ton	Paddy Rice per Head kg	Period	Rubber Output Index	Sugarcane Output Index
	1	*2*	*3*		*4*	*5*
				1890–1899	–	100
1890	21.97	4.16	189	1900–1909	–	263
1895	23.67	4.21	178	1910–1919	100	382
1900	26.15	4.47	171	1921–1925	251	491
1905	27.39	4.41	161	1926–1930	504	668
1920	34.98	6.11	175	1931–1935	600	402
1930	40.89	6.5	159	1936–1940	762	332
1940	48.42	7.84	162			
Growth Rate, %	1.6	1.3	−0.3		8.8	6 (−6.8)

SOURCE: Columns 1,2,4,5 from data in A. Booth (1988). Column 3 is derived from 1 and 2.
NOTE: Last column gives first growth rate up to 1930 and, in parenthesis, the growth rate thereafter.

rate of change was -0.3 percent per annum (table 7.3). Over the same period there was a dramatic growth of export crops: sugarcane output (base: annual average for 1890–99 = 100) increased to 668 by 1926–30 (annual average); after the agricultural depression there was a fall to 332 by 1936–40. In the case of rubber, another export crop that grew rapidly, there was no fall in output even after the agricultural depression: the index of output (same base) climbed steadily to 762 by 1936–40. The decline in paddy output per head would have been even sharper if the agricultural depression had not hit some export crops; even so it was quite substantial, only a little less than for India.

In the case of the Japanese colonies, Korea and Formosa (Taiwan), the export to Japan consisted of rice itself. Japan's net rice imports started in the 1890s, but grew rapidly from the First World War onwards after the widespread "rice riots" of 1918, and reached one-fifth of all imports and over one-fifth of domestic production by 1936. By the 1930s over half of Korea's rice output was going to Japan, accounting for two-thirds of Japan's total rice imports. The growth rate of retained rice output was below the population growth rate, leading to a per capita decline in rice consumption. Even though cheaper millets were imported from Manchuria to substitute for higher-value rice in the Korean diet, there was nonetheless a 15 percent decline in per capita calorie intake in Korea in the interwar period. The poorer peasants in Korea were reduced even to eating wild grasses for part of the year (Penrose 1940; Grabowski 1985).

In the case of Formosa, rice and sugarcane were both exported to Japan, but there was Japanese settlement on a larger scale and therefore larger investment, reminiscent of what had happened in the temperate region. (Sweet potato was also introduced into the local population's diet.) As a result, even though export growth exceeded the growth of foodgrain output, there was no actual decline in per capita cereal consumption.

The classic case in more recent years of production for the metropolitan market undermining food security relates to Africa. The integration of Africa as an agricultural exporter to the advanced capitalist countries was greatly strengthened under the diktat of the Bretton Woods institutions at the beginning of the 1980s, when African countries, for no fault of theirs, became indebted to these institutions because of the adverse shift in the terms of trade for their primary commodity exports vis-à-vis manufactured goods in the wake of the oil-price shocks (whose effects were passed on in the form of higher prices of the latter). This thrust on exports of agriproducts meant a shift away from food crop production.

If we take cereals (wheat, maize, barley, and millets), tubers (potatoes, cassava, and yam), and plantains (bananas and plantains) and aggregate them under the category of food crops by using the convention that 5 kg of tubers or plantain equal 1 kg of cereals, then we find that already in 1980 the 46 countries of sub-Saharan Africa had a per capita annual food crop output of about 138.5 kg gross (or if we correct for possible underestimation by revising the figure upwards by as much as 20 percent, then 166 kg). Even the higher of these figures was considerably lower than the contemporary figures for India and China (notwithstanding all definitional problems). And yet, for the entire sub-Saharan region between 1980 and 1987–89 (three-year average), there was a decline in per capita foodgrain output of 11.5 percent. For the six most populous countries of the region the decline was of the order of 20 percent (U. Patnaik 2008:64).

This decline in per capita foodgrain output was accompanied by a decline in imports net of "food aid" into these countries over this period (table 7.4). And even such increase in "food aid" as occurred over this decade (which was generally meagre except in the case of

TABLE 7.4

Change in Nutritional Level in Six Most Populous Countries in Sub-Saharan Africa

Country	Cereal Import (000 ton)		Food Aid (Cereals) (000 ton)		Change in Import Net of Food Aid (000 ton)	Change in Calories per Head (%)
	1980	1990	1979–1980	1989–1990	1980–1990	1979–1981 to 1989–1991
	1	*2*	*3*	*4*	*5*	*6*
Tanzania	399	73	89	22	−259	−2.17
Ethiopia	397	687	111	538	−137	−9.92
Uganda	52	7	17	35	−63	−6
Nigeria	1828	502	0	0	−1326	15.45
Kenya	387	188	86	62	−175	−9.86
Zaire	538	336	77	107	−232	4.54

NOTE: Column $5 = (2-4) - (1-3)$.
SOURCE: Various issues of World Development Report (World Bank) for columns 1 to 4. Column 6 from United Nations Food and Agriculture Organization, Food Balance Sheets/ Supply Utilisation Accounts (FBS/SUA). Presented in P. Patnaik (1999).

Ethiopia) was insufficient to prevent a decline in their overall per capita food availability—a conclusion that has validity for sub-Saharan Africa as a whole and constitutes the proximate explanation for its acute food insecurity.

The case of sub-Saharan Africa also highlights another form of income deflation, which we shall call "auto-income deflation." We have earlier discussed income deflation through a system of colonial "drain" and through unemployment (or deindustrialization). A third form of income deflation is imposed on the poor through the pursuit of "sound finance" together with the handing over of tax concessions and subsidies to both international capital and to the domestic corporate-financial elite (so that the resulting shift in income distribution has the effect of curtailing the overall demand for tropical products, since the "propensity to consume such products" is greater among the poor than among the rich). There is yet another way that income deflation can occur, which is exemplified by Africa in the 1980s, and it operates as follows.

Let us assume that starting from some initial situation, production of cash crops for exports suddenly becomes more attractive (maybe because of an exchange rate depreciation) compared to foodgrain production for home use. Since cash crop production typically requires credit financing, suppose a plot of land that was yielding $100 of foodgrains now offers $200 when converted to cash-crop production at existing prices, but the credit required for it, together with the interest payment at the end of the period, comes to $80. Cash-crop production therefore promises to yield $120 compared to $100 for foodgrains, and peasants will turn to it assuming confidently that they can meet their current foodgrain requirement, and more, by buying foodgrains in the market.

But when many producers turn to cash-crop production on this argument, its international price falls, let us say by 30 percent to $140. *And to keep things simple let us also assume that the international price of foodgrains also falls in sympathy to an exactly equal extent to $70.* (If it did not, then that would be an even stronger case of auto-income deflation.) The peasant's income, after repayment of debt-cum-interest, however, comes to only $140 minus $80, or $60. The peasants therefore would have to reduce foodgrain consumption by 10 dollars' worth in the new situation, or by one-seventh in physical terms, by shifting to cash crops. The burden of the decline in foodgrain production is felt by the peasants themselves who make the switch, even in the absence of any state-imposed income deflation.

Something of this sort happened to Africa in the 1980s, *both at the macrolevel to African countries* and to individual peasants. The switch to cash crops was followed by a decline in the terms of trade vis-à-vis manufactured goods. With debt-servicing burden in terms of manufactured goods equivalent remaining unchanged, this squeezed the capacity of the countries to import foodgrains from the world market to keep up the earlier level of foodgrain consumption (even in the absence of any shift in the terms of trade *between food grains and cash crops*).

This, however, did not necessarily mean any significant excess demand for foodgrains in the domestic market, because this very process of terms of trade shift had imposed an income deflation (after taking into account *individual* debt-service commitments) upon the peasants themselves. The income deflation imposed upon the peasantry in this manner, which restricts their foodgrain consumption even as foodgrain output falls, is what we call "auto-income deflation."

One of the problems with the Ricardian theory of "comparative advantage," apart from its basic fallacy, which we have already discussed earlier, is that it does not take into account this possibility of an *overall decline* in the availability of goods in one of the trading countries as a consequence of trade. This is because the theory is developed in a setting where the "market price" invariably equals the "natural price" (for which Ricardo generally took labour values as an approximation); and in addition there are no payments commitments associated with trade-induced "specialization."

If there is a fall in "market price" on account of specialization, then food security may become jeopardized, especially if specialization sets up payment commitments. This, however, does not appear to be a possibility if all calculations are made in terms of "natural prices" (which means that the importance of the *fixity* of payments commitments on account of specialization in cash crops is ignored). The case of Africa not only demonstrates this possibility but also falls into the widely prevalent pattern wherein producing for the metropolis reduces domestic food availability, given the fixed landmass.

No doubt there are many long-term problems with African agriculture, which many authors have noted. No doubt, too, that the high rate of population growth in Africa has an effect on per capita food availability. But the *proximate* cause for the loss of food security in Africa lies in neither of these factors but in its allowing the pattern of land use to be affected by the pull of metropolitan demand. And yet this is an aspect that is scarcely ever mentioned in discussions on Africa's crisis of food security.

IV

Evidence on Growing Absolute Poverty in the Periphery

We argued earlier that the growing demand of the metropolis on the limited tropical landmass has the effect of increasing absolute poverty in the periphery by lowering foodgrain availability in the latter. However, the question arises: Does an *observed* decline in net per capita foodgrain availability necessarily indicate an increase in absolute poverty? This is an issue that has been much debated in India.

Poverty in India is defined with respect to a calorie norm of 2,100 per person per day in urban India and 2,200 per person per day in rural India (the original norm for rural India was 2,400 calories but this was scaled down in actual application). Consumption expenditure data per month per household are obtained regularly under the National

Sample Survey (a large sample is canvassed every five years and a smaller sample every year): the data comprise a basic vector of physical quantities of food items and quantities or numbers, as applicable, of other goods and services consumed by each household (whose size and age-sex composition is also available). This physical vector generates on one side the vector of expenditure with all items valued at actual prices; on the other side the food quantities part of the physical vector generates the vector of calorie, protein, and fat intakes, or nutritional intake for short. Thus, expenditure and nutritional intake are both obtained from the same basic data on physical quantities and are presented in terms of average per capita spending and nutritional intake for twelve fractile groups. A clear positive monotonic relation has been found in every survey, as may be expected, between the spending per capita per month on all goods and services, and the daily per capita nutritional intake when we compare across fractile groups.

These data can be used for estimating poverty in two possible ways. One is to arrange for each point of time a table for the twelve fractile groups, which contains the actually observed current average level of spending on all goods and services for each group, the associated average nutritional intake levels for each group, and the proportion of persons falling below the (upper-end) value of spending for each group. That particular observed spending level that satisfies the calorie intake norm is then the poverty line, and the proportion of persons who fail to reach this level constitute the poor. This was the method followed *officially*, though only for the initial estimate relating to 1973–74, not for any later years although all relevant data were available. One of the authors (U. Patnaik 2007, 2013), applying this same official definition to every five-year data set to obtain the poverty level spending, found that the percentage of the poor was stable up to the end of the 1980s at below 60 percent but started rising thereafter, reaching around 75 percent by 2009–10. In short, the proportion of persons unable to spend enough on all goods and services to maintain the nutritional standard rose quite sharply in both rural and urban India, *precisely during the period of the implementation of neoliberal policies* (see table 7.5).

The other method, followed by government agencies after the initial 1973–74 estimate, was to take the level of per capita expenditure in this base year at which these calorie norms were met and then to adjust this poverty line to later years by using a price index. The proportion of the population falling below the "poverty line" so defined in any

TABLE 7.5

Trend in Rural and Urban Poverty, 1973–1944 to 2009–2010, All-India (percent of persons)

Rural	1973–1974	1983	1993–1994	2004–2005	2009–2010
A) Below 2400 calories poverty line	72	70	74.5	87	90.5
B) Below 2200 calories poverty line	56.4	56	58.5	69.5	75.5
Urban					
Below 2100 calories poverty line	49.6	58.8	57	64.5	73

SOURCE: Calculated after 1973–1974 from NSS reports on consumer expenditure and nutritional intake; NSS rounds for the years specified. Presented in U. Patnaik (2006, 2007, 2013).

year is the "poverty ratio" for that year, and it has been declining particularly rapidly during the period of economic reforms. A Laspeyres index concept is being applied here since the base-year basket is taken to be fixed and the notion of poverty line is no longer linked to whether nutrition norms are actually satisfied.

In brief, the very first official estimate, as well as the U. Patnaik (2007, 2013) estimates for subsequent years, take the nutritional norms as fixed and derive the spending at which these norms are satisfied, as the poverty line spending at each point of time, from which the percentage of persons falling below these poverty lines is determined. By contrast, the official estimates after the initial year, take the initial basket as fixed, and merely index its cost *without any reference at all to either actual spending or nutritional intake data over the last four decades!*

Using the data for seven surveys up to 2009–10, it has been shown by U. Patnaik (2007, 2013) that in the second method, the official poverty lines (obtained merely by price-indexing) corresponded to lower and lower nutritional intakes over time. In effect, poverty was being measured not by a constant, but by a declining nutritional standard, thus violating the official definition itself. It followed that the decline in poverty ratios arrived at by the official method was spurious, since the standard itself was being lowered, and in many states lowered quite drastically.[7]

It is not surprising that by contrast, applying constant nutrition norms over time—which is the correct method—shows a rise in poverty, because the sample survey data on consumption show directly a *decline in the average per capita calorie as well as per capita protein intake of the population over time (though fat intake shows a rise).*

How is this divergence in the movements of the two measures to be explained in terms of economic factors? Those who swear by the official claims of declining poverty explain the decline in calorie intake through a change in tastes and preferences of the people. Here three different strands of thought are brought in. One claims that the decrease in the amount of manual labour that is put in now compared to earlier implies that a lower calorie intake is required now, and this allows scope for buying other goods. The observed decline in calorie intake therefore is a symptom of people being freed from the drudgery of manual work, not of an increase in absolute poverty.

The problem with this explanation, however, is that it runs completely counter to observed cross-country experience: the calorie intake is much higher in advanced countries than in the periphery, even though the magnitude of manual work undertaken in the former is much less than in the latter. Hence the proffered inverse relationship between actual calorie intake and freedom from manual work has little basis in facts.

The second strand within this argument talks of a shift away from foodgrains in the consumption pattern as real incomes of the consumers improve. As they become better off, people consume less staple grains and more of other goods in the food basket. The decline in calorie intake that may follow from this is therefore evidence not of immiseration, but, if anything, of an improved living standard through a diversification of food consumption. But this claim also runs counter to observed behaviour. True, *direct* consumption of foodgrains per capita first goes up from very low levels and then goes down as incomes increase, but *total* consumption of foodgrains per capita, which includes both direct and indirect consumption (the latter through processed foods and animal products into which foodgrains enter as feedgrains), *increases* with per capita real income (until it plateaus at a very high level of real income). The more diversified the diet is with regard to animal products, the greater is the demand for grain and the higher is the share of grain used for feed. Thus per capita cereal consumption *for all uses* is found to range from only 175 kg in India to around 500 kg in European countries to 900 kg in the United States.[8]

This behaviour is visible not only in cross-section data across countries, but also across income groups within a country; it is visible too in pooled time series and cross-section data for countries including India (Krishna 2013). Since there is no reason to believe that Indian consumers would behave differently compared to others (even though the *level* of their average per capita foodgrain consumption may be lower), this explanation also does not stand scrutiny.

The third strand talks of people preferring to spend more on health and education in lieu of foodgrains in contemporary India. But as table 7.5 makes clear, significant increases in the proportion of population below the calorie norms have occurred even over periods as short as five years, which are in fact too short to witness such sharp shifts in *consumer preferences* as this explanation requires. It is more likely, therefore, that the decline in calorie intake, in tandem with an increase in health and education expenditure, reflects a rise in the price of health and education services (owing to privatization of such services under neoliberalism). This implies that the decline in calorie intake does reflect genuinely growing deprivation, although this growth in deprivation is camouflaged in official data showing declining poverty because of the inadequacy of the price index used to bring forward the poverty line, which does not take into account this rise in the cost of important services owing to privatization.

An example will make the point clear. Suppose between the base year and the current year there is zero change in hospital charges in government hospitals, but while in the base year there were no private hospitals, so that everyone went to government hospitals, in the current year government hospital facilities have dwindled under neoliberalism, and most people go to the far more exorbitantly priced private hospitals. Suppose also for the sake of simplicity that all other prices remain unchanged between the base and the current year. Then a price index weighted by base year quantities (used for obtaining the official "poverty line") will not take into account the new element of private hospitals, and will show zero inflation between the base and the current years and hence an unchanged "poverty line."

As a matter of fact, however, there has been a substantial increase in the cost of living because people are forced to access the more expensive private healthcare facilities instead of the less expensive government ones. With an unchanged poverty line in nominal terms, the poverty ratio is likely to show a decline. But because people are pushed from a less expensive government healthcare system to a more expensive private one, they are bound to have skimped on some other purchase, notably of food grains, and hence obtained reduced calories. The poverty line based on actual calorie intake would then show an increase in the poverty ratio, while the official measure, which estimates the poverty ratio by using a base year poverty line blown up in accordance with the consumer price index, will show a decline. Something of this sort has been happening with respect to poverty estimates in India and elsewhere. Notwithstanding claims of declining poverty on the basis of official measures, hunger, and hence poverty, even as officially *conceptualized* (though no longer measured using the official concept itself), has been increasing.

To say this is not to suggest that people in India and elsewhere in the periphery actually live worse than before in every respect. As mentioned earlier, scientific advances, especially the availability of affordable medicines, control of disease-bearing vectors, and greatly improved possibilities for surgery have increased longevity and improved the quality of life. But all that has nothing to do with, and does not negate, the basic proposition being presented here—namely, that absolute poverty manifesting itself in hunger increases when the limited tropical landmass is called upon to meet growing metropolitan requirements, which entails a reduction in per capita foodgrain output and, related to this, in per capita foodgrain availability.

CHAPTER EIGHT

The International Monetary System

Some Issues in Political Economy

IN THE PRECEDING CHAPTER we saw how the increase in exports of primary commodities to the metropolis for meeting its growing requirements has been historically associated with a decline in per capita food availability in the periphery—a relation that continues to hold to this day. In the present chapter we shall examine, again historically, the relationship between obtaining such exports and the viability of the international monetary system.

I

General Observations on International Monetary Systems

In a world knit together by the flow of commodities and capital across countries, a major role of the international monetary system is to provide wealth-holders, with a stable medium for holding their wealth. Or, put differently, a major element of any international monetary system is an arrangement for the creation of "world money," which can function both as a medium of circulation and also, as a result, as a form of holding wealth.

If world money, whose quintessential form under any particular international monetary system is the key reserve currency of that system, is to function as a stable medium for holding wealth (which is required for it to act even as a medium of circulation in the world economy), then its *expected* price in terms of commodities must be stable. This does not rule out *actual* price changes, but these must not give rise to any expectations of sustained price changes.

A standard procedure for ensuring this has been to tie the price of the key reserve currency to that of gold; since gold is generally expected to move in sync with commodity prices, this constitutes an attempt to ensure the fixity of expected commodity prices in terms of the key currency, so that it can function as a stable medium for holding wealth.

The gold standard, whereby the prices of all currencies, including above all the key reserve currency (the pound sterling), were fixed in terms of gold, was an obvious example of such tying. The Bretton Woods system, in which the price of the key reserve currency, the U.S. dollar, was fixed in terms of gold, while other currencies could change their parity vis-à-vis the dollar in certain specific circumstances with the permission of the International Monetary Fund (IMF), also fell into the same genre. (The post–Bretton Woods system, in which there is no gold backing for the key currency, will be examined later.)

But fixing the currency value in terms of gold is only a *formal* act. Unless a set of real relationships prevail underlying this formal act, this act in itself cannot create a stable medium for holding wealth. These real relationships must ensure that, first, there should be no rise in prices of goods produced in the leading capitalist economy, whose currency is typically the key reserve currency, through an autonomous money wage-push. (An autonomous wage-push in a non-leading capitalist economy will be typically accompanied by a depreciation of its currency vis-à-vis the key reserve currency, but if the currency of this non-leading capitalist economy is also to function as a medium in which wealth is held, then such wage-push must also be avoided.) Second, there should be no rise in the prices of commodities imported from the periphery through an autonomous wage-push in the latter. Third, there should be no rise in the prices of commodities produced in the periphery through an excess demand for such commodities. Excess demand for metropolitan commodities is a rarity, as Kalecki (1971:168) pointed out long ago, except in situations of war. And fourth, there should be no excess supply of the key reserve currency itself; i.e., its supply must not exceed what people are willing to demand at any time for transaction and wealth purposes.

The question may be asked here: If our third condition above is satisfied and there is no excess demand for commodities produced either in the periphery or in the metropolis, then does that not automatically ensure the absence of excess supply of the key reserve currency? Does the fourth condition become unnecessary if the third is fulfilled? The answer is "no" because an excess supply of the leading currency may be associated not with an excess demand for commodities, but with an excess demand for gold (which may arise for independent reasons) or for some other capitalist currency.

Let us now see how these conditions have been historically fulfilled. The first two of these conditions are fulfilled by having a reserve army of labour both in the metropolis and also in the periphery. Since this has been a common and well-known feature of capitalism, we need not dwell upon it here. It is in their arrangements for meeting the other two requirements that different international monetary systems have differed from one another. Let us therefore examine the different international monetary systems in this light.

II

The Gold Standard

A. *The Mechanism of Appropriating the Colonies' Export Earnings*

Underlying the gold standard was the entire system of colonial exploitation, which had two basic characteristics. One was the imposition, through a trade regime that has been described as "one-way free trade" (Bagchi 1989) of a pattern of international division of labour whereby the metropolis produced manufactured goods and the periphery produced primary commodities; this imposition in turn created large labour reserves through what we have earlier called "deindustrialization," which ensured the absence of any significant autonomous money wage-push in the periphery.

The second characteristic was a system of taxation of the people of the colonies, wherein taxes were a substantial part of the economic surplus, and a large part of these tax proceeds was used to "pay" local producers of goods comprising the export surplus. Thus, this part of economic surplus was "drained away" in the form of a merchandise export surplus to the world, whose foreign exchange proceeds remained with the particular metropolitan centre and were not permitted to flow back to the colonised countries. The producers in the latter were "paid" in local currency out of the budgetary revenues—namely, out of the taxes they themselves had handed over to the government. Thus they were only apparently paid, but were actually not paid at all: the export surplus goods were the commodity form of taxes extracted from them!

In the Indian case the countries in the world paid for the goods they imported from it by depositing gold, sterling, and other currencies to the value of their imports with the secretary of state for India in Council, who issued bills that could be cashed only in rupees. These bills were sent (by post or telegraph) by foreign importers to the Indian exporters who, on submitting the bills, got rupees from the exchange banks, where these rupees in turn came from the treasury out of the sums earmarked in the budget as the rupee equivalent of government's sterling expenditure abroad.

We earlier stated that the huge export surplus earnings of India from the world magically "seemed to disappear" as far as India's external account was concerned. Of course, these foreign exchange earnings did not actually disappear: they were entirely swallowed up in the account held in London in the Bank of England by the secretary of state for India. These earnings, which should have been a large credit for India, were appropriated by Britain by showing every year administered sterling debits vis-à-vis Britain, which always added up to a sum that was equal to, or a somewhat larger than, the total export surplus earnings, thereby obliging India to borrow. The sterling debits were in large part fictitious, manipulated, and far in excess even of the sum of "Home Charges"[1] and direct merchandise import surplus with Britain. Thus Saul's table on the 1910 balance of payments of Britain with India shows a massive sum of £60 million as the credit claimed by Britain from India (somewhat higher than the latter's entire global export surplus), of which merchandise debit with Britain was £19 million while "Home Charges" were about £15 million (Pandit 1937:65). The available data from the United Nations on the matrix of global trade show that by

1928 India's global export surplus was £106 million, entirely claimed as Britain's credit, while the Home Charges were about £28 million[2] and the debit on merchandise account with Britain, £22 million.

Thus, the "drain" obviously did not announce itself as a "drain" in the trade data: it was offset by, and hence camouflaged by, the sum of a large number of items shown on the debit side of the colony's balance of payments (not just the well-known Home Charges), which for convenience we shall call "drain-associated payments," whereby these entire exchange earnings were siphoned off. These same items also appeared in the colony's budget as the rupee equivalent of sterling expenditures abroad, as earlier mentioned. (It may be noted that after World War I, whose later years saw extra foreign earnings by India, one such debit item of payment was a "gift" of £100 million by British India to Britain, a 'gift' no Indian knew about. At current prices and at 3 percent interest, this alone would amount to at least £1,920 billion today.)

India was a classic case of "drain," and a large literature exists on the subject.[3] The "drain-associated payments" figured both in the colonial government's budget and in the balance of payments. This means that leaving these payments out, the colonial government ran a fiscal surplus that paid for the current account surplus (again leaving these payments out). The primary commodities and manufactures exported by India and other economies of the colonised periphery, in other words, were partly paid for through the imports of manufactured goods like textiles the colonies could well produce, which caused deindustrialization, but the bulk was not paid for at all since the "payment" came out of taxes. In fact the invisible debits imposed through "drain"-related items often even exceeded the entire merchandise export surplus earnings, which forced the colony to borrow, and hence face increased future interest burdens. During the period 1922–38, for example, India's cumulated total export surplus earnings, taking merchandise and gold, from the whole world (including the managed trade deficit with Britain) was £1,022 million, while largely manipulated invisible debits with Britain alone totaled £1,170 million and necessitated borrowing by India to the extent of £148 million (Banerjee 1963).[4] In the "through the looking glass" world of colony and metropolis, relations were transposed: the trade-surplus colony was obliged to borrow from the trade-deficit metropolis. For no sovereign country would we find the invisible debits with one country alone thus systematically exceeding the positive earnings with all other countries.

One implication of this arrangement, as we have seen, was the imposition of income deflation, which "released" the limited tropical land for producing export crops. The other implication was that these crops were obtained by the colonial power mainly gratis, being paid for by the tax revenue obtained from within the country itself. But that was not all. Since the magnitude of the "drain" could be adjusted (with additional items to the budgetary provisions), a situation of excess demand for commodities could be eliminated, as could, correspondingly, any situation of excess supply for the key currency, the pound sterling, arising from this source.

There was an additional factor as well. All the British colonies were obliged to hold the gold and foreign exchange reserves backing their currencies in London with the Bank of England. Much of the reserves was in the form of pound sterling, but such reserves that were held in other foreign currencies were also held in London. In effect, Britain was therefore sitting on a mountain of colonial-earned gold and foreign exchange reserves with which it could counter any tendency on the part of any other metropolitan economy to move away from pound sterling to some other currency. Any *ex ante* excess supply of the key currency, the pound sterling, matched by an excess demand for some other currency therefore, could be countered by Britain.

This arrangement was further facilitated by the fact that colonies like India had rising trade and current account surplus vis-à-vis continental Europe and the United States, while being obliged to run a current account deficit vis-à-vis Britain mainly through the imposition of administered invisible liabilities, namely the "drain-associated payments" mentioned already, over and above importing deindustrializing manufactured goods. By 1913 just over 70 percent of India's global export surplus earnings were from North America and continental Europe combined (United Nations 1962; U. Patnaik 2013). The colonies were therefore earning other metropolitan currencies, as well as gold, which were held in London either directly or converted to pound sterling. The fact that the colonies were earning other metropolitan currencies meant that at the margin any excess demand for such currencies arising within the system, on account of a movement away from the pound sterling, could be countered by making a movement into pound sterling from such other currencies (since it was the metropolitan power in association with the colonial governments that decided on the pattern of foreign currency holdings earned by the colonies, but held in London).

This entire arrangement therefore meant that any *ex ante* excess supply of pound sterling, whether caused by an excess demand for commodities or by an excess demand for some other currency, could be countered by Britain. This preserved the role of the pound sterling as a stable medium of holding wealth and did not even give rise to any tendency to move away from pound sterling (until the system itself came unstuck for reasons we discuss below).[5]

B. The "Balancing Role" of the Colonies' Exchange Earnings in the International Payments System

India earned the second largest merchandise export surplus in the world for at least four decades up to 1928, second only to the United States, according to the available League of Nations (1942) and United Nations (1960) data on the matrix of world trade. Had India not been in thrall to Britain but a free and sovereign country, these huge export earnings could have been used to import technology to build a modern industrial structure, as Japan was doing in this period. What the exchange earnings were actually used for was to help offset Britain's global current account deficits and to permit it to invest on the European continent, in North America, and in recent European settlement regions, with no balance of payments worries.

This arrangement thus had an additional advantage of great importance. Britain could maintain its leading position only to the extent that it accommodated the ambitions of the newly industrializing countries of the time by keeping its own markets open for them. The newly industrializing countries, however, were necessarily more competitive than Britain because of their more modern technologies (Britain, as mentioned earlier, had to pay, as many economic historians have put it, the "penalty of an early start"). Its keeping its markets open to the products of the newly industrializing countries meant therefore that it had to run a persistent current account deficit vis-à-vis those countries, which it did towards the end of the nineteenth century. In the event of its not doing so, they would have revolted against the gold standard, which would have therefore become unsustainable.

But colonies like India ran large and rising current account surpluses vis-à-vis these economies, notably with Continental Europe, the United States and Canada, and Japan, to whom they exported their primary commodities, as well as simple manufactures like cotton yarn in the case

of Japan. Since Indian exports were raw materials and foodstuffs required by the newly industrialising countries, they were free of tariffs,
whereas Britain's own exports faced barriers. Britain settled its deficit
with these late industrializing economies in large part by appropriating the exchange earnings of India and its other colonies and by running
a current account surplus with them. As Marcello de Cecco (1984:71)
puts it, "India's foreign trade was so structured that it realized a large
deficit with Britain and a large surplus with the rest of the world." However, the political economy of the apparently "large deficit" of India
with Britain, which is the same as a "large surplus" of Britain with India,
is not discussed by the author since no reference is made to the key
factor, Britain's political control over the Indian budget and its direct
linking to trade. The large deficit of India was manipulated to be so
because the local producers of export surplus were "paid" out of their
own tax contribution to the budget—namely, they were not paid at all
—while their exchange earnings were appropriated by imposing administered invisible liabilities on the external account to the required
amount.

This "current account surplus" of Britain with its colonies would not
have existed at all without direct political control. It arose in some part
from the deindustrializing exports that Britain made to colonies.
S. B. Saul (1960) calls the Indian market for Britain a "market on tap,"
which could be turned on at will; but it arose in much larger part from
the invisible liabilities that Britain heaped on the colonies by way of
"drain-associated" items, including munificent "gifts" it took from
the colonies for itself. Not only did Britain balance its current account
using the colonies' global export earnings through this managed triangular settlement, but so large were these earnings in certain periods
that they could be used for making capital exports as well, including to
the newly industrializing countries.

*Britain was exporting capital to the very countries with which it had
current account deficits, thus running up very large balance of payments
deficits with them.* By 1913 its combined balance of payments deficit with
the European continent and the United States reached £145 million—
quite an unsustainable sum if it had to be financed by normal means.
Britain could incur such large capital exports and resulting balance of
payments deficits with impunity because it could appropriate at will the
enormous gold and foreign exchange earnings from the global export
surplus of its colonies, while "paying" the colonised producers of the

export surplus in local currency out of the taxes raised from these very same producers. (A large part of gold inflow from foreign importers was monetary gold, and not commodity gold, though all of it is treated as commodity gold in the existing literature.)

The more complex system thus retained the essence of the earlier one, obtaining the export surplus earnings gratis since the goods were the commodity equivalent of taxes. The "drain" from the colonies was, as earlier mentioned, not merely large enough to finance a very substantial part of Britain's current account deficits vis-à-vis the newly industrializing countries; in many periods it was large enough to finance a substantial part of Britain's capital exports to the temperate regions of white settlement. As Saul (1960:58, 88) writes, "The key to Britain's whole payments pattern lay in India, financing as she probably did more than two-fifths of Britain's total deficits," and furthermore, "This was by no means all, for it was mainly through India that the British balance of payments found the flexibility essential to a great capital exporting country."[6]

This both gave rise to a tremendous diffusion of industrial capitalism and also kept up the level of demand in the world economy, which made possible the "Long Boom of the long nineteenth century." If, for instance, the colonial markets had not been available to Britain, then since British goods were not much in demand in the newly industrializing countries, Britain would have been forced either to protect its economy or to abandon pound sterling's parity with gold. In either case the gold standard would have become unsustainable, and the uncertainties that would have followed, including a spate of beggar-my-neighbour policies of exchange rate depreciations (such as actually occurred when the gold standard was finally abandoned), would have truncated the "Long Boom."

The stranglehold it had on the internal finances and export earnings of the colonies thus conferred a number of advantages on Britain and therefore upon the metropolitan capitalist system as a whole. First, it ensured that the role of the British pound sterling as the key currency, and hence as a stable medium for holding wealth, was maintained without any problems, with neither commodities (or gold) nor any other metropolitan currency posing a threat to the pound sterling. Second, it brought about a tremendous diffusion of industrial capitalism across the globe, excluding the colonies. Third, it kept up the level of aggregate demand for world capitalism, not in the sense emphasized by Rosa Luxemburg—namely, that exports to the colonies (or export surpluses) boosted demand for the capitalist sector of the world in a simple direct manner—but in the more complex sense that while diffusion of capitalism boosted world demand—the "open frontier" argument that Alvin Hansen (1938) was to underscore later—this diffusion itself could occur because of the possibility of triangular trade through the colonies.

It follows that not only was the success of the gold standard based on the existence of an empire, but the role of the empire was more complex and intricate than even theories of imperialism, such as Rosa Luxemburg's, which discuss this issue at all, suggest. The role of the empire, not surprisingly, has been missed not just in the analysis of the gold standard and of the "Long Boom" associated with it, but also in the genesis of the Great Depression of the 1930s.

It is clear from the above that a complex and intricate arrangement, based on the colonies, was involved in the international monetary system sustaining the "Long Boom." This arrangement could get unstuck by new developments, and in such a case a revival of the arrangement would be difficult, which would then prevent the emergence of a new boom until a whole new arrangement had been put in place. This is exactly what happened in the interwar period. The emergence of Japan as a competitor for Britain in its Asian markets, which had served the entire metropolis well until that time, was the first such new development. The emergence of the world agricultural crisis, whose origins need not detain us here, was another.

Japanese competition, which became serious from the 1920s, meant that Britain's colonial markets like India were no longer "on tap." Its ability to run a merchandise surplus with colonies by imposing its goods on the colonial markets was undermined, and to that extent, the possibility of sustaining very large balance of payments deficits vis-à-vis continental Europe and the United States (by investing in them while running current account deficits with them) was also undermined—though the quantitatively much larger drain-related extractions continued to sustain the system for a few years longer. The old market arrangement, in short, simply could not be revived (and British attempts to form an alliance with the domestic bourgeoisie in colonies like India, *against* the encroachment of Japanese capital, still meant conceding ground to such bourgeoisies by way of protective tariffs, which prevented a revival of the prewar scenario.)

The clearest proof of the fact that the pre-war scenario could not be revived was the fiasco of Britain's return to the gold standard at the prewar parity, which could not be sustained and led perforce to the attempt at wage deflation in Britain, and the resulting General Strike of 1926. (Interestingly the changed position of colonial markets as an explanation of this fiasco has also received little attention.) Britain's unemployment rate had already touched 10 percent by 1929; and this was before the Great Depression, not in the sense of the stock market crash but in the authentic sense of a piling up of unemployment, had begun in the United States.

Explanations of the Great Depression have been many, from Alvin Hansen's (1938) theory of the closing of the frontier, to Schumpeter's (1939) theory of the coincidence of the troughs of the three types of cycle, the Kondratieffs, the Juglars, and the Kitchins, to Baran and Sweezy's (1966) theory of the rise of monopoly capitalism with its inherent tendency towards stagnation. All these postulate independent demand side factors for explaining the slump. But even if none of these factors had operated, the very fact of Britain's not being able to meet its current deficit to the same extent because of the loss of its colonial markets would have meant in any case a decline of the gold standard, which eventually did occur, and hence enormous uncertainty in a capitalist world left without an international monetary system; this would have choked off investment and precipitated a slump anyway. Thus, simple aggregate demand-based explanations for the Great Depression that do not take into account the role of the empire in sustaining the "Long Boom" and the changed scenario in which this role could no longer be played are seriously inadequate.

A very important and generally ignored part of this changed scenario was the impact of falling agricultural prices from 1926, which sharply reduced the export surplus earnings of the colonies from the world (in India, these earnings collapsed to one-fifth of the 1925 level within six years by 1931); distress gold outflow from India, while cushioning the impact on Britain, also ceased soon while export earnings did not recover. As a result, it finally became impossible for Britain to continue to export capital to the industrialising countries or even to shore up demand by meeting its current account deficits with them in the new situation (U. Patnaik 2014). The agricultural crisis had exactly the same sort of effect, only more intensively so, as the competition from a newly emerging Japan; both undermined the gold standard by making

Britain's position untenable within it. While perceptive observers like Charles Kindleberger (1987) have seen the changed position of Britain as contributing to the Great Depression, this changed position has not been analysed in the entire literature on the subject with reference to the changing economic conditions of the British *empire.*

Despite the worsened position of the colonised population owing to depression, another massive round of surplus extraction from India by Britain took place from 1941 to 1946, and this substantially cushioned the impact on Britain itself of the war. War-related Allied expenditure in the South Asian theatre over this period (totaling over £2,500 million, while the prewar annual budget was about £140 million) was charged to the Indian budget. These swollen sums were raised in minor part through greatly increased direct taxes, but in major part through profit inflation, with forced savings being extracted through the Keynesian mechanism described earlier. This compressed the real incomes of peasants and artisans in India generally, but did so with particular severity in Bengal, the main base area of Allied forces. The profit inflation led to the death by starvation of 3.1 million persons in Bengal during 1943–44 and reduced another half a million families to destitution (Lokanathan 1946; Sen 1981; U. Patnaik 1991).

III

The Bretton Woods System

Even though the Bretton Woods system came into being before the process of decolonization got going, much of its life coincided with the post-decolonization world. And the basic weakness of the Bretton Woods system arose, as suggested in an earlier chapter, from the fact that unlike the gold standard, it was not founded upon an empire.

Interestingly, decolonization *per se* did not create any problems arising from the phenomenon of increasing supply price of tropical products and other primary commodities. This is because for a change the newly independent countries in the periphery adopted significant land-augmenting measures under the aegis of their states, uninhibited, in the new situation characterized by the hegemony of Keynesianism and the practice of Keynesian demand management, by the doctrine of "sound finance." For the first time, as we have seen, agricultural output increased to a point where, notwithstanding the continuation of primary commodity exports, per capita foodgrain availability in the countries of the periphery showed a significant increase. And the competition between the newly independent countries of the periphery to earn foreign exchange for their industrialization drive also meant that the prices of the commodities were kept down. Contrary to what authors like W. A. Lewis had expected (see Kaldor 1976), postwar inflation, after the Korean War boom, was remarkably low, and the terms of trade between primary commodities and manufacturing moved against the former (Spraos 1980; Chakraborty 2011) despite the fact of decolonization, which opened up possibilities for cartel-like organizations among primary producing countries of the periphery. The danger of any threat to the value of the key currency from an increase in commodity prices was thus kept at bay, *despite the absence of any mechanism for the imposition of income deflation upon the population of the periphery.*

At the same time there was no other currency that was strong enough to challenge the hegemony of the U.S. dollar. Inter-imperialist rivalry, which had become serious since the beginning of the twentieth century, was muted, with the United States being the undisputed leader of the capitalist world both in terms of economic might and above all in terms of military strength. Other major capitalist countries, enjoying the military protection offered by the United States were willy-nilly forced to accept the supremacy of the dollar. And it is significant that when the challenge to the dollar emerged, which led to the collapse of the Bretton Woods system, it was from gold rather than from any other capitalist currency.

The period of the Bretton Woods system that coincides with what has been called the "Golden Age of Capitalism" was marked above all by far higher growth rates and far lower levels of unemployment in the metropolis than had ever been historically experienced by capitalism (Armstrong, Glyn, and Harrison 1991). Low unemployment was a product *inter alia* of Keynesian demand management, or of what has been called "military Keynesianism" in the United States, as well as some welfare state measures under the aegis of social democracy, in a conscious bid to ward off the socialist challenge, in Europe. But it exposed metropolitan capitalism to the "danger" of "too small" a reserve army of labour. And this "danger" manifested itself in the worldwide wage explosion in 1968.

Much has been written on why this explosion occurred: some (Turner, Jackson, and Wilkinson 1970) have argued that the high taxation on account *inter alia* of the welfare state measures kept post-tax wages relative to labour productivity subdued and produced the upsurge in demand for money wage increases. Others (for instance, Kaldor 1976), to our minds more plausibly, have drawn attention to the excess demand pressures that were built up when the Vietnam War escalated: this caused some erosion in the real wages of advanced-country workers, which produced a response in the form of higher wage demands in 1968. But whatever the *stimulus* for money wage demands, the *success* of such demands owed much no doubt to the sustained levels of low unemployment rate that characterized advanced capitalist economies.

The collapse of the Bretton Woods system, however, did not occur on account of this wage-push inflation. Had inflation been the only factor at work, the advanced capitalist countries could have reached some agreement to curtail aggregate demand and restabilize metropolitan capitalism by pursuing a lower growth–lower inflation trajectory. *The collapse occurred because this inflation was accompanied by an enormous increase in the supply of dollars.* It was, in other words, the combination of inflation with an enormous outpouring of dollars from the United States that persuaded the world's wealth-holders to move away from the dollar to gold.

The United States, which traditionally had a trade and current account surplus, first moved to a current account deficit in the 1960s owing to large-scale expenditures on military bases all over the globe which it had to maintain because of its position as the leading capitalist power of the world. But since the Bretton Woods system decreed the dollar to be "as good as gold," with its price being officially fixed at $35 per ounce of gold, the United States simply printed dollars to meet its current account deficit and to make capital exports, including through American firms taking over European companies by using money printed back home. This flood of printed dollars became a torrent as the Vietnam War escalated, and the United States basically financed the war through an enlarged current account deficit. Other advanced capitalist countries, which were forced thereby to maintain a current account surplus, were obliged to hold on to this torrent of dollars emanating from the United States. When inflation began to appear in the late 1960s, the first cracks in the Bretton Woods system became visible; with the acceleration in inflation owing to the wage explosion, the system began to crumble.

Interestingly, the worldwide explosion in commodity prices was a result, not a cause, of the collapse of the dollar. It was people moving away from the dollar and into commodities that caused the worldwide price explosion in commodities. Soon this explosion subsided, except in oil, where a cartel had meanwhile come up and jacked up prices.

We have covered this ground in earlier chapters. The real point is the following. If the United States had had access to colonial "drain" in the era of the Bretton Woods system, as Britain had during the gold standard, then there would have been no outpouring of dollars, no build up of claims against the United States, just as there had been no build up of claims against Britain during the gold standard years despite its running persistent current deficits vis-à-vis other metropolitan powers. No doubt, as radical opinion held (e.g., Frank 1975; Amin 1977; Emmanuel 1972), there was an outflow of surplus from the periphery to the metropolis, including especially to the United States, even during the Bretton Woods period on account of "unequal exchange," "transfer pricing," and other such means, but these were not comparable to the politically imposed "drain" of the colonial period.

Our argument should not be interpreted to mean that the United States' "deprivation" consisted *simply* in a lack of access to political colonies. Even if the United States had political colonies, the fact remains that the surplus from these colonies, taken out in the commodity form of what they produced, *would simply not have been enough*, especially in view of the already low prices paid for such products (owing precisely to factors like "unequal exchange"), to counterbalance the current account deficit of the United States. In other words, the point is not simply that Britain had political colonies, which the United States lacked. The point additionally is that *what had sufficed during the long nineteenth century would no longer suffice now*.

It is in this sense that Rosa Luxemburg's basic insight that the process of "development" unleashed by capitalism on the world economy has the contradictory effect of removing the very props upon which such development rests, has an abiding relevance, though not exactly the way she envisaged it. The drain that can be imposed on the people of the periphery by the leading capitalist power today would take a commodity form whose price has been so pushed down (with the possible exception of oil), that it would no longer suffice to pay for the current account deficit that such a power must run in order to play its role of being the leader and allowing access to its markets by its rivals.

The Bretton Woods system, in short, had two basic weaknesses, both of which arose from the fact that it was not based on an empire of the sort Britain had. The first was that it had no means of imposing an income deflation, a weakness that became apparent only towards the fag-end of the system; the second was that it did not rest on a situation where the leading capitalist power, the one with the key currency, could use colonial "drain" to offset its current account deficits vis-à-vis its rival newly emerging economies. *The system that followed the Bretton Woods system and that characterizes contemporary capitalism has overcome the first of these weaknesses but not the second. And this fact continues to make contemporary capitalism vulnerable.*

IV

The Post–Bretton Woods World

The post–Bretton Woods system is less different from the Bretton Woods system than appears at first sight. True, the formal differences are formidable: there is no gold-dollar link; there are no fixed exchange rates; and currency values are supposedly "market determined." But the substantive differences are less significant. The dollar continues to be the key reserve currency in terms of which the bulk of international transactions are carried out and which provides the stable medium for holding wealth.

For it to play this role, however, it is essential that commodity prices, including the price of gold in terms of the dollar, should not be expected to increase significantly (for otherwise wealth-holders would simply shift to gold at the expense of the dollar). It is not necessary that they should be absolutely stable in terms of the dollar, but whatever increases do occur should not give rise to any persistent expectations of a price increase. Hence the absence of a gold link does not mean that the dollar is free to take on any value in terms of gold.

Likewise, the absence of fixed exchange rates does not mean that the major currencies of the capitalist world, in terms of which the bulk of the world's wealth is actually held, can simply take on any value vis-à-vis the dollar; for if there is an expectation of a persistent decline in the value of any of them vis-à-vis the dollar, then wealth-holders would simply move away from that currency (and currency-denominated assets) to dollar (and corresponding dollar-denominated assets). The other major capitalist countries therefore pursue deflationary domestic policies if necessary to maintain the value of their currencies vis-à-vis the dollar.

The differences between their currencies, the U.S. dollar, and the currencies of the periphery, can be seen as follows. The United States does not *have to* pursue any deflationary policies to maintain the value of the dollar since, as of now, when there are no serious inflationary threats to it, whatever dollars are made available to the world economy by the United States are simply held. Put differently, the dollar is the only currency (and there is none other like it, which is why it continues to be the key reserve currency) whose fall in value relative to other currencies creates expectations among wealth-holders that this fall will reverse itself even without any domestic deflation in the U.S. economy.

In the case of the other major currencies, any similar fall does not necessarily create such expectations, which is why, to preserve the role of those currencies as wealth-holding mediums, their economies *do* have to pursue domestic deflationary policies from time to time, in *a move that actually succeeds in keeping them as wealth-holding mediums.*

In the case of currencies of the periphery, however, there is an additional factor: namely a tendency *over time* for the parameters underlying any short-run equilibrium in the exchange market to change in a manner that expresses an unfolding preference of wealth-holders for metropolitan currencies and metropolitan currency–denominated assets, compared to the currencies of the periphery and assets denominated in them.[7] This change typically gives rise to either one, or a combination, of the following: an intensification over time of income deflation on the people of the periphery and a secular decline in the nominal, and real effective, exchange rates of the currencies of the periphery.[8] Such a secular decline, owing to the wealth-holders' growing preference for metropolitan currency–denominated assets compared to the peripheral currency–denominated assets, if it occurs, then becomes an important reason for the decline in the terms of trade of commodities produced by the countries of the periphery vis-à-vis the commodities produced by the metropolis, i.e., of primary commodities vis-à-vis manufactures, and of lower-end manufactures, such as what several developing countries produce for the world market these days, vis-à-vis

higher-end manufactures such as what the advanced capitalist economies produce.

Put differently, there is a hierarchy of currencies in the world economy in the post–Bretton Woods system consisting of the dominant currency, which is the U.S. dollar; other major currencies, which also
constitute permanent wealth-holding mediums but only through the
imposition of deflationary measures when necessary in their respective
countries; and the currencies of the periphery, from which there is always a tendency over time for wealth-holders to flee to the dollar or
other metropolitan currencies. This last assertion may appear odd in
view of the fact that China has been such a successful exporter and so
prominent an example of an "emerging economy." But even the upper
echelons of the Chinese bureaucracy, like those in contemporary
Russia, reportedly shift their private fortunes out of China systematically, which only underscores the point being made here.

This development of a hierarchy among the world's currencies becomes possible only because of the possibility of cross-border capital
flows. If there were capital controls, as under the Bretton Woods
system, then wealth-holders' preferences for one currency (or currency-
denominated assets) over another (or assets denominated in terms of
the latter) would have remained unrealized, taking the form at best
of illicit cross-border flows.

The transition from the Bretton Woods to the post–Bretton Woods
system therefore is important because of the change in context, of the
fact that the latter system is based upon a regime of freer cross-border
flows of capital, not because *among the major capitalist currencies* there
is any tendency towards a secular change in their relative values vis-à-
vis one another or even vis-à-vis gold, notwithstanding the formal possibility for such secular change under the new system.

One effect of this change in context has been widely recognized:
namely, the denial of scope for Keynesian demand management under
the new system. This arises for the following reason. Finance capital
typically favours "sound finance" and is also opposed to heavier taxation, certainly of the rich. Hence, in a world where finance is globalized while states continue to be nation-states, these demands of
globalized finance must be acceded to by the government of each
nation-state for fear that otherwise finance would leave its shores for
other countries, precipitating a severe financial crisis for the nation-state.
But acceding to these demands in turn means that state intervention

in demand management becomes impossible, since neither the weapon of a fiscal deficit nor the weapon of a "balanced budget multiplier" can be used by the state for stimulating demand. In other words, an increase in government expenditure for enlarging the level of activity, whether financed by a fiscal deficit or by larger tax-financed state spending, becomes a virtual impossibility.

This logic, strictly speaking, should not apply to the leading capitalist power, whose currency is *de facto* still considered to be "as good as gold" even if not *de jure* as under the Bretton Woods system. With the dollar considered to be "as good as gold," fiscal policy within the United States should not frighten finance capital into leaving for other shores (which in fact is the hallmark of the key reserve currency under the present system, as discussed earlier). Even in the United States, however, there is pressure to pursue a policy of "sound finance" (or capping the fiscal deficit) for two obvious reasons.

One reason consists in the fact that the demand-stimulating effect of a U.S. fiscal deficit "leaks out" to a considerable extent to other countries through larger imports from them. An increase in the fiscal deficit entails to that extent therefore an increase in the foreign indebtedness of the United States for the sake of generating larger employment abroad; and this engenders opposition within the United States to an increase in the fiscal deficit. In other words, the U.S. state is constrained to act not as a surrogate world state stimulating global demand but as a nation-state, of the United States; and this fact prevents an increase in the fiscal deficit.

The second reason is the political-ideological hegemony that finance capital exercises over the U.S. administration. The sheer pervasiveness of the doctrine of "sound finance," the proximity of the U.S. administration to the dominant financial interests of Wall Street which espouse this doctrine, the bluster of agencies close to financial interests who even on occasion "downgrade" the credit rating of the U.S. government itself—all these together ensure that the U.S. administration is under thralldom to this ideology.

This has the effect of keeping the unemployment level larger and the growth rate lower on average in the metropolis under the post–Bretton Woods system than earlier. A second factor contributes towards this same end. While fiscal deficit caps are the "norm," the major capitalist currencies other than the U.S. dollar, as we mentioned earlier, have to maintain their parity vis-à-vis the dollar from time to time by pursuing deflationary policies. This means an even lower level of aggregate demand than would ensue if fiscal deficit caps alone were being adhered to. The level of activity therefore is even lower than if all metropolitan countries were simply pursuing "sound finance" as defined in the contemporary context. It is not surprising, then, that the average growth rate of the advanced countries' economies taken together has been lower and that the average unemployment rate has been higher, despite the "bubble"-based booms that have characterized the United States, and hence, by implication, the world economy, in the period since the mid-1970s, than during the so-called "Golden Age" years.

It is the second implication of the globalization of capital, however, especially finance capital, that has received less attention. The removal of capital controls, we have suggested above, makes possible a secular decline in the nominal and even real effective exchange rate of the peripheral economies, even as they impose increasingly strict measures of deflation. The basic reason for this is an unfolding preference of the wealthy in the periphery to locate their wealth in the metropolis, which is the home base of capitalism. This means that there is no *long-term* "equilibrium" level of the exchange rate, even for a given level of money wage rate in the domestic currency and even in the absence of "increasing supply price" of tropical commodities coming into play, at which these economies can settle.

This point should be distinguished from the central concern of our book. Our concern has been: What happens to the value of the currency in the event of "increasing supply price"? The point here however is: What happens to the value of the currency, even when increasing supply price does not come into play, because of the long-term desire of the rich in the periphery to flee to the currencies of the metropolis?

Such preference for the metropolitan currencies over the currencies of the periphery does not mean that the value of the latter, even in the absence of specific countervailing measures such as intensified income deflation, would necessarily zoom down to zero in any period. This danger, we suggested earlier, is serious if "increasing supply price" is allowed to come into play. But the unfolding preference for the metropolitan currency is qualitatively different from, *and operates more gradually than*, the response to increasing supply price. It may make the currency of the periphery drift downwards *over time* (and when it does, it further reinforces itself); but this is a more long-term threat.[9] At any rate, this unfolding "absolute preference" is the difference between the currencies of the periphery and even the non-leading metropolitan currencies.

Some may argue that if the peripheral economies became clones of the metropolitan ones, then this tendency on the part of the wealthy in the periphery to shift their wealth to the metropolis would disappear. But notwithstanding the high rates of growth that some economies of the periphery have experienced of late, this denouement of their becoming clones of the metropolitan economies does not seem to materialize. The "advantage" that Europe had, of the possibility of vast amounts of emigration of its population to the temperate regions of white settlement, is not available to countries like India today, in whose case therefore even high growth will not come anywhere near depleting the enormous labour reserves. (Even stories of the exhaustion of China's labour reserves, though possibly true in coastal pockets, have to be taken with a pinch of salt if the focus is on the country as a whole.) The persistence of vast labour reserves and hence of poverty and misery essentially gives rise to a capitalist development whose social base remains forever shaky, and hence creates a desire on the part of the wealthy to "flee" the country for the more secure home base of capitalism, which is the metropolis.

There is perhaps an additional factor here. The bourgeoisie in the periphery, for reasons that Franz Fanon (2001) underscored, is forever keen to be "counted" in the metropolis, to join the "high table" as it were. And holding one's wealth in the metropolis is one way of joining the "high table." An indication of this desire to join the "high table" is given by the fact that the richest Indian businessmen prefer to donate money to Harvard University or to Cambridge University rather than to cash-strapped Indian universities.

The only way to prevent such flight of capital is for the peripheral economies to have capital controls as a permanent feature. In short, "globalization" in the contemporary context, which means above all the globalization of capital, including finance capital, must be avoided by the peripheral economies, no matter how high their statistically measured GDP growth rates are, if they are to have a modicum of concern for their poor and working population.

Let us, however, come back to our main discussion. We argued earlier that the Bretton Woods system had two basic problems. The first was that it had no mechanism for imposing income deflation on the peripheral economies. While the post-decolonization dirigiste regimes in these economies carried out land-augmenting measures, the problem of increasing supply price was kept at bay; and since there was intense competition between these economies, with each being keen to earn as much foreign exchange as possible for importing the wherewithal for industrialization, there was no question of their colluding to jack up their prices. The absence of the scope for income deflation therefore did not immediately matter. But the moment there was excess demand, buttressed by a "rush to commodities" in the aftermath of the collapse of the Bretton Woods system, this failing became obvious. Any revival of Bretton Woods was ruled out.

The second problem of the Bretton Woods system arose from the fact that the leading capitalist country had no way of settling its current account deficit, which it had to necessarily incur as the leader vis-à-vis newly industrializing economies if the system was to be acceptable to all, without simply getting into ever-growing debt. Since others demand dollars, this does not matter up to a point, but it does make the system fragile.

The post–Bretton Woods arrangement, which has been associated with a removal of capital controls and hence entails the globalization of capital, including finance capital, has dealt with the first problem but not with the second. The pursuit of "sound finance," with its reduced taxation of the rich, has squeezed purchasing power in the hands of the domestic working population to make a range of commodities produced on the limited tropical landmass available for exports. This has entailed reduced domestic per capita foodgrain availability. And the emphasis on "inflation targeting" has also meant a calibration of domestic income deflation in a manner that prevents the leading metropolitan currency from becoming "debauched."

But while we are back to a regime of income deflation on the periphery, the current account deficit of the leading country continues to be a problem with the new arrangement and makes the system fragile. A repeat of British experience during the gold standard years when despite having a current deficit vis-à-vis the newly industrializing countries of the time, Britain used colonial surpluses appropriated gratis not only to avoid getting into debt but even to make substantial capital exports, is not possible today. And that, as we have suggested earlier, is not because the United States does not have formal political colonies or lacks the might to appropriate surpluses gratis from the countries of the periphery; rather, it expresses the fact that capitalism, having already exploited the periphery to the hilt, has significantly exhausted the possibility of using it any further to stabilize itself.

V

Concluding Observations

The mode of exposition above may suggest that the shift from one international monetary system to another was a well-planned, consciously thought-out operation. But capitalism is not a planned system. The transition from one monetary system to another neither occurs in a planned way nor for reasons having to do directly with the problems encountered in the original system. The time lag between the collapse of the gold standard and the coming into being of the Bretton Woods system was a decade and a half. True, the war intervened, but even before the war, eight years had elapsed with the capitalist world having no international monetary system and yet being submerged in a depression.

While the current international monetary arrangement came into being with the collapse of the Bretton Woods system, globalization of capital that provides the setting for it and underlies the income deflation imposed upon the people of the periphery was a result of "centralization of capital," that is, the coming into being of larger and larger blocs of capital, *which is a spontaneous tendency under capitalism* not willed by anybody. The end of dirigisme in the periphery and the imposition of income deflation, in other words, is a result not of any conscious effort to overcome the "lacunae" (from the point of view of metropolitan capital) of the earlier Bretton Woods system, which, as we have noted, had no mechanism for imposing income deflation, but of a spontaneous tendency of capitalism. These complexities, which our brief presentation may not make clear, must be borne in mind.

Likewise, our discussion of the international monetary systems has been motivated entirely by the desire to see how the basic structural contradiction with which this book is concerned—namely, how the requirements of expanding capital are met on the basis of supplies from a fixed tropical landmass, without jeopardizing the value of money in the metropolis—has been resolved under each of these systems. The other implications of these systems, though occasionally touched upon, are not the central theme of this chapter.

We are not even concerned with the different ways in which the people in the periphery are "exploited" by metropolitan capital. Our focus has simply been to highlight one particular structural relationship of "exploitation" that metropolitan capitalism cannot do without. This relationship, notwithstanding its essential nature, has not received any attention in the literature, including in the literature on imperialism. Our effort has been to rectify this lacuna.

CHAPTER NINE

Some Concluding Remarks

I

A Restatement of the Argument of the Book

The purpose of this book has not been to discuss the contemporary conjuncture in world capitalism, which is what Lenin had done in his classic work. Nor has it sought to provide an account of the multifarious ways in which metropolitan capital, whether or not with the support, connivance, and collaboration of the capital of the periphery, exploits the people of the periphery, which is typically what postwar theories of imperialism tended to focus on. Its purpose has been altogether different and rather *sui generis*. It has asked the question: Is it *necessary* for metropolitan capital *always* to enter into a structural relationship with the people of the periphery, which entails a subjugation of the latter?

This question by its nature constitutes a departure from Rosa Luxemburg's perception, since in her view the people of the periphery would not remain forever in their pristine state: with the spread of capitalism at the expense of the precapitalist sector, the people of the periphery according to her would merely become the proletariat (or the reserve army of labour in the usual sense) of expanding capitalism. Our very question therefore entails a nonacceptance of the Luxemburg perception. But this nonacceptance, which does justice to real history (since the precapitalist producers lingered on in real history as a subordinate mass in the periphery without becoming assimilated into the capitalist workforce), is precisely what makes our question pertinent: Given the fact that the people of the periphery linger on as a miserable mass and do not simply become the proletariat (or the reserve army as usually understood) of an expanding capitalism, is there any *necessity* for capitalism to exploit them nonetheless on a *continuous* basis?

An obvious affirmative answer can be given to this question according to the following reasoning. It is in the nature of capital not to leave any quarter of the globe untouched. Its subjugation of the people of the periphery therefore is an integral part of its modus operandi. Such subjugation is embedded in its very behavior, and any question of its functional necessity for the working of capitalism is beside the point.

This argument amounts to saying that metropolitan capital subjugates the people of the periphery because "they are there." While we do not dispute this argument, it does raise a pertinent question: If perchance a segment of the periphery became unavailable to metropolitan capital, then would metropolitan capital carry on without any inconvenience to it, as if that segment had simply never existed? True, it would try and snatch for itself whatever happened to become unavailable to it, for fear that not doing so would encourage other regions also to make themselves unavailable; but apart from such *strategic* considerations, are there any *economic* reasons why metropolitan capital simply cannot do without the periphery?

We can put this question differently. Joseph Schumpeter argued that the tendency of capitalism was to look for possibilities of carrying out "innovations" (in the sense defined by him) within whatever space was available to it, not to expand that space. Other than *strategic* considerations (which Schumpeter himself never recognized) that may dictate that capitalism must expand the space under its control as much as possible, are there also any *economic* reasons why it should do so? In other words, are there any *economic* reasons why the Schumpeterian argument that capitalism simply adjusts to the space available to it cannot be valid? If there are any such reasons, and if they hold for all phases of capitalism, then the claim that imperialism has become an obsolete category in the contemporary epoch must be wrong.

The purpose of this book has been to argue that there is indeed a compelling economic reason for metropolitan capital to subjugate, and to maintain continuous ascendancy over, the people of the periphery; and that reason, to recapitulate the argument of the preceding chapters, is as follows.

Metropolitan capitalism requires a large range of commodities that are necessary for it (including not only for the subsistence of the workers it employs but for consumption by all classes) but that it cannot produce in the geographical space within which it exists; nor can it develop substitutes for all of these commodities. It must obtain them from outside of its space, i.e., from the periphery constituting the global South, where they are produced by a host of precapitalist petty producers and typically in conditions that entail an "increasing supply price." Of course the phenomenon of increasing supply price (always defined with a given money wage or money income of producers) affects many commodities required by metropolitan capitalism, including exhaustible resources like oil; but in the present study we have taken as our archetypal case the commodities produced on the fixed tropical landmass, though our argument holds equally well for exhaustible resources (for the overwhelming bulk of known reserves of these resources lie outside the geographical space the capitalist core occupies). Since land-augmenting investment can be done primarily by the state located on such land mass, and since state activism in undertaking investment is typically frowned upon by capital (which prefers "sound finance"), the supply of such goods cannot be augmented, *ceteris paribus* to match the growing demands of metropolitan capital, as accumulation is undertaken.

An increase in the prices of such commodities, on the other hand, would threaten the value of money in the metropolis, making it impossible for wealth to be held in money or money-denominated assets. To maintain the value of money and yet obtain its requirements of products from the tropical landmass, metropolitan capital must impose "income deflation" upon the people of the periphery, entailing compression of their demand, so that commodities are snatched away from being absorbed by them for use in the metropolis. The structural arrangement for such income deflation is an essential component of imperialism and is as central today as ever.

Other than in the immediate aftermath of decolonization, when imperialism was in retreat and income deflation was eschewed by the newly independent states in the periphery, such income deflation has been a necessary feature of capitalism at all times. In the post-decolonization dirigiste phase, while income deflation was eschewed, land-augmenting investment was undertaken by the new states, which, in tandem with metropolitan states undertaking Keynesian demand management, rejected the doctrine of "sound finance." But this absence of any mechanism for income deflation in the periphery was a "weakness" (from the point of view of metropolitan capital) of the Bretton Woods system, which came to the fore in the early 1970s. Globalization, though arising for reasons that do not necessarily concern this particular issue but rather lie in the phenomenon of centralization of capital, once more reestablished a mechanism for income deflation.

Imperialism is concerned in short with the imposition of income deflation by metropolitan capital on the people of the periphery in order to squeeze out larger and larger supplies of a range of commodities required in the metropolis, without bringing into play the problem of increasing supply price that would threaten the value of money in the metropolis.

II

A Recapitulation of the Main Objections to the Argument

The immediate objection to this argument would be that the value of periphery's goods imported into the metropolis is so small that to imagine that a rise in the prices of such goods owing to increasing supply price (or to forced savings on the part of the people of the periphery in the absence of income deflation) would threaten the value of money in the metropolis is to defy credibility.

Of course the fact that the value of such goods is small is itself an outcome of imperialism, which has kept the value small, even though the use value of such goods in the metropolis is enormous. But even leaving aside this aspect, our argument is that a persistent rise in prices, even of goods of the periphery, would make wealth-holders shift to gold in lieu of money, which would jeopardize the value of money in the metropolis. Even if the wealth-holders in the metropolis do not shift to gold, wealth-holders in the periphery would, and that would raise gold prices relative to all currencies, destabilizing the value of money in the metropolis. And even if wealth-holders in the periphery did not shift to gold but to the metropolitan currency so that there is no threat to the latter, the collapse of the periphery's currency that would follow would make *the system as a whole* nonfunctional.

For all cases of nonvanishing excess demand, whether for gold or for the metropolitan currency within the periphery, the argument may be made that there would eventually be rationing in the concerned market, and that this would lead to a stabilization of the value of money everywhere. But rationing of this kind is not the way that capitalism in its spontaneity has functioned. Its "rules of the game," except in periods of dirigiste regimes or of war, have allowed freedom of choice, of the sort that matters for our argument, to wealth-holders with regard to currency and gold holdings.

The second objection that can be raised against our argument is that since prices have after all increased sharply throughout the twentieth century, why should we imagine that such price increases hold any terror for the system? The answer is simply that the price rise occurred predominantly during the war years and in the postwar period of dirigisme. A persistent and significant price rise becomes particularly difficult to sustain without serious threat to the value of money and hence to the entire financial architecture of metropolitan capitalism, in a regime where capital controls have been lifted, where controls over the flow of gold have been lifted, in short in a world where wealth-holders are free to choose the form in which they hold their wealth. Such freedom generally characterized the gold standard, just as it characterizes the current international monetary system resting upon "globalization." The war period and the period of dirigisme were not characterized by such unrestricted freedom of asset choice. This is not to say that any amount of inflation could be sustained under these regimes; we have seen from their experience that they could not be. But certainly more inflation could be tolerated when there were restrictions on asset choice than when there were none.

In fact, even when the restrictions on asset choice are removed, it is not as if all wealth-holders immediately act on the basis of such removal. Old habits persist; besides, even among the bulk of wealth-holders, especially in countries where the spirit of capitalism has made only a belated entry, hedonism is far from being rampant. The response of asset preference to inflation that has been postulated by us may not therefore be as prompt as we have assumed, which also means that inflation may occur to a greater extent without bringing the system to a standstill than suggested by us.

By the same token, however, as hedonism, or "economic rationality" as some would prefer to call it, gains currency *over time*, the analysis of this book should become even more relevant. To say this is not to suggest that it has not been; but even the distance that may be said to exist between real world phenomena and the reasoning of our book is likely if anything to shorten over time.

Another factor working in the same direction is the enormity of the financial architecture that has been developed of late. Its intricateness and complexity, far from making old-fashioned imperialist coercion over the people of the periphery irrelevant, actually makes it even more urgent, since the defence of the value of money becomes even more necessary because of the complexity and nontransparency of this architecture, which make for more proneness to financial crises. The irony of capitalism is that the more it changes, the more it stays the same; the greater the sophistication it acquires, the more urgently it requires the old practices of coercion. All this only underscores the basic theme of this book: namely, that imperialism, far from becoming unnecessary in the current era of capitalism, remains indeed even more necessary today than it has ever been. Let us now turn to some issues surrounding the argument we have presented.

III

Capitalism's Differential Treatment of the Peasantry

The fact that capitalism undermines precapitalist petty production is well understood. The real question relates to what ensues as a consequence. Rosa Luxemburg, as noted earlier, was of the view that such undermining led to a supplanting of petty production by capitalism (though occasionally in her opus one does get a somewhat different impression of the denouement she visualized). As a matter of fact, however, while such supplanting did occur in history in the case of the artisans and other petty producers of *manufactured goods*, which were the sectors where capitalist production made its entry, "supplanting" as a general rule was far from being the case for the bulk of the petty producers, especially the peasantry.

One can see the impact of capitalism on the precapitalist petty producers, especially the peasantry, in terms of two sharply contrasting scenarios. In the heartland of capitalism, namely within the metropolis itself where capitalism first developed, the peasantry was largely destroyed as a class (with certain obvious exceptions like France where it survived but kept reducing in relative size over time); the erstwhile peasants along with other segments of the workforce, including displaced artisans, who were not absorbed by capitalist activities at home, migrated to the temperate regions of white settlement. They set up as "farmers" there at the expense of the local inhabitants whose resistance was suppressed and who were driven off their land and herded into special areas and reservations.

In the case of the metropolis, in other words, the process of undermining of petty production led to a large scale relocation of the displaced petty producers; but this relocation itself was made possible by an imperialism that entailed conquest of distant lands to set up "colonies of settlement." These colonies themselves were later to throw off the metropolitan yoke, without relenting at all in their drive against the local population.

But in lands far from the cold temperate metropolis, the dispossession of local petty producers in the tropical and subtropical regions was *not accompanied by a destruction of the peasantry as a class.* It was effected through the setting up of "colonies of conquest," to which relatively little migration took place from the metropolis. The object of the expropriation of peasants in such colonies of conquest was not to *introduce capitalist agriculture* in lieu of peasant agriculture. On the contrary, the peasantry in these countries lingered on, even when losing its rights over land and being reduced to the status of inferior tenants. The peasantry in these colonies of conquest was not supplanted but was further suppressed and reduced to an inferior status. It was made to produce crops to meet the demands of the metropolis, and these were appropriated gratis through the system of colonial taxation of which the peasants themselves were major victims.

In fact, the pressure on the peasants to produce for the metropolis was itself often exerted through the very cash taxation system that took away what they produced gratis. The peasants who paid directly to the colonial authority were made to pay the cash taxes by certain fixed dates.

And when they were reduced to the status of tenants having to pay their dues to landlords, these landlords in turn had to pay their cash revenue to the colonial authority by a certain date. The entire system of payments, in short, became rigid; and nonpayment meant forfeiting whatever rights the peasants still had on land.

To meet their payment dues, they had to borrow from merchants who doubled as moneylenders and gave them advances. The condition for such advances was that they should grow certain crops and sell them to the merchants at precontracted prices. The production decision was thus related to market conditions, but the decisions themselves were not necessarily taken voluntarily by a group of optimizing peasants. Rather, they were taken by merchants and middlemen who responded to market signals, but made their responses effective by coercing the peasants to produce certain crops and taking advantage of the colonial system of taxation.

Thus, while the peasantry was destroyed in the metropolis and was reincarnated at best as "farmers" in the "new world" who carried on mechanized agriculture and who, despite not employing much hired labour (owing to such mechanization) could still be called "capitalist farmers" (Lenin 1964), the story was entirely different in the tropical and subtropical colonies of conquest. Here the peasantry lingered on and was made to produce increasingly for meeting the demands of the metropolis. Such production, however, did not give rise to the problem of "increasing supply price" because of the imposition of income deflation, of which the peasantry itself ironically was a major victim.

There was thus a basic difference in the treatment meted out by capitalism to the peasants in the tropical and subtropical lands and to those in the temperate regions. In the latter, they were destroyed as a class to be reincarnated in another avatar, while in the former, they continued to linger on despite the fact that their incomes were increasingly compressed by capitalism.

The Bengal famine of 1943–44 illustrates the last and extreme case of compression of income of the peasantry under colonial rule in India— a compression so intense that three million people starved to death. The peasants, fishermen, artisans, and rural labourers were made to bear the brunt of war financing through an engineered *profit inflation*, which raised prices much faster than the incomes of these self-employed petty producers, thus extracting the forced savings required to finance the enormously swollen war-time spending.

IV

Asymmetry between Tropical and Temperate Regions

Let us go back to the asymmetry we mentioned in an earlier chapter, that while the major products of the cold temperate regions such as wheat, summer fruits, and vegetables could also be produced in the larger tropical and subtropical countries in winter, those goods that were specific to the latter, such as stimulants, fibres, cane sugar, some edible oils, tropical fruits, and vegetables, could not be produced in the former. This asymmetry has two implications. First, obtaining a large range of goods that simply could not be produced in the temperate regions from the tropical landmass, and doing so in growing quantities because of capital accumulation, was, and remains, a perennial necessity for capitalism. And if increasing supply price is to be avoided, then there is no alternative to obtaining such goods at the expense of their local absorption. This in short remains a perennial feature of capitalism.

Second, insofar as goods that are produced in the temperate regions are concerned and that can pose a similar threat to the value of money in the metropolis, there is no need, *even in principle*, to impose any similar income deflation upon the people in the temperate region, since these goods, being producible in the tropical and subtropical region as well, can be obtained through the same process of income deflation that is imposed on the tropical population. *There is therefore something very specific about the structural relationship between the capitalist segment and the people of the tropical and subtropical regions. It is this structural relationship that we cover under the term "imperialism."*

Imperialism as an actual historical phenomenon no doubt entailed many things, including the dispossession of Amerindians, the original inhabitants of the temperate lands of the new world, so that the displaced petty producers and peasants of the metropolis unabsorbed by metropolitan capitalism could migrate there. But even though these particular phenomena, such as the dispossession of the original populations, may come to an end, as it did after a while, the phenomenon highlighted by us, namely, the imposition of income deflation on the periphery so that tropical goods (and temperate goods in winter) can be obtained by the capitalist sector without any threat of an increasing supply price, continues unabated. This is a relationship that existed at the inception of capitalism, that exists today, and that will continue to exist as long as capitalism remains. Hence this relationship constitutes in our view a basic defining characteristic of imperialism.

The foregoing also explains the asymmetry between the temperate and tropical regions: income deflation *has* to be imposed upon the latter and not necessarily upon the former. This is not just a matter of differential treatment of different *groups*. In other words, the basis for the asymmetry is not that the capitalist sector has a particular antipathy towards the people of the tropical and subtropical lands, while it has less antipathy towards the people of the temperate region. That may or may not be the case, but it is not germane to our argument. The basic reason is that *while temperate goods can be produced in the tropical and subtropical regions, the opposite is not true*. Hence income deflation in the periphery can meet the needs of capitalism for *both* kinds of goods.

This remains true even in a world where there is no actual import of temperate region goods into the tropical lands. It remains true, in other words, not because reduced *absorption* by the population of the tropical and subtropical region of goods produced on the temperate lands helps the metropolis. It remains true because with *temperate region goods being producible on tropical and subtropical lands*, an income deflation imposed upon the people of the latter region would cause a diversion of land use to produce even the temperate region goods on their lands, and thereby negate any threat to the value of money arising from their potential shortage. Any asymmetry in the treatment of *groups*, in other words, becomes possible because of the difference in the capacities of temperate and tropical lands.

The tropical and subtropical regions *were both historically self-sufficient* and are potentially capable of being self-sufficient even today. The temperate regions neither were historically self-sufficient nor are potentially self-sufficient even today. The living standard of people living in the temperate region simply cannot be met through the production within this region alone. They have to rely on imports of tropical and subtropical products. The same, however, is not true of the latter regions, which do not have to rely on imports of temperate products.

The foregoing discussion should absolve us of the charge of advancing just a "geographical" theory of imperialism. Imperialism being a *spatial* phenomenon does bring in geography. But, though founded upon certain geographical differences, it is a relation between *classes*. And the fact that the spread of capitalism to the periphery implies that the class of bourgeoisie or proto-bourgeoisie of the periphery switches sides, as it were, in the contradiction between metropolitan capital on the one side, and the peasants and petty producers of the periphery, together with the agricultural and other labourers dependent upon them, on the other, merely facilitates the persistence of this contradiction.

V

Transcending Capitalism

The fact that capitalism necessarily imposes income deflation and poverty upon the peasants and petty producers of the periphery underscores both the need for transcending the capitalist system for human progress and the difficulty of doing so. This difficulty arises from the fact that a *world-level* worker-peasant alliance for overthrowing the system is not practicable in the foreseeable future. International working-class organizations are virtually nonexistent, and international peasant organizations even more so. And given the differences in the *levels* of material conditions and consciousness between the working people of the metropolis and those of the periphery, forging such bonds poses formidable practical problems in the immediate future.

Hence the alternative scenario of transcendence of capitalism that might be visualized is one where in *particular* countries, especially of the periphery, worker-peasant alliances are forged and advance politically by de-linking those countries from the web of globalization, and hence from the hegemony of international finance capital. But such delinking makes these attempts extremely weak and vulnerable to imperialist counterattacks. In addition, given the fact that the peasantry in these countries often carries over a precapitalist feudal consciousness that is premodern and reeks of superstition, caste, and patriarchal attitudes (which the development of capitalism in those countries does little to demolish), the advance of such a worker-peasant alliance towards socialism remains fraught with difficulty.

Imperialism, in short, not only oppresses the working people in the periphery but also makes any challenge to such oppression by its victims that much more difficult. But imperialism is bringing the world to such an impasse at present—an impasse characterized by economic crisis, stagnation, and unemployment both in the metropolis and in the periphery; by unprecedented and intolerable levels of oppression of peasants and petty producers in the periphery (of which the mass suicides of peasants in India is one indication); and by an acute threat to our ecosystem—that mass resistance to it, as had happened in the context of the world wars that provided the backdrop to the previous round of revolutions, can suddenly erupt anywhere. That could usher in a whole new era of resistance and revolutions through which all existing social conditions, including levels of consciousness, could alter with astonishing rapidity.

A Commentary on
A Theory of Imperialism

DAVID HARVEY
CUNY Graduate Center

THE THEORY OF IMPERIALISM that Utsa and Prabhat
Patnaik propose depends on the idea that tropical regions have a natural monopoly over the supply of certain crucial goods required for the
functioning of metropolitan capitalism by virtue of the physical geographical (climatic) conditions required for the production of those
goods. There is, they claim, a fundamental asymmetry: anything that
the temperate region produces can be produced on the tropical landmass, but the converse is not true. Imperialism is defined as a set of non-
market coercive political and economic mechanisms designed to prevent
tropical producers from ever exercising their potential monopoly powers in global trade. If they were ever able to do so, then prices in the
metropolis would skyrocket, the value of money in the metropolitan
capitalist economies would be destroyed, and the capitalist system
would crumble. Imperialist domination over the tropical landmass is,
therefore, a necessary condition for the reproduction of capital.

During the colonial period there were obvious ways in which colonial powers accomplished this goal (and the Patnaiks provide an interesting account of how this was done in India and with what effects).

After a brief flirtation with postcolonial dirigisme after World War II, the tropical landmass has been brought back into line by neocolonial and market-driven structures of domination that produce "income deflation." The inhabitants of tropical regions are prevented from acquiring the purchasing power to buy their own products. This keeps the prices of tropical products artificially low for the benefit of the metropolis. It is on this basis that metropolitan capitalism survives intact.

This interpretation of how imperialist practices worked in the past allows us to see the continuity of those practices, though under changed political and economic conditions and through new mechanisms, into the present. The idea that contemporary globalized capitalism is no longer characterized by or dependent upon this continuous undercurrent of imperialism is, they argue, profoundly mistaken. The superexploitation of the tropical landmass through imperialist practices has always been and still is a constant and necessary feature of the reproduction of capital. Without it, capital would simply cease to be.

In advancing this thesis, the Patnaiks characterize the agrarian system prevailing in the tropical regions in the following way. It consists broadly of noncapitalist peasant social relations underpinning an agrarian mode of production where what they call any large scale "landaugmentation" is politically if not technically impossible. By this they mean that the land is already fully occupied and exploited mainly by noncapitalist producers and that the prospects for any dramatic increases in productivity are limited. Agrarian resources are, in short, maxed out on the tropical landmass, and imperialism is about squeezing as much labour and product out of these noncapitalist producers as possible for the benefit of metropolitan capitalism.

Economics, they claim, "has not looked at capitalism as it has really existed" and "has not come to terms with the fact that obtaining goods at nonincreasing prices from petty producers located on the tropical landmass, whose products are not producible within the capitalist sector itself that has grown up in the temperate region of the world, is simply not possible under the normal rules of market exchange. It has therefore not accepted the fact that capitalism is unsustainable under the normal rules of exchange. It requires coercion to be exerted on this outside world, a coercion we call imperialism."

The material basis of this argument rests on the physical character and capacities of the tropical landmass in relation to metropolitan capitalism's requirements. There is, however, a damaging looseness in the way they articulate this physical proposition. In some instances they write about "the periphery," "the third world," or sometimes simply "outlying regions" and "distant lands" as if they were all the same as the tropical landmass. By the end of their essay, for example, the language is mostly about "the periphery" (wherever that is). This would not matter were it not for the fact that it is the very specific productive capacities of the tropical landmass that grounds what their theory of imperialism is all about. They also suggest—implausibly—that the exploitation of mineral and energy resources can be handled in the same way as agrarian products. "The case of mineral extractions is in principle no different," they claim, but this is obviously wrong. The limitations imposed upon agricultural production by climatic conditions on the tropical landmass have no parallel when it comes to the extraction of oil and mineral resources. Oil from Alaska, Russia, Nigeria, and Angola enter into the same global market system as equivalents in ways that are not so for cacao, palm oil, coffee, tea, and cane sugar. The Middle East, the world's major oil producer region, is not part of the tropical landmass and it would be strange to exclude it from imperialist influences given its historical geography.

Extractivism (as the Latin Americans define it) is certainly a problem when it comes to energy and mineral resources. Bolivia and Ecuador articulate their own distinctive anti-imperialist politics via a struggle against capitalist extractivism, but the limiting physical conditions that prevail in the agrarian case and are crucial to the Patnaiks' argument do not apply. Oil, I repeat, can equally well be and is extracted from Arctic and temperate regions.

So where is this "tropical landmass" and what are the climatic conditions that create the monopoly over the supply of certain agricultural inputs to metropolitan capitalism? Again, there is a lot of looseness of definition here. Sometimes the Patnaiks talk exclusively about tropical regions, while elsewhere they include the subtropics. So where is this region exactly and what are its geographical characteristics? Checking on the Köppen classification of tropical and subtropical climatic regions, I see a band of countries that encompasses most of sub-Saharan Africa (apart from South Africa), much of South Asia (with the exclusion of Northern India, though that may be controversial) and all of Southeast Asia, the southern part of China and Taiwan, and Central and South America, including most but not all of Brazil, with the Andean Region and the Southern Cone of Chile and Argentina excluded. The

Caribbean lands and Florida are also included. Where to put what is conventionally referred to as the "Middle East" in all of this is not quite clear but it is definitely not tropical or subtropical in the conventional sense, given the aridity that generally prevails. Most definitions treat it as a continental extension of the Mediterranean climatic zone bordering on the desert regions that clearly demarcate the northern and southern borders of the tropics and subtropics in many parts of the world.

There is some awkwardness in this classification because many states (like China, Brazil, Argentina, Mexico, the United States, and even India itself) straddle climatic zones, and the trading patterns occurring between countries and currency blocks do not correspond to climatic configurations. This is particularly the case in China, where a vast subtropical southern zone contrasts with a temperate continental climate north of the Yangtze River. China is one of the biggest producers of both rice (in the south) and wheat (in the north) as well as cotton, but most of that is for domestic consumption and is hardly subject to imperialistic designs. In the United States the super-efficient and highly subsidized production of sugar, rice, cotton, and citrus allows for a subtropical component within a metropolitan capitalist economy, and this component is highly competitive with tropical producers both at home and abroad. And if one looks in more detail, the Mediterranean regions also have certain monopolies on agrarian production—olive oil, wine, nuts, and other elements in the famed Mediterranean diets—and of course they too (e.g., Israel) produce citrus fruits for export to the metropolitan regions. Here the incredible productivity of Californian agribusiness (producing fruit, nuts, and vegetables that can outcompete in global markets) ought surely to feature. California produces 80 percent of the world's almonds, for example, and the recent drought and partial failure of the almond harvest there has wrought havoc in the world's bakeries, including those in the tropics.

But laying aside the details, there are a number of questions that have to be posed concerning the validity of the Patnaiks' challenging presentation. Is all the land in the tropical landmass already used up? The answer is a resounding "no." There is abundant "open land" in sub-Saharan Africa, and the recent pace of invasion of Amazonia by the soybean planters, the cattle interests, and the loggers defines a vigorous frontier of conversion of tropical rainforests to commercial agriculture (if soil fertility is not too rapidly depleted, which it usually is). There are still major regions in Southeast Asia that are "open," as indicated by the pall of smoke that emanates from Sumatra in the dry season to cause major pollution problems in Singapore as more and more of the tropical rain forest is burned down through illegal logging and agrarian conversions. I use the scare quotes around "open" because in many of the instances I cite, there are indigenous populations or even traditional cultivators, cattle grazers, and in the Brazilian case rubber tappers—sometimes even a peasantry as conventionally defined—who will need to be displaced or transformed such that commercial goods can be produced.

The tropical frontier for agrarian conversions is undoubtedly closing rapidly, so the scenario painted by the Patnaiks of full capacity utilization could become true in the future. But there is still some way to go. This brings us to the proposition that the agrarian systems of the tropical landmass are being worked at their maximum capacity under noncapitalistic social relations.

Tropical agrarian systems are heterogeneous in the extreme. The variation is partly a reflection of different adaptations to different environmental conditions. The environmental contrast between, say, West Africa (e.g., Senegal) and East Africa (e.g., Tanzania) is substantial and produces very different agrarian regimes and potentialities. But much also depends on social organization, cultural presuppositions, colonial histories, and the like. The problem in many parts of sub-Saharan Africa, for example, is a traditional form of agrarian organization (and it is not really accurate to call it "peasant") that does not conform to capitalistic standards of labour efficiency and optimal use of inputs and still has a substantial element of self-subsistence in its mode of life. Many areas still have very little access to mechanization or irrigation techniques. The uneven penetration of "green revolution" techniques (whatever one thinks of them) must also be factored in. State pressures for social reorganization and agrarian reform have been around for a long time (backed by international agencies like the World Bank and the IMF) but often resisted (for good and bad reasons) in ways that block the transition to capitalist forms of development. It is true, though, that over many years there have been agrarian transitions towards the production of more and more commercial products—such as cotton in West Africa and the Sudan—to be sold in metropolitan markets. The recent dispossession of large tracts of land in Africa by foreign interests—conventionally referred to as "land-grabbing"—is proceeding apace.

Local populations are ruthlessly chased off the land to make way for large scale industrialized agriculture mainly, it seems, to produce bio-fuels, palm oil, or whatever.[1] In other instances, it has proven more efficient to revert to smaller-scale but capitalistically organized agricultural production of export crops (flowers, fruits, vegetables, coffee, and bananas, though usually under the monopolistic supervision of merchant capitalists). It is certainly not true that most of the agrarian production is noncapitalistically organized in tropical regions (e.g., Brazil). Temperate region crops (such as wheat) can be grown in some places on the tropical landmass, but good luck with trying that in Amazonia, the Congo River Basin, or Sumatra, and even where wheat is grown (as in parts of India and Mexico), competition with the United States and Canada is impossible.

So where, then, do we find tropical and subtropical land that can grow temperate region crops and is fully occupied under conditions of noncapitalistic, peasant agrarian production? The best answer I can come up with is much (but by no means all) of the Patnaiks' India (and perhaps the African Sahel zone). If all the tropical world were like India, then they might have a case, but it is not.

The dependency of metropolitan capitalism on products from tropical and subtropical regions produced by petty commodity producers is nowhere near as significant as the Patnaiks claim. I cannot imagine that the Indian peasantry is producing much for the metropolitan markets, for example. And quite a lot of the crops exported to metropolitan regions—e.g., palm oil—are not produced by peasants but by corporate forms of capital. Only about 8 percent of imports into the metropolitan North come from the tropics. The Patnaiks concede this low proportion as measured in value terms, but claim that it conceals the hidden subsidy of artificially low prices of tropical products created by the imposition of a politics of income deflation, through, for example, typical structural adjustment mechanisms of the IMF and the politics of the WTO. There is a certain truth to this. It is, they say, the use value of the tropical goods for both industrial inputs and wage goods (primarily food) that is critical to the survival of metropolitan capitalism. This assertion is unwarranted. The idea that metropolitan capitalism will collapse because of price inflation in the strawberries and blackberries that come from Guatemala in winter and the cut flowers that come from Ecuador and Colombia or that the lack of haricot vert from Kenya in Paris markets will bring the French economy to its knees is farfetched. Some seemingly crucial tropical and subtropical products, such as sugar, are substitutable. Ever since the Napoleonic Wars taught the peoples of the metropolis how vulnerable they might be to the disruption of sugar supplies from tropical and subtropical regions in times of war, a subsidized sugar-beet industry has been organized in temperate regions to provide an alternative.

The case of cotton (not really a tropical crop but one that requires warm production conditions) is by far the most interesting. It can be produced in both the United States and China (the world's largest producer). The highly subsidized U.S. industry is now the world's largest exporter. The United States lost a case recently brought by Brazil before the WTO regarding unfair competition by way of agricultural subsidies to U.S. cotton producers. The United States settled the case with a buyout of Brazil, which has left the West African cotton producers at a serious price disadvantage. But it would cost Burkina Faso several years of its total national income to pay the legal fees to bring a case against the United States before the WTO. The artificially low global prices of cotton are maintained by policies within the metropolis. The politics are simple: keep the global price of cotton (and other primary products) as low as possible while compensating domestic producers with subsidies. But there is another problem with cotton—its use is substitutable with artificial fibers in much the same way that the once-upon-a-time exclusive reliance on the tropical landmass for rubber (that led Ford to create a failed Fordlandia in the Amazon) has been displaced by oil-based synthetic rubber.

If we are to speak of imperialist strategies in general and the power exercised by the United States in particular, then surely this is the sort of thing that we should be examining. There has been and still is a definite tendency for the more powerful nations in the global economy to hold the price of primary products down. But the impact of this strategy (which is not always successful) is global and by no means confined to tropical regions. The fact that the terms of trade for primary producers have been negative for much of capitalism's history (though recently they did improve under the impact of burgeoning Chinese demand) is relevant, and to the degree that tropical regions have been forced into the production of raw materials in order to gain access to metropolitan products, this does create an effect that looks something like that which the Patnaiks describe. But such effects are not confined to the tropical landmass.

There are only a few products like cacao, palm oil, coffee, tea, and citrus fruits (many of which can of course be grown in Mediterranean climates very well) that may be critical for metropolitan capitalism. Among the food grains, we have rice as the only crop of global relevance (with millet and yams important in tropical regions but not to metropolitan capitalism). Rice is successfully and competitively grown in South Korea, Spain, and the United States, which are not exactly tropical. And while it is useful as a supplement to have imports of beef from Costa Rica and Brazil, it is certainly not the case that metropolitan capitalism depends upon such trade. Indeed, the shift towards meat-based diets in tropical regions on the part of those who can afford such products is sparking dependency in the other direction. Cattle and chicken feed coming from temperate regions supports beef and chicken production on a large scale in many tropical regions (e.g., southern China and Indonesia). Depriving the metropolis of coffee, tea, bananas, cacao, peppers, and spices might provoke revolutionary thoughts in metropolitan populations who are used to such products, but this is hardly a convincing basis for a theory of imperialism. The claim that the agrarian use values extracted from tropical regions are physically critical to metropolitan capitalism does not wash. And the energy and mineral resources taken from tropical regions are not, as we have already established, specific to those regions and cannot be analyzed in this way.

Indeed, if anything, the imperialism problem—if such there is—arises from forces arranged the other way round. A highly efficient and powerfully subsidized agriculture in North America and Europe is destroying peasant production systems where they still exist through competition over a whole range of crops. Taiwan's vegetable growers cannot compete with imports from California under WTO rules, and the super-efficient agribusiness (armed with explicit as well as hidden subsidies) makes the United States a major exporter of food (both raw and processed). We have already mentioned the case of cotton, the depressed price of which has been destructive particularly for West African producers. The point here is not to deny the transfers of wealth and value that occur through global trade and extractivism, or from geo-economic policies that disadvantage primary producers. Rather it is to insist that we not subsume all these features under some simple and misleading rubric of an imperialism that depends upon an anachronistic and specious form of physical geographical determinism. To take such a path reminds me of the disastrous turn within Marxism that occurred with Karl Wittfogel's *Oriental Despotism* and his theory of the geographical distinctiveness of the oriental mode of production. This is not, of course, Patnaiks' specific argument, but they at times appeal to the same kind of crude environmental determinism found in Jared Diamond's *Guns, Germs, and Steel* or in Jeffrey Sachs's *The End of Poverty: Economic Possibilities for Our Time*.[2] Being good Marxists, they claim, of course, that the foundation of their whole analysis lies in class relations. But, they say, these class relations play out across the immutable and fixed geographical environment of the tropical landmass in such a way as to make its imperialist domination and exploitation both necessary and inevitable to the survival of capitalism.

The Patnaiks here equate materialism with physicality, which is a common error in reading Marx. It eliminates the history that distinguishes Marx's historical materialism from the physical materialism of the natural sciences. Marx could not abide social theories that depended on so-called natural conditions or forces to explain anything about capitalism. But the Patnaiks here choose to follow a whole line of economists who conceive of "geography" in purely "natural" physical and immutable biotic terms as if the social production of space and the long history of human modifications of environments do not matter. Our relevant geographical environment has in large measure been modified and produced by human action and, particularly over the last few centuries, by capitalist imperatives. The economists have staged in recent times an intense and entirely bogus debate over whether (physical) geography matters. Jeffrey Sachs, who says it is the physical environment that matters, is pitted against Acemoglu et al. (who insist that institutions are key, as if institutions of the state are not geographical facts identifiable on the ground).[3] All of this presumes a clear distinction between "nature" on the one hand and "culture, institutions, and economy" on the other. Marx, however, was not a Cartesian. He had a far more dialectical understanding of the relation between economy and nature. We can only change ourselves by changing the world, and when we change the world and our environment through human labour, we change ourselves. The dialectical metabolic relation to nature is in constant evolution and much of that evolution has been dictated by human action so that we now live in a world profoundly modified by that human action in general and capitalism in particular. In exactly the same way that ants and beavers modify their environments to reproduce themselves and meet their needs, so capital does the same. The historical has to be reinserted into materialism. The contradictory unity between human action and natural evolution has to move to the center of our thinking. The conditions of agrarian production (to take just that sector for the moment) are not fixed by nature but defined by historical transformations in land, technology, culture, economy, and politics. The tropical landmass as it is now constituted is completely different to that of the last century. Flowers, fresh fruits, and vegetables come to the metropolitan regions from tropical regions because revolutions in transport have dramatically reordered the relative spaces of the global economy to make metropolitan markets accessible to tropical producers. The steamboat and the railways did this in the nineteenth century and the internal combustion and jet engines along with innovations like containerization have done much the same over the last fifty years. The "annihilation of space through time" that Marx spoke of in the *Grundrisse* has produced a radical bout of time-space compression in global economic relations, and the tropical landmass has been absorbed within that process.[4]

From this perspective we see that the temperate regions have accumulated distinctive monopoly powers far beyond those claimed by the Patnaiks for the tropical landmass. And it is from this that a lot of contemporary asymmetries derive. Humanly constructed physical infrastructures are a fundamental feature to the nature we have produced. There is a stark contrast between what that produced nature looks like on the tropical landmass, largely constructed under conditions of colonial rule, and the nature that has been produced in the advanced capitalist economies of temperate regions. Look at a map of the transportation system of West Africa and you see a north-south orientation in the rail and road system that is designed to drain wealth from the interiors down to the port cities that then ship that wealth to the metropolis. The rivers drain a bit in the same way, but the difference is that the rivers existed before colonialism, while the rail and road systems were built by human activity engaging in extractivism. To this day, the lineaments of this produced physical geography have profound effects on economy and culture, just as the territorial divisions of the colonial administrations did when they became the basis for the formation of states in much of the tropical world—of states that thus had no basis whatsoever in nature, culture, or even any history apart from extractivist colonialism. Contrast this with the pattern of infrastructural

development and state formation in the metropolitan capitalist economies, and we see two very different worlds defined not by raw nature
but by differentially produced "second natures" shaped by a history of
uneven processes of application of economic and political power. There
is nothing unnatural about New York, San Francisco, and Chicago.
They are physical geographical facts in the North American landscape
of production and consumption.[5] Capital is drawn to locate in such cities rather than in Mogadishu because of the agglomeration economies
that can be realized in such advantaged locations. It is not only the
physical but the social infrastructures that play a crucial role in where
capital locates. The monopoly power that accrues to capital based in the
United States by virtue of the outstanding system of research universities created there is just one element of a competitive advantage of the
region that has been created and most certainly not given by nature.

Metropolitan capitalism has a great deal of accumulated monopoly
power over knowledge production, research and development capacity, organizational forms and social infrastructures (to say nothing of
military power). The United States and Britain may not be able to produce cacao and palm oil, but the state apparatuses on the tropical
landmass cannot easily produce anything equivalent to the social and
physical infrastructures available to capital in the metropolitan temperate regions. It was the genius of Lee Kuan Yew to create Singapore as
the exception to this rule (with Brazil, China, and India lurking rather
far behind). The tropical landmass may be able to produce many of the
agrarian products available to metropolitan capitalism (though as we
saw in the case of the U.S. export of cotton and rice even this perspective must be challenged), but it has to confront the monopoly power
of metropolitan capital when it comes to advanced automotive or aero-
spatial engineering, electronics, pharmaceutical technologies and products, and biomedical engineering. Ecuador may have a part role in the
tropical "monopoly" of cacao and banana production, but Germany
has Siemens and BMW, while the United States has big pharma, Boeing,
Monsanto, Caterpillar, and Apple. Pharmaceuticals are now protected by
TRIPS agreements and the WTO. All of this confers monopoly powers within metropolitan economies, which are hard to break, no matter
how hard India and Brazil might try in the production of, say, generic
drugs. If there is any asymmetry here, the balance has to be on the
side of the monopoly power lodged in metropolitan regions. Tropical
regions are even more subjected to the monopoly power of Monsanto

and Cargill than their temperate region counterparts. Furthermore, to the degree that the populations of the tropical landmasses need and desire the cars, computers, cell phones, and other electronic goods largely invented, designed, and produced in the metropolitan regions (though with branch-plants in the tropical landmass), they are forced to give in to extractivism to get the foreign exchange to survive. Ecuador and Bolivia both articulate an anti-extractivist anti-imperialist politics, but both have to allow their hydrocarbons and their agrarian base to be exploited in order to acquire the foreign exchange they need to fund social welfare and alternative economic development strategies while everyone buys cell phones.

The Patnaiks do, however, have some important observations on the conditions of the labour reserve on the tropical landmass. In many respects I think this is their most important contribution, although they fail to recognize its full implications. Samir Amin has long pointed out, for example, that Africa constitutes the last vast labour reserve for capital that has yet to be exploited. The Patnaiks fudge somewhat because again it is sometimes the reserve on the tropical landmass and at other times the reserve in some ill-defined periphery (that would presumably include the massive labour reserves in China, Turkey, North Africa, and elsewhere) that counts. The tropical and subtropical land mass has a huge labour reserve living under conditions conducive to super-exploitation. Over the last forty years (and this is new), capital has increasingly sought to mobilize this labour reserve in search of higher profits through industrial development. If there is any one map that confirms the distinctiveness of the tropical landmass, it is one that shows the location of export processing zones, 90 percent of which are on the tropical landmass. And it is the labour reserve that is the lure not the agrarian base (though the partial proletarianization that occurs as social reproduction is taken care of on the land while capital just exploits the labour at a less than living wage is undoubtedly important).

The Patnaiks correctly note that Marx's theory of the production of an industrial reserve army and a consequent increasing immiseration of the proletariat in Volume I of *Capital* assumes a closed-space economy (it also assumes no problems of effective demand and no impacts of the division of the surplus among rent, interest, taxes, and profit of merchant's capital).[6] The existence of a vast reserve of labour in the colonies and in noncapitalist social formations is excluded from consideration in Marx's theorization in part because at that time it was too difficult to exploit that reserve except in plantation labour. They also argue, correctly in my view, that the distinction between the reserve in the metropolitan center and in the periphery has been much reduced by globalization in recent times, such that we can reasonably think of the capital-labour confrontation as being more unified now across the spaces of the global economy. Income deflation (and export processing zones) in the periphery now exercise a considerable drag upon labour conditions in the metropolis. One of the resulting complications is that as income deflation spreads back into metropolitan regions, a trend towards underconsumption becomes an issue (partly mollified by extensions in the credit system). Unfortunately, the Patnaiks largely ignore the industrialization occurring on the tropical landmass in favor of their obsession with agricultural production.

In this regard they correctly note that the increasing need to allocate land to export crops to earn foreign exchange in peripheral regions tends to reduce local food supplies. As a consequence, as they show convincingly from their Indian data, the supply of food energy to populations on the tropical landmass and in the periphery more generally is much diminished, producing rising malnutrition in an environment rich in agricultural potential. There are many examples of such a decline in per capita food production as a result of these processes of developing export-oriented agricultural production, but these are not confined to the tropical land mass, nor are they universal to it. Under conditions of income deflation, people are often, as the Patnaiks correctly point out, faced with the ugly choice of paying for decent medical care and education or securing an adequate food intake. The conditions of life of the labour reserve on the tropical landmass are indeed a major issue and in many respects anchor an alternative view of imperialist practices to those that the Patnaiks emphasize.

Geography, I insist, is far more than a bunch of data about climate and soil types, and I object strenuously to the Patnaiks' antiquarian conception of it. The geography I study is dynamic and not static. It is perpetually evolving, and there are a few basic principles underlying that evolution. The relative spaces of the global economy are perpetually being revolutionized by innovations in transport and communications (how many of the major innovations in the history of capital are about overcoming spatial constraints and accelerating turnover times?). The potentiality for capital mobility has consequently increased dramatically, but it is now money that is the most mobile compared to commodities, and both are typically more mobile than production itself. But with accelerating turnover times, even an auto plant can be erected and abandoned in a dozen or so years. Capital is therefore better positioned to take advantage of small differences in the qualities of places (e.g., its labour supplies) such that those place qualities (labour skills and cost, access to resources and markets, taxes, and infrastructures) are more important now than ever before. The labour reserve in tropical and subtropical regions can now be mobilized with dire consequences as we have seen in Bangladesh. The capitalist state, furthermore, is now obliged to lure capital to town with subsidies and tax relief (hence the emphasis upon special economic zones, which suddenly became all the rage in India with often disastrous results). The capacity to produce places and modify environmental qualities is much enhanced by technological and political changes. The flows of capital around the world are constantly changing direction, and labour seeks to follow suit. In spite of all manner of barriers, population movements are very strong across the spaces of the global economy. Meanwhile, environmental issues and stresses are taking their toll, to become a major issue threatening global security.

The geography I study encompasses the changing human use of the earth and what humans have done to it. Humans have made a differentiated environment and landscape in which, as Gunner Myrdal long ago pointed out, rich regions tend to grow richer by virtue of the agglomeration economies and cumulative synergies they generate and the social and physical infrastructures they build up. Poorer regions decline because of their cumulative lack of such advantages.[7] This process can happen at local levels (contrast Detroit with San Francisco or London with Newcastle), but it also happens on a world scale by a process that may or may not be reinforced by what is conventionally referred to as "imperialist practices." The fertility of the tropical landmass, to take another example, has been depleted by decades of soil degradation and erosion, a history from which it has been hard to recover. Yet the tropical landmass is a dynamic space in the full flood of rapid evolution. Contemporary Brazil or the export-processing zone in Mauritius looks nothing like the kind of space that the Patnaiks describe.

So how, then, might we best characterize the processes of uneven geographical development in today's capitalism, and what role do these play in the reproduction of capital? There are undoubtedly imperialist practices and geopolitical strategies deployed within the framework of this uneven development of contemporary capitalism. So how might we best theorize them?

The Patnaiks here make an extraordinary claim. Theories of imperialism, they say, have hitherto been "detached from any spatial location," and this has prevented economists from understanding imperialism as "a system of spatial exploitation." While this may be the case with Marxist economists, this is certainly not true of the sociologists and geographers who have long addressed the problem of the geographical and spatial development of capital and advanced all manner of theoretical formulations from dependency, unequal exchange, and variants of world system theory to theories of the production of space and nature and of uneven geographical development.[8]

I have, for example, been studying and writing on these questions for over forty years. I do not propose to go over my arguments in any detail here. But some elements are I think foundational to understanding the lineaments of what contemporary imperialism (if that is what we still choose to call it) might be about.

Let me begin with an example that illustrates a conundrum. There are multiple forms of extractivism occurring around the world, depending upon who is doing the extracting where. Indian and Chinese corporations currently dominate the exploitation of Zambian copper, for example, and their practices seem not much different from North American or Australian mining companies.[9] Brazilian soybean producers have been invading Paraguay, converting it into a vast soybean plantation for the China trade. So can we meaningfully speak of Chinese, Indian, and Brazilian imperialisms? I would prefer not to. Furthermore, the tropical regions have in recent times been invaded, precisely because of their labour reserves, by industrialization (and export processing zones) such that "made in" Indonesia, Bangladesh, Guatemala, the Philippines, Vietnam, and Cambodia, as well as in Turkey and Egypt, can be found in all the shops in the metropolitan countries. There has been massive industrialization in subtropical Southern China and an increasing preoccupation in India for setting up special economic zones in which foreign capital—be it subcontractors from South Korea, Taiwan, Indonesia, Japan, and even China—are given free reign. This industrialization has accelerated the tendency to launch yet another round of primitive accumulation against the peasantry that is left. Yet it does not generate much local wealth. Foxconn, which makes Apple computers under super-exploitative labour conditions for immigrant labour in Southern China, registers a 3 percent profit while Apple, which sells the computers in the metropolitan countries, makes 27 percent.

It is not only industrialization that has penetrated into the tropical landmass. Massive urbanization has produced cities like Sao Paulo, Lagos, Mumbai, Jakarta, Shenzhen, and Shanghai, which have absorbed huge amounts of surplus capital while acting as a problematic destination for increasingly dispossessed rural populations. The industrialization and urbanization that have occurred on the tropical landmass, accompanied by a lot of rural-urban migration, is totally ignored in the Patnaiks' account.

Those of us who think the old categories of imperialism do not work too well in these times do not deny at all the complex flows of value that expand the accumulation of wealth and power in one part of the world at the expense of another. We simply think the flows are more complicated and constantly changing direction. The historical draining of wealth from East to West for more than two centuries has, for example, been largely reversed over the last thirty years.

In order to track the cross-cutting currents of exploitation, we need to look at where capital surpluses are produced, how they are geographically dispersed, and in search of what. When South Korea suddenly found itself with masses of surplus capital in the late 1970s, followed a few years later by Taiwan, then flows of surplus capital out of those countries at first into China and Southeast Asia and later across the whole globe produced a pattern of exploitation in one place to the benefit of capital originating somewhere else. South Korean and Taiwanese subcontractors have been responsible for some of the most ghastly and exploitative labour practices all around the world (particularly on the tropical landmass) as they have sought to absorb the surplus capitals piling up in their home countries by moving their operations abroad. I hesitate to call this "imperialism" in the old fashioned sense. But it certainly entails geo-economic exploitations. If this is a form of imperialism, then it is perhaps best we dub it "sub-imperialism" since it is the Taiwanese and South Koreans who provide the goods for merchant capitalists (such as Nike, Walmart, the Gap) located mainly in the metropolitan regions.[10]

It is precisely the uneven geographical development of these patterns of exploitation and super-exploitation that I would argue must be the focus of our studies, rather than cramming everything that is going on into some simplistic theory of imperialism of the sort that the Patnaiks propose.

I am not resorting to an argument here of "it is more complicated than that" in response to the Patnaiks' propositions. There are some basic forces at work that help explain the pattern of capital flows around the world and the current hyper-activity of capital in searching out new opportunities for surplus value extraction. In my own work I have relied mainly upon a theme that can be traced from Marx via Lenin to the contemporary situation. This rests on the dilemmas that arise out of the persistent trend within capitalism to produce more and more surplus capitals that thereby pose perpetual and escalating problems of capital surplus absorption. This tendency underpinned Marx's conclusion that capital must ultimately conquer the whole world for its market and Lenin's focus on capital export as the most important lever for imperialist practices. These positions led me to think in terms of capital's incessant pursuit of what I have called a "spatial fix" to its overaccumulation problems.[11] The tendency towards perpetual overaccumulation of capital is relieved by perpetual geographical expansion and/or geographical reconstruction (e.g., the conversion of formerly industrial cities such as Sheffield, Essen, and Pittsburgh into consumer and commercial hubs). The quest for a perpetual "spatial fix" internalizes a fascinating contradiction between fixity and motion in the theory of capital accumulation. Part of the overaccumulated capital has to be fixed in space as place-bound physical and social infrastructures embedded in the land (including those of state apparatuses) in order to facilitate the free and continuous flow of the remaining capital across space.[12] The geographical mobility of one part of capital is facilitated by immobilizing part of the total capital in a produced and fixed physical and social landscape (of transport and communication infrastructures, for example).

But capital mobility differs considerably depending upon whether it exists as money, as commodities, or as productive activity. Money is the "butterfly" form of capital that can flit around the world without any constraints other than those imposed by human decisions (e.g., capital controls on artificially constructed state boundaries). The liberation of finance capital from many constraints after the 1970s (mainly with the intent of disciplining labour), along with the long-standing attempts to reduce barriers to cross-border trade both by tariff reductions and lower transport costs, has changed the whole spatial dynamic of capital accumulation. Finance capital became a major instrument for engineering the deindustrialization of metropolitan capitalism and the simultaneous industrialization of selected sites on the tropical landmass. It also introduced a new impetus for deepening the contradictions between, for example, the geographical fixity of the state versus the fluidity of money flows such that the latter now exercises a much stronger disciplinary authority over state policies (the power of the proverbial bond-holders). On the other hand, the larger and more powerful states or collections of states (e.g., the European Union) typically use their collective political and police powers on the global stage to weld highly mobile capital to their particularist agendas. It is out of this contradiction that a diversity of quasi-imperialist practices flow—e.g., the United States' power of seigniorage of the global currency, its power to dominate the policies of the IMF and the WTO (a topic that the Patnaiks take up towards the end of their essay), and its capacity to extend its own regulatory regime like a blanket over much of the world.[13] But this power is contested, even as it is hard to break. For this reason, I think it useful to take up Giovanni Arrighi's preference to abandon the idea of imperialism (along with the rigidities of the core-periphery model of world system theory) in favor of a more fluid understanding of competing and shifting hegemonies within the global state system.[14] But while I am increasingly inclined to accept Arrighi's view, I would want to insist upon a better understanding of the contradiction between the territorial logic of state interests and the molecular logic of capital flow (particularly in its money form), which cannot easily be (if at all) corralled within the logic of the state system.[15]

Investigations into uneven geographical developments, shifting hegemonies, and the fluid movement of extractivist practices and of accumulations by dispossession through, for example, land grabs in the global economy would be deemed as irrelevant if we accepted the Patnaiks' formulation. All such questions would be swept aside as "not germane to the argument," as happens throughout their text whenever they encounter an awkward conundrum. Their arguments would not be valid even if the whole world looked like India (which it does not). Living conditions are indeed dire in many parts of the tropical landmass (with some exceptions of course), and those conditions need to be analyzed, addressed, and acted upon by way of the kind of capitalist development logic identified with "emerging markets" (the so-called BRICS, along with other rapidly growing economies such as those of

Turkey, Mexico, Chile, and Indonesia), which, far from threatening the future of metropolitan capitalism, might save it from its more self-destructive impulses. But the Patnaiks' argument does not, I fear, help us understand any of this.

So why, in the face of all this evident dynamism in the global economy do the Patnaiks insist on the unreal concept of a fixed and immutable "dead" agrarian space of a tropical landmass populated by noncapitalist peasant producers destined for perpetual exploitation of metropolitan capital as the latter's primary lifeline to survival? Only the Patnaiks can answer that question. But what is clear is that without this prop, their theory of imperialism fails. From this we should not conclude that there are no geo-economic threats to the reproduction of capitalism or that spatial specificities do not matter. They plainly do, but theirs is no way to theorize how and from where such threats might materialize. Unfortunately, they get their concepts of space, place, environment, and geography all wrong. It is crucially important for them and for us to get them right.

A Response to David Harvey's Comments

UTSA PATNAIK
PRABHAT PATNAIK

WE WELCOME THE FACT that David Harvey has taken the time and trouble to read through our book and write a comment. We will take this opportunity both to expand on some of our propositions, which are stated somewhat tersely in the book, and to respond to some of the more important comments that Harvey has made.

We regret that we have not been able to make our theory of imperialism clear to Harvey, let alone persuade him of its worth. Central to our theory is not some geographical determinism but the concept of *increasing supply price*, which implies an undermining of the value of money under capitalism, and reflects the fact that certain commodities under certain circumstances are producible only at an increasing supply price—a fact that no economist can deny and that even Keynes underscored in his classic *The Economic Consequences of the Peace*. Harvey appears to be under the misconception that we have made some absurd claim that oil is a tropical product, but we have not, and this would be clear from a careful reading of our argument. It is a material reality that the overwhelming bulk, nearly nine-tenths, of known oil and natural gas reserves lie outside the borders of advanced countries, that can no longer directly control their supply. While it has already been pointed out that U.S. attempts to control oil supply was "closely linked to the monetary stability of the capitalist world" (P. Patnaik 2009: 219), the present book is concerned with exploring the impact of asymmetric agricultural production capacities of countries, which can give rise to increasing supply price. If increasing supply price is allowed to manifest itself, whether for oil or other primary products, then it poses a serious threat to the value of money under capitalism, which is why capital does not allow it to manifest itself by imposing income deflation on the working people in the periphery, and this is a phenomenon central to imperialism.

Even with regard to increasing supply price, we are suggesting that *it could be warded off in other ways—namely, through state efforts, which require state expenditure*; but capitalism in its spontaneity insists on "sound finance," rejects this route, and prefers income deflation instead. Imperialism in short is linked to capitalism as a social system; it is not an inevitable product of geography. Put differently, capitalism as a social system overcomes its deprivation of certain natural resources, which arise not exclusively but *inter alia* for climatic (geographical) reasons, in a specific manner involving income deflation, and that is the hallmark of imperialism. That is our position; and it is a caricature of our theory of imperialism to read into it a "capitalism-would-collapse-if-spices-are-not-imported" view.

On the issue of the products of the tropical and subtropical landmass in particular, which we take for highlighting increasing supply price, there is a significant lack of knowledge as well as a significant obfuscation of material facts in the theoretical literature. Before reiterating our theory of imperialism, therefore, we would like to make the factual position clear.

LOW PRODUCTIVITY IN EUROPE AND EXTERNAL EXPANSIONISM

The existing literature in academia of the global North abounds in questions like "Who will feed China?" and discussion of "the origins of third world food dependence." The impression conveyed is that today's developing countries have difficulty in feeding their own populations and this arises from their large populations or low productivity. Much of the discussion is both fallacious and tendentious. The basic fact that is conveniently ignored is that the origins of food dependence for some third world regions today (Africa, the least developed countries) lie in the first world's centuries-old and continuing heavy dependence on developing countries for both raw materials and foodstuff imports, leading to diversion of area under foodgrains to export crops and reduction in local food availability. Today's developing countries, which are located mainly in tropical to subtropical areas, were perfectly capable of feeding their own populations in the past and this remains true today. But they were obliged under direct colonial subjugation in the past, and are continuously pressurized through the Bretton Woods institutions, the WTO, and bilateral agreements at present, to "open up" to trade and devote an increasing part of their limited land and resources to providing advanced-country populations with the primary goods that *the latter's own cold countries cannot ever produce but that have become an essential part of their consumption baskets whether for direct consumption or for productive use.*

These goods include today not only the traditional imported crops (such as cane sugar, spices, tea, coffee, cereals, and fibres) but also all those perishable vegetables, fruits, and flowers that cold temperate lands can grow only in their summer but not in their winter when the land is frozen, hence, the necessity of imports to avoid seasonal lack of supply. So fresh carrots, tomatoes, fruit, and flowers in December–January are, analytically speaking, to be conceptualized as "tropical goods" for northern populations.

The importance of external expansion in the rise of capitalism dates from the end of the fifteenth century, when the West European countries engaged in the greatest land grab in history. While Spain and Portugal vied in destroying Central and South American civilizations and seizing their resources, the French and the British fought over the vast land resources of North America, seized from indigenous inhabitants who were decimated and whose remnants were driven into reservations. The British later ousted the Dutch from control over South Africa and had an uncontested run in taking over Australasia from the indigenous population. Ireland was conquered with violent campaigns during Cromwell's Commonwealth period: the local farmers were dispossessed and turned into pauperized tenants of the English settler landlords. Under the pressure of heavy rent payments, they exported wheat and animal products to Britain while being forced by poverty to subsist on potatoes alone. The great potato blight famine of 1846–47 killed one million Irish, out of a total population of eight million at most, while wheat and livestock products continued to be forcibly exported.

This insensate drive by a handful of West European maritime nations to acquire by force the very conditions of existence of the peoples of other preindustrial societies, separating small producers forcibly from the free ownership or usufruct of their own lands and in many cases enslaving them for production, cannot be understood without some knowledge of the low productivity of late medieval European agriculture and the very poor standard of life of the European population—a standard that started rising only after these countries acquired control over the superior productivity of biodiverse tropical lands.

If we study the historical origins of the first world's agricultural dependence on today's developing countries, several interesting facts emerge. First, agricultural productivity in medieval Europe and food availability were clearly extremely low compared to Asia or Central America during the same period, and this was owing to a combination of factors detailed in the magisterial study by B. H. Slicher van Bath (1963), among other sources. There was only a single growing season in the year, with land too frozen to grow anything in winter (which continues to this day); a very high seed-to-yield ratio ranging from one-third to two-fifths, which correspondingly lowered the net grain output; a high rate of fallowing, with one third to one half the arable left uncultivated to restore fertility; and the necessity of using half of the actually cultivated land for raising feed crops. What resulted was an "atrocious competition" between humans and animals over sharing the inadequate grain output as food and feed. When crops failed in successive years and famine ensued in Europe, as it did in the fourteenth century, many cases, documented in the chronicles, of *collective cannibalism* occurred. As Slicher van Bath (1963:83) put it, "People did not shrink from appeasing their hunger in strange fashions."

The violent outward expansion of a handful of maritime West European nations is easier to understand in the light of the extreme poverty of late medieval life and the absolute necessity of obtaining spices to preserve meat through the winter months to avoid starvation. A pattern of global specialization was initiated and forcibly imposed by today's advanced countries under colonial systems using slave labour, indentured labour, and taxation of peasants. This entailed the industrializing countries' increasing dependence on primary imports (food-

TABLE I

Structure of Britain's Total Imports by Commodity Groups,
1784–1786 to 1824–1826

Period	Manufactures %	Foodstuffs %	Raw Materials %	All %	Total Value of M (£mn.)	Share of Colonies in Total %
1784–1786	14.2	42.2	43.6	100	22.76	52.3
1794–1796	10.7	48	41.3	100	37.92	51.5
1804–1806	6.8	43.1	50.1	100	55.56	45.6
1814–1816	3.8	44.6	51.6	100	71.80	49.5
1824–1826	5.9	39.7	54.4	100	66.39	43.7

SOURCE: Calculated from Davies (1979) Appendix Tables. (Current values, three-year annual averages).
NOTE: Colonies are Asia, West Indies, and Ireland.

stuffs and raw materials) mainly from tropical and subtropical countries. The first industrializing nation, Britain, imported more primary products—four-fifths of which were from its colonies—than it produced by the mid-nineteenth century (Davis 1979: table 31.51). The North American colonies won independence at the very beginning of the first Industrial Revolution, so the only cold temperate country that remained a colony for any length of time was Ireland.

The combined imports from Asia, the West Indies, and Ireland amounted to half of Britain's total imports over the entire crucial period of Industrial Revolution as table 1 shows. Merchandise import surpluses from Asia and the West Indies, combined, rose rapidly to comprise over 6 percent of Britain's GDP. Most importantly, these trade deficits created no external liability and did not have to be paid for by the metropolis because they embodied taxes, slave rents, and land rents extracted from the subjugated populations. A vast flow of foodstuffs and raw materials was extracted completely gratis, a fact that continues to be not only ignored but actively obfuscated to this day by the leading economic historians of Britain, who try to project a purely internal dynamic for the first capitalist industrialization. They go to the extent of eliminating a large part of colonial trade entirely when estimating Britain's early trade, and give incorrect, grossly underestimated trade figures.[1] France and the Netherlands followed similar patterns of exploitation. Smaller northern countries that had no colonies sourced their tropical goods requirements from the major powers.

The basic reasons for imposing by force such a pattern of specialization lay first in the inability of the first industrializing countries to meet their food, energy, and raw material needs from their own agriculture, and second in their cold countries' *permanently* poor range of crop production, dictated by a climate that no degree of capitalist technical progress can alter, at least up to the present, compared to the highly diversified productive capacity of tropical and subtropical lands. (We have to remember that agriculture was the main source of energy in that it provided feed grains for oxen and horses used in cultivation, traction, and transport until the 1840s when fossil fuels came into wider use. Advanced countries are once more reverting to agriculture for biofuels today.)

The fact that per capita corn output actually declined in Britain during its so-called "agricultural revolution" in the eighteenth century has emerged from the recent empirical work of a number of economic historians of that period.[2] With growing nineteenth-century grain and meat imports from the Americas, there should have been a decline in the pressure on colonies for grain exports to the first industrial nation, but the reason the latter continued into the twentieth century (to the detriment of local food security) was that such imports were financed from locally raised taxes, and hence came free for the metropolis, involving no external liability for it, while imports from the Americas did not.

The term "crop rotation" has completely different spatial meanings, a fact that is seldom understood: in the North it refers to crops grown over *successive years* on the same piece of land; in the South it refers to crops grown over successive seasons *within the same year* on the same piece of land. The output vector in warm lands includes a large range of crops that can never be grown in the cold temperate North, but the converse is not the case: most summer temperate land crops can be grown in winter in warm lands. This is a very important material reality that is never taken into account in economic theory, which on the contrary fudges the argument in the most intellectually disingenuous fashion and tries to hide this reality in three ways: by pretending that land productivity is higher in developed compared to developing countries; by positing necessary mutual benefit from specialization and trade; and by making the factually baseless assumption that the North's dependence on the South was of no great importance either historically or at present.

ELEMENTARY FALLACIES IN THE
RECEIVED LITERATURE

The first fallacy, that land productivity was historically higher and continues to be higher in developed countries, is clearly subscribed to uncritically by Harvey as well, since he repeatedly refers to the "super-efficiency" of northern agriculture. This is a misconception, for, as we discuss below, advanced-country agriculture is in reality the most "super-inefficient" in the world. The fallacy of allegedly higher land productivity in the North was expressed decades ago by W. Arthur Lewis in his Princeton lectures titled *The Evolution of the International Economic Order* (1979), and his incorrect argument is worth recapitulating.

Lewis compared the Indian farmer's wheat yield per acre in 1900 of 700 lbs unfavourably with the European farmer's wheat yield of 1600 lbs, and this allegedly lower Asian land productivity was made the basis for arguing that emigrating Indians and Chinese accepted a low "product wage," thereby ending up as "coolies"; but the emigrating Europeans, given their higher yields, would not accept anything but a higher "product wage."

But an incorrect statement of fact leads to a material fallacy in the argument since Asian land productivity was not lower, but was considerably higher than European land productivity. *The period of production for measuring output has to be the same*, and we cannot, as Lewis did, compare output that the European farmer produced over an entire year with output that the Indian farmer produced in only four months. (This means succumbing to a variant of the "fallacy of composition," since the part in one case is taken as equivalent to the whole in the other.) Over the entire year the Asian farmer produced on the same acre of land, not only wheat or an oilseed in the minor *rabi*, or winter season, but also a second crop (another food grain like rice, or cotton) in the major *kharif*, or monsoon season, and sometimes grew a third crop of a pulse, gram, or groundnut. The fact that nineteenth-century emigrant Europeans had a high income had nothing to do with any allegedly higher "product wage" in their home country since no such higher annual yield in fact existed on their cold single-crop lands. Their relatively high income had much to do with their successful decimation of indigenous populations in the Americas, Australia, and elsewhere and their seizure of rich resources—land, timber, water, minerals—*to a far greater extent than they commanded in their home countries.* The fact that migrant Indians and Chinese served as "coolies" had nothing to do with any allegedly lower "product wage," since annual yields in their home countries were in fact higher than in Europe; their "coolie" status was the outcome of their pauperization under military conquest followed by colonial or semicolonial[3] exploitation, as was the starvation status of Irish peasants who emigrated to the tune of a million persons in a single year after one-eighth of the population perished in the great famine of 1846–47, while wheat exports to Britain continued. In Lewis's exposition, however, colonial or semi-colonial subjugation by some European or Asian nations of other nations never existed, or if it did, played no role worth mentioning for explaining the increasing economic distance between nations. Lewis is not unique in this respect: his analysis mirrors the sanitized approach of what goes by development theory at present.

Many elements of earlier low land productivity have been successfully overcome in modern agriculture in the North, including in Europe: the seed fraction of yield has been lowered greatly, artificial fertilizing permits nearly all arable land to be cultivated, grain is now produced far in excess of domestic absorption needs as food and feed, and a large part of grain output is exported, as table 2 shows (the difference between production and domestic supply is mainly exports). *But over much of the North, single-cropping imposed by climatic constraints cannot be overcome.* We do not enter into definitions of what is north and what is south, what is the centre and what is the periphery—matters with which Harvey makes much play. As Joan Robinson famously remarked, it is possible to define a point in mathematics in one sentence, but we cannot so define an elephant; it hardly matters, however, for we know an elephant when we see it—unless we happen to be blind.

As table 3 shows, to this day the annual *total output in physical units per hectare, taking all food-crop groups,* in China is more than two and a half times the level in the United States; in India it is 52 percent more than in the United States. No amount of technological change under capitalism in its most advanced centres is able to negate the effects of the more favourable natural conditions under which farmers in the global South operate, or the efficacy of their cultivation practices tested

TABLE 2

Cereals Supply/Demand per Capita and Utilisation for Selected
Countries/Regions for year 2011 (unless specified otherwise)

Country/Region	Population (millions)	Total Production (kg)	Total Supply/ Demand (kg)	Food (kg)	Feed (kg)	Other Use & Food Manufacture (kg)
			Per Capita in Kilograms per Annum			
India	1221.2	192.7	176.5	152.1	9	0.42
India (2001)	1059.5	185.3	175.9	156	6.8	0.42
Least Developed Countries	773.5	197	216.2	148.4	26.9	19.5
Africa	971.2	158.3	225.7	150.5	40.5	12.6
China	1368.4	330.2	330.7	152.5	121.7	34.3
West Asia	230.3	217.5	351.6	178.4	119	16.3
Russian Federation	143.4	637.5	514.1	149.5	254.7	31
European Union	507.4	577.6	549.1	124.9	330.5	61.6
USA	314.9	1219.5	1032.9	105.8	396.3	521.4
USA (2001)	287.5	1118.9	877.9	112.7	571.4	179.1
World	6887.31	340.6	336.6	147.2	118.9	46.1
World (2001)	6122.51	311.5	313.2	148.7	117.8	22.1

SOURCE: Food and Agriculture Organization, Rome, faostat3.fao.org/faostat-gateway/go /to/download/F/FO/E.
NOTE: "Supply," which is identical to actual use for all purposes, is obtained by the FAO by adjusting the output figure for net import and change in stockholding. The last column, "Other Use and Food Manufacture," includes conversion of cereals to ethanol. Use of cereal as seed and waste is not shown but can be obtained as a residual. For India, USA and the World the values for year 2001 are also shown.

TABLE 3

Annual Food Crops Output per Hectare in China, India, and the
United States, 2011

	Arable + Permanent Crop Area (million hectares)	Food Output (million tons)	Output per Ha (tons)	Index A Comparative Output per Ha, base USA value	Index B Comparative Output per Ha, base India value	Index C Comparative Output per Ha, base China value
USA	166.93	645.778	3.87	100	65.7	38.2
India	157.4	927.911	5.89	152	100	58.1
China	152.83	1549.879	10.14	262	172.2	100

NOTE: "Food Output" includes all the vegetal food groups shown in tables 4 and 5, but not foods of animal origin. Area total above includes the area under fibre crops (cotton, jute, etc.) and rubber, but output does not include these. The index for India and China is higher than shown relative to United States, since the latter does not produce jute or rubber. Area figures are from official government data on land use in each country.
SOURCE: Output calculated from United Nations Food and Agriculture Organization, Food Balance Sheets/ Supply Utilization Accounts (FBS/SUA), available at faostat3.fao.org /faostat-gateway/go/to/download/F/FO/E.

182 A Response to David Harvey's Comments

over centuries. The Mekong delta today produces 11 crops in four years, or has an annual cropping intensity of nearly three.

Harvey's statement that advanced-country agriculture is "super-efficient and highly subsidized" involves a glaring contradiction. If U.S. agriculture was even of average efficiency, it would not need any subsidies at all, let alone high subsidies. Under capitalism, "efficiency" is always defined in terms of unit cost of production relative to unit output value. This must necessarily be much higher in the United States and Europe than the global level since heavy subsidies are present, and indeed we find that unit costs are so high that in many years there is negative value added in some crops; i.e., the global market price does not cover even unit material cost, let alone give a return to labour. The reason for high unit production cost is the enormously high dependence on fossil fuels used directly and embodied in manufactured inputs. Many authors, including David Pimentel and Marcia Pimentel (2003), have shown that the meat-based diets of northern populations are extremely resource- and energy-intensive in terms of very high feedgrain, pasture, and water demand, while others have found that the energy balance ratio is not only unfavourably high in northern agriculture but rising over time. (The energy balance is the proportion of the total energy embodied in the inputs required to produce a unit of output to the energy that unit of output provides).

Chinese, Indian, and Egyptian farmers produce at a much lower unit cost and could competitively decimate the United States on global markets in cereals, cotton, and virtually any other product (other than perhaps maple syrup), if U.S. farmers were not state-supported through unbelievably large subsidies. The U.S. cotton subsidy is globally notorious, amounting to over $110,000 annually per full-time farmer during the period 1997–2012, and is carefully calibrated to swings in global production conditions, with the bulk of subsidies going to the largest one-tenth of farming enterprises. Over the same period the resulting artificially lowered and volatile price of cotton has contributed to the average annual tally of nearly 18,000 farmer suicides in India and has undercut incomes of cotton farmers in African countries. Harvey can take some comfort from the fact that European and Japanese agriculture require even higher subsidies than U.S. agriculture and are the most "super-inefficient" of all. Since mechanization has raised labour productivity to such an extent that less than 5 percent of their workers and an even lower share of their GDP is attributable to agriculture and allied activities, the advanced industrial countries can afford to, and do, give as subsidy out of the budget, up to half or more of the entire value of their agricultural output, and thus can dominate global markets despite their inefficiency.

The second fallacy, that international specialization and exchange necessarily lead to mutual benefit for trading partners, is embodied in David Ricardo's illogical and hence incorrect theory of comparative cost advantage, which is the mantra for free traders to this day. As discussed already in this book, Ricardo's conclusion of mutual benefit follows only if the assumption of his model, that "both countries produce both goods" (indeed his unstated assumption is that "all countries produce all goods") is satisfied, since without this assumption, relative cost and comparative advantage cannot be defined. But material reality tells us that "both countries produce both goods" is a very special premise that did not hold for the bulk of global trade, in particular trade in tropical products with temperate lands. When Kenya imported Lancashire cloth and exported tea to England, the relative cost of production could be defined for Kenya (the number of units of cloth producible by redirecting to it the labour released by reducing tea output by a unit) since it could and did produce both cloth and tea. But the relative cost of production could not be defined at all for England, where cloth output was positive but tea output was and will always remain zero. If a good cannot even be produced, the question of *any* definable cost of production does not arise, let alone the matter of relative cost, without which no comparison of costs and hence of advantage is possible. Ricardo's ignoring material reality gives rise to what logicians call the "converse fallacy of accident," meaning that from a very restricted premise a general conclusion of mutual benefit is improperly drawn and applied to situations where the premise is not satisfied.[4] The conclusion of mutual benefit no longer follows.

Indeed trade became positively harmful for the colonies obliged through extra-economic coercion to specialize in primary products for export, which reduced both their high value-addition manufacturing activities and their domestic grain availability. The same outcomes are seen today as advanced countries directly, and via the international financial institutions and the WTO, constantly badger developing countries to "open up" and specialize to the benefit of advanced countries on the false promise of mutual benefit explicitly quoting Ricardo's fallacious theory. The latest effort of the Doha round is to restrict public stockholding for food security purposes in the developing countries, never mind that it was the diversion of grain to ethanol in advanced countries that precipitated a major global food-price crisis in 2008 and undermined welfare.

The third fallacy arises from the deep, almost deliberately cultivated ignorance in northern academia regarding the specific conditions of global trade and investment under which their countries developed from the last quarter of the nineteenth century, the heyday of the gold standard. They choose to have no inkling that *their capitalist development was substantially dependent on colonial exploitation even when their countries had no colonies themselves.* The system worked as follows: Britain and France were the important net capital exporting nations in this period, Britain as the world capitalist leader being far ahead of France. Over four-fifths of export of capital from Britain went to developing continental Europe, North America, and regions of recent white settlement such as Argentina, South Africa, and Australia. Further, Britain kept its markets open to imports from these regions and thereby kept up their level of activity. It thus ran large *current account deficits* with these regions at the same time that it exported capital to the very same regions thereby incurring rising *capital account deficits with them* (since capital export is a negative item in a country's balance of payments). These two deficits summed to very large and increasing *balance of payments deficits with them,* which by the eve of the First World War had reached what would normally have been a totally unsustainable percentage of Britain's GDP. Nor did Britain have offsetting surpluses with other regions of the world to pay for these deficits, if *normal* items of trade and services are considered.[5]

The mechanism through which it avoided any balance of payments difficulties and gold outflow was ripping off its tropical colonies. Given the insatiable demand of the then-developing countries for food stuffs and raw materials, India earned the second largest export surplus in the world for over four decades up to 1928 (the largest surplus earner was the United Sates); and in the year 1928 earnings reached the peak of half a billion U.S dollars. But all its foreign exchange earnings were systematically appropriated by Britain every year to pay for Britain's own balance of payments deficits with the above-mentioned developing regions, including the United States, while local colonized peasant and artisan producers of export goods were "paid" out of the budgetary tax revenues raised from them—which means that they were apparently paid, but were not actually paid at all. This compression of their incomes permitted export goods, including grain exports, to be released at the expense of a fall in their own consumption. The exchange earnings from their export surplus piled up in London and, for accounting purposes, were offset by showing government-administered invisible liabilities on the colony of an unwarranted and fictitious nature to at least an equal extent.[6]

The fact that the pound sterling was considered "as good as gold" rested on the material basis that Britain obtained gratis the commodity equivalent of taxes squeezed out from over 400 million abysmally poor persons in the colonies. It was finally toppled from this position in only 1931, when the agricultural depression starting from 1926, led to a collapse of colonial exchange earnings. The rapid diffusion of capitalism in Europe and North America through capital exports by Britain simply would not have been possible without its wholesale appropriation of the exchange earnings of its colonies that were disguised as its own earnings. The fact that the dollar today does not have the same rock-hard status as the pound sterling, despite desperate attempts by the current world capitalist leader, the United States, to control the supply of vital global primary products including oil, has to do with lack of direct political control as in the colonial era, and the fact that the periphery has already been so "drained" for so long that its capacity for providing further "drain" to pay for the deficits of the capitalist leader is much less now.

When Harvey comments that India hardly exports much to the United States, he evidently has little idea of the actual historical facts: the United States alone accounted for nearly a quarter of all India's export surplus earnings by 1928, while continental Europe accounted for 40 percent. Not a single dollar earned from export surplus to these fast-developing regions was allowed to flow back to the tropical colonies. A long history of direct political control has habituated advanced countries to getting tropical goods free, as the commodity equivalent of taxes and rents: in the present era that is no longer possible, but it is approximated by unremitting pressure on developing countries to devalue their already undervalued currencies so that their exports are constantly cheapened in dollar terms.

Harvey remarks on our "obsession with agriculture," a charge we gladly accept, while hoping that he would spare a thought for the reason, which is the past and present *implacable obsession of global capitalism with accessing the lands and primary resources of the South,* at the expense of inflicting famine in the past, increasing hunger in the present era, and denuding these lands of mineral resources.[7] The ideologues of global capital seek to camouflage these realities: while urging income deflation and larger exports from the South—which both compress local mass demand and reduce food output growth— they typically claim massive reduction in hunger and poverty there by using the simple expedient of quietly lowering over time the nutrition standard against which hunger and poverty are measured. Indeed, an important part of the modus operandi of imperialism is in the intellectual domain, where it promotes incorrect theories of trade and of unemployment combined with illogical methods of measuring poverty to show a decline when deprivation is actually on the rise.

CURRENT DEPENDENCE OF ADVANCED COUNTRIES ON AGRICULTURAL IMPORTS

The advanced countries' import dependence on the ex-colonial countries has not declined; on the contrary, import dependence has intensified since air-freighting now permits imports of highly perishable products and seafood, not possible in the earlier era of slow sea transport. The method of securing the products that the northern countries want has necessarily changed, however, since direct political subjugation is no longer possible. Instead, incessant pressure is exercised on developing countries, directly and through international organizations, to remove all protection to their producers and engage in "free trade" while altering their output mix towards exports via systems of contracting with local farmers by their food business corporations.

The cost to developing country populations as their scarce land is diverted to export crops, is falling grain output per capita and falling nutritional levels. This inverse relation is extremely well established and the evidence has been summarized in our book already.[8] As table 2 shows, by 2011 the absorption of grain per capita in all forms was below 225 kg annually in India, the least developed countries, and Africa, compared to over 1,000 kg in the United States. In developing countries undergoing trade liberalization and fiscal contraction, grain output per head has been falling as more resources are diverted to export crops, and so has nutritional intake, in a manner that replicates the situation of colonial "one-way free trade."

Advanced countries have always urged developing countries to give up domestic food security systems and import food grains from them. Food imports may not actually take place to compensate for falling domestic output, however, for this depends on whether domestic demand is permitted to grow through expansionary public policies or constrained by the deflationary macroeconomic policies so universally implemented in this neoliberal era. As we have shown, while taxation in the past squeezed out export goods at the expense of declining consumption, the income deflating policies of finance serve the same purpose today of restricting the growth of indigenous demand in order to release products for export to the North. And it is the institutions located in the North that insist on income deflation and free trade: the IMF, the World Bank, and the WTO.

Harvey is not factually correct in asserting that "the dependency of metropolitan capitals on products from tropical and subtropical regions . . . . is nowhere as significant as the Patnaiks claim." Perhaps overnight all products from nontemperate lands have to disappear from the supermarket shelves to make it clear how significant these products are in underpinning the highly diversified consumption basket to which rich consumers in the North are complacently habituated. If tea, coffee, cocoa, cane sugar, chocolate or vanilla flavoured ice-cream and confectionery, fresh vegetables, fruits and flowers, and imported seafood all disappeared, their supermarket shelves, especially in winter, would be bare except for cereals and dairy and meat products, which are all that northern countries can produce in abundance. The unit supply price of agricultural products would shoot up without their access to the superior productive capacity of developing lands.

We require a complete matrix of world trade to establish sources of and destinations for the major traded primary goods, but such a matrix is not available at present. Data from the United Nations Food and Agriculture Organization's database allow for at least a partial picture of the comparative import dependence of developed and developing countries. From table 4, which covers a total of twenty food groups, we see that for advanced industrial countries like Germany and the United Kingdom, there is zero domestic output for at least three food groups; hence import dependence approaches infinity, as has been the

TABLE 4

Imports as a Percentage of Domestic Production for All Food Groups, Selected High-Income Countries and Regions, 2011

Imports/Production (M/Q), percent	Germany	United Kingdom	Italy	United States	European Union	Russian Federation	Japan	W. Asia
Cereals	27.2	19.3	63.2	2.3	28.6	1.5	390.3	86.1
Pulses	63.5	31.6	203.5	22.4	43.9	1.7	209.9	73.4
Starchy Roots	11.9	29.2	99.2	18.1	25.6	5.5	40.7	13.9
Sugar Crops	0.9	0.1	0	0.4	0.7	0	0	0
Sugar and Sweeteners	40.7	108.3	261.1	22.8	73.9	46.9	87.2	279.2
Oil Crops	183.8	44.3	44.4	2.2	72	9.6	2363	78.6
Vegetable Oils	111.4	172.1	225.3	39.5	132.1	33.6	64.1	175.5
Vegetables	172.6	159.2	13.9	24.1	42	22.8	26.1	8.4
Fruits	338.1	1882.8	15.7	30.9	89.9	282.1	150.2	22.7
Stimulants	→∞	→∞	→∞	98200	→∞	→∞	854.9	332.2
Spices	→∞	→∞	→∞	31600	339.2	200	194.1	123.2
Alcoholic Beverages	35.7	45.1	19.2	22.8	27.3	11.5	24.9	35.3
Meat	31.6	69.7	43.1	3.7	36	28.1	100.8	43.4
Offals	18.4	42.4	20.1	3.3	27.6	58.2	24.6	6.8
Animal Fats	23.4	60.2	48.4	1.8	39.3	35.9	36.8	84.6
Eggs	65.2	12.7	5.2	0.1	19.7	1.2	2	15.4
Milk	25.4	39.5	71.7	4.3	33	7.1	25	24.4
Fish and Seafood	1128.5	47.6	417.6	90.3	275.7	31.7	95.6	121.3
Aquatic Products, other	→∞	→∞	3100	180	310.7	100	15.6	100
Tree Nuts	4446.7	→∞	106.7	40.7	320.4	1246.2	1094.7	45.7

SOURCE: United Nations Food and Agriculture Organisation. Calculated from Food Balance Sheets/Supply Utilization Accounts, (FBS/SUA), available at faostat3.fao.org/faostat-gateway/go/to/download/F/FO/E.

NOTE: where a country's output of a particular food group is zero and there are positive imports, the output is treated as tending to zero and the import to output ratio is shown as tending to infinity using the symbols →∞

case always for two of these groups, namely, the stimulants (coffee, tea, and so on) and spices. For six more food groups in Germany and four more in the United Kingdom, *imports exceed domestic output, in some cases amounting to a multiple of home output.* These food groups include sugars and sweeteners, fruits and vegetables, oil crops and vegetable oils, fish and seafood. Interestingly Germany exports spices and stimulants to a substantial extent, though it produces none at all: it re-exports one-third of its spices imports and two-thirds of its stimulants imports. Germany imports three times more fruit than it produces, and its exports are more than its own production, again indicating re-exports.

Even a warm temperate Mediterranean country like Italy, endowed with the gifts of the olive and the vine, is very substantially import-dependent. As in cold temperate countries, its output of stimulants and spices is zero, so import dependence tends to infinity. *For six food groups, Italy imports more than its domestic output.* Despite an extensive coastline, it imports more than four times the fish and seafood that it produces domestically. Additionally for cereals, starchy roots, and milk its imports exceed 60 percent of domestic output.

The United States, a country of continental dimensions with some subtropical land and the largest arable area under cultivation of any country in the world, is less import-dependent than the European countries. However, it imports nearly one thousand times the stimulants and over three hundred times the spices that it produces, and it engages in re-export of these items. Despite its relatively more varied output, it is a net importer for ten out of the twenty food groups, and it imports more than 30 percent of domestic output in the case of vegetable oils, fruits, fish and seafood, aquatic products, and tree nuts. It is also a substantial importer to the extent of between 20 and 30 percent of domestic output, of pulses, sugar and sweeteners, vegetables, and alcoholic beverages. For many product groups, although the ratios are lower, the absolute import volumes for the United States are close to or more than double that of Germany (sugars and sweeteners, vegetables and fruit, alcoholic beverages, fish and seafood). In spite of its extensive coastline, the United States imports fish and seafood to the extent of 90 percent of its domestic production.

Japan, the first Asian industrial nation with an even greater land constraint than Britain, became food-deficient, like that country during its industrial transition and relied heavily on tax-financed rice imports from its colonies—Korea and Taiwan—in the interwar period. Unlike the northern industrial nations, it remains today a large importer of food grains, four times and double its domestic output for cereals and pulses respectively. For another seven food groups, it imports more than its domestic output. Another, newer import-dependent region is comprised of the oil-rich countries of West Asia, which have medium-high per capita income, while many of them face severe climatic constraints on production. This region is also substantially dependent on imported foodgrains, in addition to having higher import volumes than domestic production for sugars and sweeteners, vegetable oils, and fish and seafood.

As soon as we compare the import dependence of regions and countries of the global South, we see a very striking difference: namely, that for only one or two food groups is there any substantial import, and even for these groups import is never more than domestic output (table 5). For thirteen out of the twenty food groups, India imports zero or 0.5 percent and less of domestic output; for another three groups its import dependence is below 5 percent. Only for three groups—pulses, vegetable oils, and tree nuts—is the import to output ratio high, for pulses nearly one-fifth and for tree nuts and vegetable oils above four-fifths. Tree nuts are of small importance in absolute terms, but imports of edible oils, mainly palm oil from Southeast Asia, have increased rapidly in recent years.

After three decades of trade liberalisation, China shows higher import ratios than India, but much lower than the advanced countries. Import dependence is below 5 percent for ten food groups and for another four groups it is below one-fifth. The most important import is of oil crops, which almost equals domestic output, and vegetable oils, at nearly half of output, but a substantial part is imported from neighbouring Southeast Asian countries.

Africa and the least developed countries show high import dependence only for sweeteners and edible oils. With per capita cereals output falling as exportable crops rose under the debt-conditional trade liberalisation regimes of the early 1980s onwards, Africa has come to have a severe cereals deficit, relying on imports at present to the extent of nearly half of domestic output.[9] South America shows consistently low import dependence in all food groups compared to the advanced countries, below 5.1 percent of domestic output for 11 groups and its

TABLE 5

Imports as a Percentage of Domestic Production for All Food Groups, Selected Low- and Medium-Income Countries and Regions, 2011

	India	China	Indonesia	Southeast Asia	Least Developed	Africa	Brazil	South America
Cereals	.04	1.2	20.9	17.1	18.1	47.5	12.9	19
Pulses	18.3	18.8	0	5.2	5.5	9.9	7.8	14.1
Starchy Roots	0.16	11.5	8.7	7.2	0.6	0.44	1.91	2.3
Sugar Crops	0	Neg	0	0	0	0	0	0
Sugar and Sweeteners	0.48	27.9	121.4	33	116.1	104.7	0.01	5.1
Oil Crops	0.13	96.9	9.4	13.4	4.3	11.9	0.28	0.78
Veg. Oils	86.8	47.2	0.4	9.9	167.2	116.8	6.6	12.9
Vegetables	0.01	0.3	8.1	7.6	5.2	4.4	5	6
Fruits	0.88	4.2	5.3	5.7	3.7	3.4	1.9	3.2
Stimulants	9.4	21.2	9.1	34	22.4	19.6	2.5	9.4
Spices	2.3	3.4	23.1	27	1.3	14.4	33.3	14.3
Alcoholic Beverages	1.4	1.5	0.3	7.1	4.7	3.6	4.1	4.2
Meat	0.03	4.9	2.9	10.6	9.5	11.6	0.18	2.4
Offals	0	4.4	8.1	15.2	1.3	13.4	0.6	1.8
Animal Fats	0.05	24.2	27.2	37	21.6	48.8	3.9	20
Eggs	0	0.4	0.4	0.3	5.9	2.6	0	0.3
Milk	0.04	13.4	165	165.5	9	20.1	3.4	5.1
Fish and Seafood	0.06	20.9	8.5	15.8	5.5	63	53.5	17
Aquatic Products, other	0	0.2	0	0.1	0	0	150	1.9
Treenuts	83.1	14.1	2.7	6.3	18.3	5.7	23	23

SOURCE: See table 4.

highest ratio does not exceed one-fifth (for animal fats, of no great absolute magnitude).

We present data for 1992–94 on import dependence for some of the more important food groups in table 7.1 of our book. Comparing that with the more detailed tables 4 and 5 for 2011 given here, we clearly see that advanced country import dependence has increased greatly over the two decades and remains far higher than that of developing countries. U.S. import-dependence for spices and stimulants (and seafood) is now far higher, as is U.K. and German import dependence for fruits. Not only does import dependence as regards the traditional nonperishable goods continue; rich populations have now become habituated to a year-round supply of perishable vegetables and fruit, fish and seafood. Without intensive trade with the South, the standard of living of populations in the North would collapse to levels certainly better than in late medieval times since grain supply is not a constraint, but their consumption basket would become extremely seasonally limited, monotonous, and unhealthy. The incessant current pressure on developing countries to "open up" to the pull of global (read: advanced country) demand is the outcome of this material reality of asymmetric production capacities and the one-sided demand from rich populations on the products of warmer lands.

THE THEORY OF IMPERIALISM

The theory of imperialism we advance is set within this context. Given the overwhelming dependence of the advanced countries on products of the tropical and subtropical landmass—a dependence that is not even recognized in much of conventional literature—an increase in the demand for such products, which is inevitable if there is positive all-round growth in world incomes, could be met without any increase in their prices, if appropriate "land-augmenting" measures could be undertaken. But these require activism on the part of the state, and this is what was ruled out under capitalism in the colonial period and is ruled out under capitalism in the neoliberal period, i.e., under capitalism *other than in the post-colonial dirigiste period*. That period in our view represented a special situation *of weakening of imperialism*: the Second World War had left the hegemony of capital in the metropolitan economies, and of metropolitan capital in the colonies, under severe challenge; and the socialist threat loomed large. It is this that made possible not only the adoption of Keynesian demand management policies for the maintenance of high levels of employment in the advanced economies, but also "decolonization" and a degree of autonomy of the post-colonial states in the periphery in pursuing expansionary fiscal policies, including those for "land augmentation"; some of them even embarked on "national planning" in an effort to emulate the successes of the Soviet Union.

The process of centralization of capital, leading to the formation of an international finance capital, which was mobile across countries and which gradually forced all countries to open their doors to its free movement, has brought that period to an end. And in the era of neoliberalism, as in the era of colonialism, the tendency of finance capital to prevent any state activism *except what directly promotes its own interests*, once again manifests itself; "fiscal responsibility," which entails among other things a withdrawal of the state from undertaking "land-augmentation" measures, is an outcome.

Growing demand for products of the tropical land mass under these circumstances—in the absence of income deflation imposed on the users of such products to curtail their demand, and above all on the populations of the periphery where such products are produced—will necessarily cause a rise in prices (as happened once in the early 1970s), and this rise will pose a threat to the value of money. This is anathema for international finance capital; and hence the pervasive imposition of income deflation.

Our theory of imperialism therefore is based on the recognition of a basic trait of capitalism: namely, when it is faced with two alternatives, one of which can be described as a "cooperative solution" effected through state activism to the benefit of all, and the other at the expense of the working population, *it invariably chooses the latter*. This trait is pervasive: it has manifested itself in the imposition of "austerity" in the midst of the current recessionary crisis; it has manifested itself in the intransigence over the renegotiation of the Greek debt; and it is the diametrical opposite of what John Maynard Keynes believed was possible within capitalism, namely an acquiescence of the system to state activism benefiting all in a non-zero-sum game such as was possible in a recession.[10] *We see imperialism as a manifestation of this trait, which insists invariably on the "income deflation route" for ensuring that metropolitan demands for tropical products are satisfied without a rise in their prices and without state activism for "land augmentation."*

Our theory of imperialism is about capitalism as it behaves in the context of certain undeniable facts relating to production possibilities of different regions. *It is about capitalism not geography.* So Harvey's comments about the fact that "production can be improved on the tropical landmass" (of course it can be improved, that is precisely our point, but is not permitted to improve), and about space and time and such like, are entirely irrelevant to our theory.

Similarly we fail to perceive the relevance of his comments about capital being drawn to locate production in metropolitan centres rather than in the periphery ("Mogadishu") to our theory of imperialism. Certainly, in understanding the phenomenon of "underdevelopment," this fact plays a role (P. Patnaik 1973). One can for instance argue as follows: while capital located in the metropolis destroyed precapitalist production elsewhere in its quest for markets and thereby perpetrated "deindustrialization" and mass unemployment in the periphery, *it did not locate production in the periphery, notwithstanding the low wages caused by such unemployment,* because of its tendency to locate production where it is already located and hence the "physical" and "social" infrastructures, to use Harvey's words, are already available. This is what creates "development" at one pole and "underdevelopment" at another (as Gunnar Myrdal (1957) pointed out in the context of "regions" and one of us has argued in the context of the world economy [P. Patnaik 1973]). And in case such "spontaneous" reproduction of the "development-underdevelopment" dichotomy is sought to be deliberately broken by a country of the periphery, as happened after decolonization when the postcolonial dirigiste State worked to build up its own physical and social infrastructure to make it conducive for the location of modern industry, the power of metropolitan capital, which has monopoly over knowledge production, research and development, and technology, is invariably employed to thwart any such effort (often backed by the armed overthrow of the state that dared to challenge this monopoly).

But this entire argument, which we fully accept, is in no way counter to our theory of imperialism. Besides, such "spontaneous" reproduction of the "development-underdevelopment" dichotomy becomes undermined in the era of "globalization," when capital becomes far more globally mobile, and the much lower wages of the periphery begin to attract metropolitan capital, as it overcomes its reluctance to move out of its traditional habitat and locate plants elsewhere. But our point precisely is that *even if such relocation happens it does not overcome imperialism, because no matter where capital is located, the problem of increasing supply price for a range of goods, especially those grown on the tropical and subtropical landmass, remains.* And capital copes with that problem by imposing income deflation, above all on the working population of this landmass, which is why *no amount of locational shift of capital to this landmass will overcome the hunger and poverty of its working population.*

Likewise, we do not of course doubt that much change has taken place under capitalism. But what most authors do is to detail these changes and to conclude from the enormity of their scale that old categories, like imperialism, have ceased to be relevant today. We ask on the contrary: Are there any major *continuities* between the colonial period and now, continuities that are both rooted in the nature of capital and underlie the unquestionable poverty and degradation that exist over much of the globe? In focusing on these *continuities*, we naturally refrain from detailing the numerous changes that have occurred in capitalism. *That we do so cannot therefore be a legitimate criticism of our theory,* for if we had harped on the changes, we could not have focused on the continuities.

To detect these continuities, however, it is necessary to know what exactly colonialism entailed. And here, even the Marxist tradition has been remarkably remiss. Lenin, who was concerned with the monopoly phase of capitalism and restricted the term "imperialism" to only this phase, wrote little about colonialism *per se.* And Rosa Luxemburg, who was extremely sensitive to the issue of capitalist penetration into the colonies, visualized not the persistence of the colonies (and semicolonies and dependencies) as degraded and exploited economies that linger on in that state, but their disappearance as separate entities altogether and assimilation into a capitalism becoming a universal phenomenon. Indeed, other than Marx himself in his writings on colonialism, Marxist authors in the advanced capitalist countries have produced very little analysis of colonialism. And thus it is not surprising that there is a readiness among them to treat imperialism as no longer relevant, *because, not having analyzed colonialism, they fail to perceive any continuities between then and now.* The failure to perceive contemporary imperialism is, at its core, a failure to perceive colonialism.

The pervasiveness of the latter failure, upon which the former is based, is clear from some of Harvey's remarks. When he says that "the historical drain of wealth from East to West for more than two centuries has been reversed over the last thirty years," it is clear that he is unfamiliar with the concept of "drain." Indeed the whole of northern academia, and even the present day Marxists, with very few exceptions,[11] have systematically ignored the large literature on the drain available from the South. It refers not just to the direction of capital flows but to the phenomenon of sucking out the surplus of an economy *without any quid pro quo*. As already discussed, this is what Britain did to its colonies for centuries, and this "drain" occurred in the *form* of commodities taken out of these colonies gratis. This phenomenon *has not been reversed*, as Harvey claims it has, since the "East" is not appropriating gratis any surplus from the "West." The "West" also is no longer appropriating gratis a part of the surplus of the "East" in the same way as it was doing earlier, since decolonization has put a stop to that. The tax revenue of the colonies can no longer be used for "paying" local export goods producers while appropriating their global exchange earnings, which had thereby meant a free flow of commodities and international purchasing power to the metropolis. But there are other means of appropriation such as unequal exchange, the enforcement of "intellectual property rights," the wholly unreasonable demand that developing-country budget-spending on equipment must be globally tendered, and so on, and these still go on. The "East," on the other hand, does not appropriate from the "West" in any such way. Once we understand the meaning of "drain" and ask ourselves what it was used for, we are in a position to explore whether there are any continuities between then and now. Without understanding colonialism, we obviously cannot develop any awareness of these continuities, which is why our theory of imperialism places so much emphasis on understanding colonialism.

CONCLUDING REMARKS

Let us look at our argument from a different perspective. The fact that in a capitalist economy there may be certain sectors whose growth cannot occur without an increase in the "real price" of their goods (to use Keynes's 1919 term) has concerned economists from David Ricardo to

Keynes himself. The reason for this has typically been attributed to "diminishing returns" arising from the natural scarcity of land. We do not talk of "diminishing returns," but argue instead that "land-augmenting" investment and technological change could prevent an increase in the "real price" of the goods produced by these sectors. The fact that these do not occur—that instead, in order to prevent any price rise that may threaten the value of money in the metropolis, income deflation is imposed on the working people of these sectors—is the result of a certain immanent trait of *capitalism*. It is this trait that underlies imperialism, which is why we analyze imperialism starting with increasing supply price.

These sectors include the products of the tropical and semitropical landmass, which are less commonly discussed. But exhaustible resources also fall under the same rubric, since they too are subject to increasing supply price (though maybe over a longer period and as long as appropriate new substitutes are not found). Obviously, we do not make the absurd claim that they are produced *only* on the tropical landmass. Their analogy with products of the tropical landmass relates to the phenomenon of increasing supply price, as already explained. But recent developments involving the return to crops as an energy source in capitalist countries after two centuries of using fossil fuels underscore the historically close interaction between agriculture as source of energy and as source of food and reinforces the point regarding increasing supply price.

The material reality is that the overwhelming bulk of known fossil fuel reserves is located outside the territories of the industrially advanced countries, whose combined share is less than one-eighth in estimated remaining global reserves of oil and natural gas. Their share in global coal and lignite reserves is high, but about nine-tenths of these reserves cannot be exploited at all if there is genuine commitment to limiting global warming.[12] Hence we see the vertiginous increase in subsidy-aided conversion of corn to ethanol in the United States, which has precipitated a global food-price crisis since 2008 and adversely affected those developing countries that have become heavily food import-dependent as a result of their export specialization.

In the case of mineral resources including oil, however, there is an additional factor: ownership over them gives a monopoly, and if these monopoly owners collude, then they can earn high rents. It is for this reason that metropolitan capital has struggled long and hard to prevent these resources from being nationally owned, to the point of overthrowing regimes that dared to do so. But this aspect of imperialism is too well known to need recounting, which is why we have concentrated on the story relating to the other sphere where increasing supply price matters.

Notes

PREFACE

1. Such "land augmenting" measures, which include irrigation that increases cropping intensity and innovations that raise yields, typically require state expenditure.

2. Among the useful studies of imperialism that have come out in the last several years, mention may be made of Owen and Sutcliffe (1972), Patnaik (1986), Chilcote (1999), *The Palgrave Encyclopaedia*, edited by Ness and Cope (2015), and a special issue of *Monthly Review* (2015).

1. INTRODUCTION

1. This is the title of a very influential book by Hardt and Negri (2000).

2. "Adjusted for inflation, real wages have stagnated or fallen; a typical male worker's income in 2011 ($32,986) was lower than it was in 1968 ($33,880)" (Stiglitz 2013).

3. John Smith (2015) notes that under the current form of globalization, while competition between the workers of the periphery and those of the metropolis has increased, the same is not true of competition between the firms of the two regions. Metropolitan firms compete intensely against one another by locating plants in low-wage countries of the periphery; competition is not between the firms of the periphery and those of the metropolis.

4. An extract from Hilferding (1910) dealing with the ideology of finance capital can be found in Sweezy (1942).

2. THE THREAT OF INCREASING SUPPLY PRICE

1. A situation of increasing supply price as defined by us, i.e., for a given money wage rate per efficiency unit of labour, can, it follows, be prevented in reality if the money wage rate of a natural unit of labour is not allowed to rise with its productivity. This prevention is precisely one form of what we call "income deflation" below, that is resorted to, in practice.

2. Free trade arguments have been systematically invoked by the advanced countries during the Doha round even to put barriers against.a public distribution system in foodgrains in some of the most hunger-afflicted countries of the world.

3. For Ricardo this meant a lower amount of direct and indirect labour embodied per unit of output. Take two countries, 1 and 2, and two goods, A and B, where both goods are produced using less labour in Country 1. Reducing by one unit the output of good A and redirecting the labour released to good B, produces, say, 2 units of B in Country 1, but 1.5 units of B in Country 2. Country 1 should specialize in good B and Country 2 in good A.

4. The argument for free trade put forward by Ricardo, like the later Heckscher-Ohlin argument, presupposes the absence of any demand constraint. Ricardo, it may be recalled, was a believer in Say's Law.

5. We refer to countries in the Northern Hemisphere. Cultivable warm temperate lands in the Southern Hemisphere (parts of Argentina, South Africa, Australia) also meet seasonal demand in the North since they experience summer when the North is in the grip of winter.

6. The "fallacy of accident" argues improperly from a general proposition to an exceptional case—the premise that "all persons can see" does not mean that Homer can see. The "converse fallacy of accident" argues improperly from a special case to a general conclusion.

7. The term "vector-wise larger" is defined as follows: vector a is larger than vector b if $a \geq b$ but $a \neq b$, i.e., if some elements of a are larger than the corresponding elements of b but no element is smaller.

8. This point has been discussed at greater length in P. Patnaik (2009).

9. The point that a monetary economy in which the money price of gold is infinite, is untenable, need not be laboured. For if the money prices of non-gold commodities are finite, then the gold producers would claim their entire supply, leaving nothing for the producers of these commodities, which in turn would prevent them from producing at all; on the other hand, if the money prices of non-gold commodities are also infinite, then money has become completely worthless anyway and can play no role whatsoever.

3. COPING WITH THE THREAT

1. Marx wrote this in his article on "The British Rule in India," in the *New York Daily Tribune*, June 25, 1853; the precise words of the quotation given here are taken from Husain (2006:13).

2. For a critique of Wittfogel's theory, see Habib (1961).

3. The "rent barrier" argument was adapted for developing societies in the reference cited, from Karl Marx's discussion on the barrier of absolute ground rent to expansion of capitalist production, in *Capital Vol. 3* (1971), chap. 45. Joan Robinson (1979) referred to and appears to have accepted the argument of rent as a barrier to investment.

4. This point is discussed at length in the paper "The State Under Neo-Liberalism," reprinted in P. Patnaik (2011).

5. Evidence for India is put together in U. Patnaik (2003, 2008) and P. Patnaik (2015).

6. For a discussion of the Bengal famine as a "boom famine," see Sen (1982), and for its specific character as an engineered "profit inflation," see U. Patnaik (1991).

4. THE RESERVE ARMY OF LABOUR IN THE PERIPHERY

1. For a discussion of NAIRU and a view on it different from that of "mainstream" economics, see P. Patnaik (1997); see also R. E. Rowthorn (1977).

2. The argument being presented here is somewhat different from that of Foster, McChesney, and Jonna (2011). They refer to a "global reserve army of labour" that characterizes the new imperialism. The point being made here, however, refers to capitalism's need for labour reserves in the periphery, quite apart from the reserve army that exists in the metropolis, throughout the history of capitalism.

3. Habib (1999) even talks of troops in Mughal India being used to bring back agricultural labourers, in case they fled their habitats, to prevent the emergence of a *shortage* of labour.

5. CAPITALISM, POVERTY, AND INEQUALITY

1. The above theoretical argument can be rigorously stated as follows: *unless there are zero-elastic price expectations in the foodgrain market in the tropical country, even when current price moves up,* because of increased demand for

tropical products from the metropolis, the foodgrain price will always rule at some level higher than what prevailed initially and this will be accompanied by a corresponding exchange rate adjustment; and this happening in every period into the future would threaten the value of money. Inelastic, as distinct from zero-elastic, price expectations alone are insufficient to rule this out. But zero-elastic price expectations cannot obtain unless the state in the tropical country plays a proactive role to prevent any foodgrain price increase, which does not happen under capitalism in its spontaneity.

2. It may be thought that since under the gold standard the exchange rates were fixed anyway, the argument we have just presented has little relevance. But the argument can then simply be restated to mean that the gold standard itself would have ceased to be sustainable in the absence of income deflation. This point is discussed at length in a later chapter.

3. Whenever the term "poverty" is used below in the text, it refers to the "basket-commanded" notion of poverty.

6. FURTHER ELABORATIONS AND CLARIFICATIONS

1. Keynes (1949: chap. 17) had famously suggested that land preference might have played a role in restricting the growth of wealth in older societies, rather like liquidity preference in contemporary capitalist economies. Although in saying this he had not brought in the question of the fixity of land, his general conception of "money" as having a low elasticity of production would suggest that he thought of the fixity of land as underlying land preference. Of course, land preference *per se* may not play this role when the usual rules of market exchange do not hold, i.e., when there is a rationing equilibrium. On this, see P. Patnaik (2007).

2. Interestingly John Strachey, one-time British Communist theorist, saw Keynesian state intervention in "demand management" as making Lenin's theory of imperialism irrelevant (Strachey 1959). He was wrong in attributing an "imperialism-is-necessary-for-resolving-the-realization-problem" theory to Lenin, but he was one among many in believing that Keynesian demand management obviated the need for imperialism.

3. The data source is Food Balance Sheet/Supply-Utilisation Accounts, Food and Agriculture Organization, faostat3.fao.org/faostat-gateway/go/to /download/F/FO/E.

4. The idea that postcolonial dirigsme represented a loosening of the bonds of imperialism, which have tightened under the current neoliberal regime, may sound odd to many. In fact it is common to come across precisely the opposite view. The reason for this opposite perception could be that there were several

military interventions by the United States and other capitalist powers against dirigiste regimes, such as in Iran (1953), Guatemala (1954), Egypt (1956), Brazil (1964), the Dominican Republic (1965), and Chile (1973), while their more recent interventions do not appear openly "anti-dirigiste," thus creating the impression that imperialism as an *economic relationship* is unrelated to such recent interventions. This apparent contrast is also matched by a disappearance of the term "imperialism" from the discourse of the Left in the metropolis in recent years. On this latter point, see P. Patnaik (1995).

7. METROPOLITAN DEMAND ON TROPICAL LANDMASS

1. Such an adverse movement in the terms of trade would arise because while the prices of tropical products in terms of the money of the metropolis would be prevented from increasing (and might even fall), through income deflation, a rise *inter alia* in the "degree of monopoly" à la Kalecki (1954) would raise, relative to them, the prices of manufactured goods.

2. This inverse relationship was first discussed in U. Patnaik (1996, 2003).

3. As also in the limited temperate lands in the Southern Hemisphere, which experience summer during the Northern winter.

4. This table is from U. Patnaik (2003).

5. "Net availability" is defined as net output (obtained by deducting from gross output, one-eighth for seed, feed, and wastage) plus net import plus net reduction of stocks. The table is from U. Patnaik (2008). Note that before Independence there was no public stockholding, so net output is adjusted for trade alone

6. The discussion that follows is based on U. Patnaik (2003, 2008).

7. By 2004–05, the calorie intake accessible at price-indexed official poverty lines in some of the individual states had reached as low as 1,400 to 1,500 per day. Only the population falling below these extremely low nutritional intakes were officially "the poor."

8. Data for every year are available in *Food Balance Sheets/Supply Utilization Accounts*, United Nations Food and Agriculture Organization. The quoted figures relate to 2005. The relation between direct and indirect grain consumption as income rises was discussed by P. Yotopoulos (1985).

8. THE INTERNATIONAL MONETARY SYSTEM

1. The "Home Charges" were annual sterling liabilities put on India and included the leave allowances and pensions of British administrators, interest

on debt, outlays on purchase of government stores, and defence spending including for operations outside India.

2. D. Kumar with M. Desai (1984), table 12.10, 938.

3. See for instance S. Habib (1975), A. K. Bagchi (2005), and U. Patnaik (2006).

4. The figures are Rs.14,923 million export surplus on merchandise and gold, and Rs.17,093 million invisible debits giving a negative current account balance of Rs.2170 million. (Banerjee 1963: table 37) These have been divided by 14.6 to convert to pound sterling, taking a rough average of the exchange rate series from United Nations (1962).

5. De Cecco (1984) discusses the role of Britain's empire in sustaining the gold standard, but even he does not touch on the role of the "drain of surplus" from the empire to Britain.

6. Again, while stressing the balancing role of India's earnings in meeting Britain's deficits, Saul (1960) also does not link it to the drain, since no mention is made of the fact that colonized producers were "paid" out of taxes.

7. This can be visualized formally in the following manner: the differential risk premium that a "representative" wealth-holder in the periphery would demand for holding wealth in the periphery's currency, as compared to holding it in a currency of the metropolis, keeps increasing over time, because wealth-holders in the periphery become both more aware and more sensitive to the differential risk itself.

8. For a fuller discussion of this point, see P. Patnaik (2013).

9. The following question may have struck some: If, according to our argument, increasing supply price, when allowed to express itself, would drive down the value of the currency of the periphery to zero, making the system untenable (which is what necessitates income deflation), then how does the system survive in the face of this "absolute preference" for the currency of the metropolis by the rich in the periphery? The answer lies precisely in the fact that this "absolute preference" unfolds over time; it is a more gradual, more muted, more long-term phenomenon. Though this phenomenon is related to the factors emphasized in this book, viz., the income deflation and associated poverty in the periphery which makes it on the whole a more "dangerous" place for capital than the metropolis, it is nonetheless quite distinct from the argument of our book.

A COMMENTARY ON *A THEORY OF IMPERIALISM*

1. S. Sassen, *Expulsions: Brutality and Complexity in the Global Economy* (Cambridge: Harvard University Press, 2014).

2. J. Sachs, *The End of Poverty: Economic Possibilities for Our Time* (New York: Penguin, 2005); J. Diamond, *Guns, Germs, and Steel: The Fates of Human Societies* (New York: Norton, 1997 [2003]); K. Wittfogel, *Oriental Despotism* (New Haven: Yale University Press, 1953). For my critical view of this literature, see D. Harvey, *Cosmopolitanism and the Geographies of Freedom* (New York, Columbia University Press, 2005).

3. D. Acemoglu, S. Johnson, and J. Robinson, "Reversal of Fortune: Geography and Institutions in the Making of the Modern World Income Distribution," *Quarterly Journal of Economics* 117 (2002): 1231–94; J. Sachs, "Is Geography Destiny?," in *World Bank Conference on Development Economics*, ed. B. Pleskovic and J. Stiglitz (Washington, D.C.: World Bank, 1999).

4. K. Marx, *Grundrisse* (London: Penguin, 1973). I took up this theme in some detail in D. Harvey, *The Condition of Postmodernity* (Oxford: Basil Blackwell, 1989).

5. D. Harvey, *Justice, Nature and the Geography of Difference* (Oxford: Basil Blackwell, 1996). See also W. Cronon, *Nature's Metropolis: Chicago and the Great West* (New York: Norton, 1991).

6. K. Marx, *Capital, Volume 1* (London: Penguin, 1967), 709–10, 727.

7. G. Myrdal, *Economic Theory and Underdeveloped Regions* (London: Duckworth, 1957).

8. S. Amin, *Accumulation on a World Scale* (New York: Monthly Review Press, 1974); I. Wallerstein, *The Modern World System* (New York: Academic Press, 1974); A. Emmanuel, *Unequal Exchange: A Study of the Imperialism of Trade* (New York: Monthly Review Press, 1972); A. Frank, *Capitalism and Underdevelopment in Latin America* (New York: Monthly Review Press, 1969).

9. C. K. Lee, "Spectre of Global China," *New Left Review*, 2nd series (September–October 2014): 29–66.

10. D. Harvey, *The New Imperialism* (Oxford: Oxford University Press, 2003), 185–86.

11. D. Harvey, "The Geography of Capitalist Accumulation: A Reconstruction of the Marxian Theory," *Antipode* 7 (1975): 1–28; This, and most of the subsequent essays are collected in D. Harvey, *Spaces of Capital* (New York: Routledge, 2001); see also D. Harvey, *The Limits to Capital* (Oxford: Basil Blackwell, 1982).

12. D. Harvey, *Spaces of Global Development: Towards a Theory of Uneven Geographical Development* (London: Verso, 2006); D. Harvey, *Rebel Cities: From the Right to the City to the Urban Revolution* (London: Verso, 2013); D. Harvey, *Seventeen Contradictions and the End of Capitalism* (London: Profile, 2014).

13. L. Panitch and S. Gindin, *The Making of Global Capitalism: The Political Economy of American Empire* (London: Verso, 2013).

14. G. Arrighi, *The Geometry of Imperialism* (London: New Left Books, 1978); G. Arrighi, *The Long Twentieth Century: Money, Power, and the Origins of Our Times* (London: Verso, 1994).

15. This is the main theme of D. Harvey, *The New Imperialism* (Oxford: Oxford University Press, 2003).

A RESPONSE TO DAVID HARVEY'S COMMENTS

1. Phyllis Deane in *The First Industrial Revolution* (1965) had correctly emphasized the important part that re-exports of imports (four-fifths of re-exports were tropical goods) had played in enabling England to pay for its temperate land imports of corn, iron, and naval supplies, given that Britain's own domestic exports faced inelastic demand. But in her jointly authored book with W. A. Cole, *British Economic Growth 1688–1959—Trends and Structure* (1969, 2nd. ed.), not only was this discussion cut out entirely, the very figures of re-exports were eliminated both from imports and exports, and only retained imports and domestic exports were added up to give what they called "the volume of British trade." This is not the concept of trade in any macro-economics textbook, nor is it used by any international organization such as the United Nations, the World Bank, or the IMF, which always sum up total imports and total exports. Using the correct concept of trade applied to these authors' own data, we found that Britain's annual trade averaged over £82 million by the triennium 1799–1801, compared to the mere £51 million estimated by Deane and Cole (1969). Compared to their figure of 36 percent, the correct trade to GDP ratio was 58 percent. See U. Patnaik (2000, 2011a) for the time series for the period 1697 to 1804 and for a critique of Kuznets (1967), who reproduces the misleading Deane-Cole figures without mentioning that they are not comparable with trade estimates for other countries.

2. The references are available in U. Patnaik (2011).

3. North China (Manchuria) was occupied, and China's sovereignty was undermined by a number of old and new imperialist powers—USA, Britain, France, Germany, Japan, and Russia. They obtained under the Unequal Treaties and after WWI, extensive trade privileges, rights of extra-territoriality, access to natural resources and to markets. Owing to its loss of tariff autonomy, manufactured goods poured into China causing de-industrialization and displacement of labour as in India, while imposition of millions of pound sterling in war indemnities undermined its finances. The economic effects of semi-colonial control by numerous powers were thus similar to colonial control by a single power.

4. See U. Patnaik (2005) for a detailed discussion of Ricardo's fallacy.

5. The necessary trade data are available from the United Nations (1962) and are reproduced in U. Patnaik (2014). S. B. Saul (1960) in his pioneering work usefully discussed Britain's use of India's global export surplus to balance its own international payments, but without any appreciation of the tax-financed, hence gratis, element of Britain's appropriation of these export surplus earnings.

6. For the real and financial mechanism, see U. Patnaik (2006, 2014). No matter what heights the merchandise export surplus reached, the government-administered invisible liabilities were manipulated to be even higher, so that all exchange earnings were siphoned off, and the colony was obliged to borrow.

7. British colonial rule in India, for instance, was marked by a series of famines of which the most severe one was the 1943 Bengal famine. For a discussion of the Bengal famine see Lokanathan (1946), Sen (1981), and U. Patnaik (1991).

8. See also U. Patnaik (2003, 2008).

9. For a calculation from UN data of the extent of sub-Saharan Africa's food staples decline see "The Loss of Food Security in sub-Saharan Africa," in U. Patnaik (2008).

10. This trait is so little recognized in economics, including in Marxian economics, that to our knowledge there is no concept capturing it. The unconventional popular term "bloody-mindedness" comes closest to *describing* it. Kalecki's classic 1943 paper "Political Aspects of Full Employment" (reprinted in Kalecki 1971) is one place where it finds implicit recognition.

11. The exceptions include Paul A. Baran (1973) and André Gunder Frank (1971), already referred to in our book, and more recently, Angus Maddison (2006).

12. See McGlade and Ekins (2015). North America, Europe, and the Pacific OECD countries taken together account for 10 percent and 11 percent of oil and natural gas reserves.

References

Amin, S. 1977. *Unequal Development: An Essay on the Social Formations of Peripheral Capitalism.* New York: Monthly Review Press.

Armstrong, P., A. Glyn, and J. Harrison. 1991. *Capitalism Since 1945.* Oxford: Blackwell.

Bagchi, A. K. 1970. "European and Indian Entrepreneurship in India 1900–1930." In *Elites in South Asia,* edited by E. Leach and S. N. Mukherjee. Cambridge: Cambridge University Press.

Bagchi, A. K. 1972. "Some International Foundations of Capitalist Growth and Underdevelopment." *Economic and Political Weekly,* Mumbai, 8, nos. 31 to 33 (August): 1559–70, 1972.

Bagchi, A. K. 1989. *The Political Economy of Underdevelopment.* Cambridge: Cambridge University Press.

Bagchi, A. K. 2005. *Perilous Passage: Mankind and the Global Ascendancy of Capital.* Lanham, Md.: Rowman and Littlefield.

Banerjee, A. K. 1963. *India's Balance of Payments—Estimates of Current and Capital Account from 1921–22 to 1938–39.* Bombay: Asia Publishing House.

Baran, P. A., 1973. *The Political Economy of Growth.* Harmondsworth: Penguin.

Baran, P. A., and P. M. Sweezy. 1966. *Monopoly Capital.* New York: Monthly Review Press.

Bhattacharya, S. 2005. *Financial Foundations of the British Raj.* Delhi: Orient Longman.

Bhattacharya, S. 2006. "International Flows of Un-Free Labour." In Jomo 2006, 195–226.

Blyn, G. 1966. *Agricultural Trends in India 1891–1947: Output, Area and Productivity.* Philadelphia: University of Pennsylvania Press.

Booth, A. 1988. *Agricultural Development in Indonesia.* London: Allen and Unwin.

Boxer, C. R. 1973. *The Portuguese Seaborne Empire 1415–1825*. Harmondsworth: Pelican.

Chakraborty, S. 2011. "Movements in the Terms of Trade of Primary Commodities vis-à-vis Manufactured Goods: A Theoretical and Empirical Study." Ph.D. dissertation. New Delhi: Centre for Economic Studies and Planning, Jawaharlal Nehru University.

Chandavarkar, A.G. 1989. *Keynes and India: A Study in Economics and Biography*. London: Macmillan.

Chandra, B. 1968. "Reinterpretation of Nineteenth-Century Indian Economic History." *Indian Economic and Social History Review* 5, no. 1 (March): 35–75.

Chilcote, R., ed. 1999. *The Political Economy of Imperialism: Critical Appraisals*. Norwell, Mass.: Kluwer Academic Press.

Davis, R. 1979. *The Industrial Revolution and British Overseas Trade*. Leicester: Leicester University Press, Leicester.

Deane, P. 1965. *The First Industrial Revolution*. Cambridge: Cambridge University Press.

Deane, P., and W. A. Cole. 1969. *British Economic Growth 1688–1959: Trends and Structure*, 2nd ed. Cambridge: Cambridge University Press.

De Cecco, M. 1984. *The International Gold Standard: Money and Empire*. New York: St. Martin's Press.

Doniger, W., and M. Nussbaum. 2015. *Pluralism and Democracy in India: Debating the Hindu Right*. Oxford: Oxford University Press.

Drescher, S., and S. L. Engerman. 1998. *A Historical Guide to World Slavery*. New York: Oxford University Press.

Dutt, R. C. (1903) 1970. *The Economic History of India, Vol. 1: Under Early British Rule 1757–1837*. London: Routledge and Kegan Paul.

Emmanuel, A. 1972. *Unequal Exchange: A Study of the Imperialism of Trade*. New York: Monthly Review Press

Fanon, F. 2001. *The Wretched of the Earth*. Harmondsworth: Penguin.

Feinstein, C. H., ed. 1967. *Socialism, Capitalism and Economic Growth: Essays Presented to Maurice Dobb*. Cambridge: Cambridge University Press.

Foster, J. B., R. W. McChesney, and R. J. Jonna. 2011. "The Global Reserve Army of Labour and the New Imperialism." *Monthly Review* 63, no. 6 (November): 1–31.

Frank, A. G. 1971. *Capitalism and Underdevelopment in Latin America*. Harmondsworth: Penguin.

Friedman, H. 1990. "The Origins of Third World Food Dependence." In *The Food Question—Profits Versus People?*, 13–31. Edited by H. Bernstein, B. Crow, M. Mackintosh, and C. Martin. London: Earthscan.

Galbraith, J. K. 1963. *American Capitalism*. Harmondsworth: Penguin.

Ghosh, J., and C. P. Chandrasekhar, eds. 2003. *Work and Well-Being in the Age of Finance*. Delhi: Tulika.

Goodwin, R. M. 1967. "A Growth Cycle." In Feinstein 1967, 54–58.

Grabowski, R. 1985. "A Historical Re-Assessment of Early Japanese Development." Development and Change 16, 235–60.

Habib, I. 1961. "An Examination of Wittfogel's Theory of Oriental Despotism." *Enquiry* 6, Delhi, 54–73.

Habib, I. 1999. *The Agrarian System of Mughal India 1556–1707*. Delhi: Oxford University Press.

Habib, S. 1975. "Colonial Exploitation and Capital Formation in England in the Early Stages of the Industrial Revolution." In *Proceedings*, Indian History Congress, Aligarh.

Hansen, A. H. 1938. *Full Recovery or Stagnation?* New York: W. W. Norton.

Hardt, M., and A. Negri. 2000. *Empire*. Cambridge: Harvard University Press.

Hilferding, R. 1910. *Das Finanzkapital*. Vienna: Wiener Volksbuchhandlung.

Husain, I., ed. 2006. *Karl Marx on India*. Delhi: Tulika.

Jomo, K. S., ed. 2005. *The Pioneers of Development Economics*. Delhi: Tulika.

Jomo, K. S., ed. 2006. *Globalization Under Hegemony—The Long Twentieth Century*. Delhi: Oxford University Press.

Kaldor, N. 1968. *Causes of the Slow Rate of Growth of the United Kingdom*. Cambridge: Cambridge University Press.

Kaldor, N. 1976. "Inflation and Recession in the World Economy." *Economic Journal* 86, no. 314: 703–14.

Kalecki, M. 1971. *Selected Essays on the Dynamics of the Capitalist Economy*. Cambridge: Cambridge University Press.

Kenwood, A. G., and L. Lougheed. 1971. *The Growth of the International Economy 1820–1960*. London: Allen and Unwin.

Keynes, J. M. 1919. *The Economic Consequences of the Peace*. New York: Harcourt, Brace and Howe.

Keynes, J. M. 1930. *Treatise on Money (The Applied Theory of Money)*. New York: Harcourt Brace.

Keynes, J. M. 1940. *How to Pay for the War*. New York: Harcourt Brace.

Keynes, J. M. 1949. *The General Theory of Employment, Interest and Money*. London: Macmillan.

Kindleberger, C. P. 1987. *The World in Depression*. Harmondsworth: Penguin.

Krishna, R. 2013. "Cereal Consumption as a Proxy for Real Income." *Economic and Political Weekly* 48, no. 29 (July 20): 102–9.

Kumar, D. ed. with M. Desai 1984. *The Cambridge Economic History of India, Volume II: 1757–1970*. Delhi: Orient Longman in association with Cambridge University Press.

League of Nations. 1942. *The World Trade Network*. Princeton N. J.: Princeton University Press.

Lenin, V. I. 1964. "New Data on the Laws Governing the Development of Capitalism in Agriculture." In *Collected Works*, vol. 22. 13–102. Moscow: Progress Publishers.

Lenin, V. I. 1977. *Imperialism the Highest Stage of Capitalism*. In *Selected Works*, vol. 1. 634–731. Moscow: Progress Publishers.

Lewis, W. A. 1978. *Growth and Fluctuations 1870–1913*. London: Allen and Unwin.

Lewis, W. A. 1979. *Evolution of the International Economic Order*. Princeton N. J.: Princeton University Press.

Lokanathan, P. S. 1946. *India's Post-War Reconstruction and Its International Aspects*. Indian Council of World Affairs. Delhi: Oxford University Press.

Luxemburg, R. 1963. *The Accumulation of Capital*. London: Routledge.

Maddison, A. 2006. *The World Economy, Vol. 1: A Millennial Perspective, Vol. 2: Historical Statistics*. OECD Development Centre.

Magdoff, H. 1969. *The Age of Imperialism*. New York: Monthly Review Press.

Mantoux, P. 1928. *The Industrial Revolution in the 18th Century*. Translated by Marjorie Vernon. London: Methuen.

Marx, K. 1978. *Capital*, vol. 1. Moscow: Progress Publishers.

Marx, K. 1971. *Capital*, vol. 3. Moscow: Progress Publishers.

McGlade, C., and P. Ekins. 2015. "The Geographical Distribution of Fossil Fuels Unused When Limiting Global Warming to 2° C." *Nature* 517 (January 8): 187–90.

Monthly Review. 2015. Special Number on Imperialism with an Introduction by John Bellamy Foster, vol. 67, no. 3 (July–August).

Myrdal, G. 1957. *Economic Theory and Underdeveloped Regions*. London: University Paperbacks, Methuen.

Ness, I., and Z. Cope, eds. 2015. *The Palgrave Encyclopaedia of Imperialism and Anti-Imperialism*. London: Palgrave Macmillan.

Northrup, D. 1995. *International Labour in the Age of Imperialism 1834–1922*. Cambridge: Cambridge University Press.

Nurkse, R. 1954. "International Investment Today in the Light of Historical Experience." *Economic Journal* 64, no. 256: 744–58.

Owen, R., and R. B. Sutcliffe, eds. 1972. *Studies in the Theory of Imperialism*. London: Longman.

Pandit, Y. S. 1937. *India's Balance of Indebtedness*. London: George Allen and Unwin.

Patnaik, P. 1972. "A Note on External Markets and Capitalist Development." *Economic Journal* 82, no. 328: 1316–23.

Patnaik, P. 1973. "On the Political Economy of Underdevelopment." *Economic and Political Weekly* 8, nos.4–6, Annual Number (February): 197–212; reprinted in P. Patnaik. 1995. *Whatever Happened to Imperialism and Other Essays.* Delhi: Tulika Books.

Patnaik, P., ed. 1986. *Lenin and Imperialism: An Appraisal of Theories and Contemporary Reality.* Delhi: Orient Longman.

Patnaik, P. 1995a. "Whatever Happened to Imperialism?" In Patnaik, 1995, 102–6.

Patnaik, P. 1995. *Whatever Happened to Imperialism and Other Essays.* Delhi: Tulika.

Patnaik, P. 1997. *Accumulation and Stability Under Capitalism.* Oxford: Clarendon.

Patnaik, P. 1999. "On the Pitfalls of Bourgeois Internationalism." In *The Political Economy of Imperialism: Critical Appraisals,* edited by Ronald Chilcote, 169–79. Norwell, Mass.: Kluwer Academic Press.

Patnaik, P. 2006. "The Diffusion of Development." *Economic and Political Weekly* 41, no. 18 (May 6): 1766–72.

Patnaik, P. 2007. "Land Preference and Productive Investment: A Theoretical Note" in A. Vaidyanathan and K.L. Krishna, eds. *Institutions and Markets in India's Development: Essays for K.N. Raj,* 95–108. Delhi: Oxford University Press.

Patnaik, P. 2009. *The Value of Money.* New York: Columbia University Press.

Patnaik P. 2011. *Re-Envisioning Socialism.* Delhi: Tulika.

Patnaik, P. 2011a. "The State Under Neo-Liberalism." In P. Patnaik 2011, 125–35.

Patnaik, P. 2011b. "A Marxist Perspective on the World Economy." In P. Patnaik 2011, 259–71.

Patnaik, P. 2013. "The Secular Decline in Third World Exchange Rates." Paper presented to the Annual Conference of the Central Bank of the Argentine Republic, November.

Patnaik, P. 2015. "Neo-Liberalism and the Food Crisis." In W. Doniger and M. Nussbaum 2015, 191–206.

Patnaik, U. 1976. "Class Differentiation Within the Peasantry—An Approach to Analysis of Indian Agriculture." *Economic and Political Weekly* 11, no. 39 (September 25): 82–101.

Patnaik, U. 1984. "Tribute Transfer and the Balance of Payments in the *Cambridge Economic History of India* Vol. II." *Social Scientist* 12, no. 12; reprinted in U. Patnaik 1999, 305–22.

Patnaik, U. 1986. *The Agrarian Question and the Development of Capitalism in India.* Delhi: Oxford University Press; reprinted in *Land, Labour and Rights—10 Daniel Thorner Memorial Lectures,* edited by Alice Thorner. Delhi: Tulika, 2001, 17–57.

Patnaik, U. 1991. "Food Availability and Famine—A Longer View." *Journal of Peasant Studies* 19, no. 1.

Patnaik, U. 1996. "Export-Oriented Agriculture and Food Security in Developing Countries and in India." *Economic and Political Weekly* 31, nos. 35–37; (September): 2429–49. Reprinted in U. Patnaik 1999, 351–416.

Patnaik, U. 1999. *The Long Transition—Essays on Political Economy.* Delhi: Tulika.

Patnaik, U. 2000. "New Estimates of Eighteenth-Century British Trade and Their Relation to Transfers from Tropical Colonies." In *The Making of History: Essays Presented to Irfan Habib*, edited by K. N. Panikkar, T. J. Byres, and U. Patnaik, 359–402. Delhi: Tulika Books.

Patnaik, U. 2003. "On the Inverse Relation Between Primary Exports and Food Absorption in Developing Countries Under Liberalized Trade Regimes." In Ghosh and Chandrasekhar 2003, 256–86.

Patnaik, U. 2005. "Ricardo's Fallacy." In *The Pioneers of Development Economics*, edited by K. S. Jomo. Delhi: Tulika Books.

Patnaik, U. 2006. "The Free Lunch: Transfers from the Colonies and Their Role in Capital Formation in Britain during the Industrial Revolution." In Jomo 2006, 30–70.

Patnaik, U. 2006. "Theorising Food Security and Poverty in the Era of Neo-Liberal Reforms." *Social Scientist* 33, 7–8, 50–81. http://www.cefsindia.org/reports/secondlecturebyprofutsapatnaik.pdf.

Patnaik, U. 2008. *The Republic of Hunger and Other Essays.* Delhi: Three Essays Collective.

Patnaik, U. 2009. "Origins of the Food Crisis in India and Developing Countries." *Monthly Review* 61, no. 3: 63–77; reprinted in *Agriculture and Food in Crisis—Conflict, Resistance and Renewal*, edited by F. Magdoff and B. Tokar. New York: Monthly Review Press, 2010, 85–101.

Patnaik, U. 2011. "The 'Agricultural Revolution' in England—The Cost for the English working class and the Colonies." In *Capitalism, Colonialism and Globalization*, edited by Shireen Moosvi. Delhi: Aligarh Historians Society and Tulika Books.

Patnaik, U. 2011a. "Misleading Trade Estimates in Historical and Economic Writings." In *Excursus in History—Essays on Some Ideas of Irfan Habib*, edited by P. Patnaik. Delhi: Tulika Books.

Patnaik, U. 2012. "Capitalism and the Production of Poverty." *Social Scientist* 40, nos. 1–2 (January–February): 3–20. www.thehindu.com/multimedia/archive/00893/T_G_NARAYANAN_Memo_893967.pdf.

Patnaik, U. 2013. "Poverty Trends in India 2004–5 to 2009–10." *Economic and Political Weekly* 48, no. 40: 43–58.

Patnaik, U. 2014. "India in the World Economy 1900–1935: The Inter-War Depression and Britain's Demise as World Capitalist Leader." *Social Scientist* 42, nos. 1–2 (January–February): 13–35.

Penrose, E. 1940. "Rice Culture in the Japanese Economy." In *The Industrialization of Japan and Manchukuo*, edited by E. B. Schumpeter. 131–53. New York: Macmillan.

Pimentel, D., and M. Pimentel. 2003. "Sustainability of Meat-Based and Plant-Based Diets and the Environment." *American Journal of Clinical Nutrition* 78 (suppl.) 660S-3S.

Prebisch, R. 1950. *The Economic Development of Latin America and Its Principal Problems*. New York: United Nations Economic Commission for Latin America.

Raychaudhuri, T. 1985. "Historical Roots of Mass Poverty in South Asia." *Economic and Political Weekly* 20, no. 18 (May 4): 801–6.

Ricardo, D. 1951. *On the Principles of Political Economy and Taxation*. In *The Works and Correspondence of David Ricardo*, vol. 1, edited by Piero Sraffa, with M. H. Dobb. Cambridge: Cambridge University Press.

Robinson, J. V. 1956. *The Accumulation of Capital*. London: Macmillan.

Robinson, J. V. 1963. Introduction. In *Luxemburg*, 13–28.

Robinson, J. V. 1966. *Economic Philosophy*. Harmondsworth: Penguin.

Robinson, J. V. 1979. *Aspects of Development and Underdevelopment*. Cambridge: Cambridge University Press.

Rowthorn, R. E. 1977. "Conflict, Inflation and Money." *Cambridge Journal of Economics* 1, no.3 (September): 215–39.

Samuelson, P. A. 1970. "Market Mechanisms and Maximisation." In *The Collected Scientific Papers of Paul A. Samuelson*. New Delhi: Oxford University Press.

Saul, S. B. 1960. *Studies in British Overseas Trade*. Liverpool: Liverpool University Press.

Schumpeter, J. A. 1939. *Business Cycles*, 2 vols. New York: Mc Graw-Hill.

Schumpeter, J. A. 1951. *Imperialism and Social Classes*. New York: Augustus M. Kelley.

Schumpeter, J. A. 1952. "Karl Marx." In *Ten Great Economists*, 3–73. London: George Allen and Unwin.

Sen, A. K. 1981. *Poverty and Famines—An Essay on Entitlement and Deprivation*. Delhi: Oxford University Press.

Seton, F. 1957. "The 'Transformation Problem.'" *Review of Economic Studies* 24, 3 (June): 149–60.

Singer, H. 1950. "The Distribution of Gains Between Investing and Borrowing Countries." *American Economic Review* Papers and Proceedings, vol. 40 (May): 473–85.

Slicher Van Bath, B. H. 1963. *The Agrarian History of Western Europe AD 500 to 1850*, translated by Olive Ordish. New York: St. Martin's.

Smith, J. 2015. "Imperialism in the Twenty-First Century." *Monthly Review* 67, no. 3 (July–August): 82–97.

Spraos, J. 1980. "The Statistical Debate on the Net Barter Terms of Trade Between Primary Products and Manufactures." *Economic Journal* 90. 107–28, 357.

Sraffa, P. 1960. *Production of Commodities by Means of Commodities.* Cambridge: Cambridge University Press.

Stiglitz, J. E. 2013. "Inequality Is Holding Back the Recovery." *New York Times,* January 13.

Strachey J. 1959. *The End of Empire.* London: Gollancz.

Sweezy, P. M. 1942. *The Theory of Capitalist Development.* New York: Monthly Review Press.

Turner, H. A., D. Jackson, and F. Wilkinson. 1970. *Do Trade Unions Cause Inflation?* Cambridge: Cambridge University Press.

United Nations. 1962. *International Trade Statistics 1900 to 1960.* New York: United Nations, available at www.unstats.un.org/unsd/trade/imts /Historicaldata 1900–1960.pdf.

United Nations Food and Agriculture Organization, Rome. Food Balance Sheets /Supply Utilisation Accounts (FBS/SUA). Available at faostat3.fao .org/faostat-gateway/go/to/download/F/FO/E.

Wittfogel, K. A. 1957. *Oriental Despotism: A Comparative Study of Total Power.* New Haven, Conn.: Yale University Press.

Yotopoulos, P. A. 1985. "Middle-income Classes and Food Crises: the 'New' Food-Feed Competition." *Economic Development and Cultural Change* 33, 3. 463–83.

Index

Non-Accelerating Inflation Rate of
Unemployment (NAIRU),
49–50, 201n1 (chap.4); derived
from the idea of "inflationary
barrier", 49; distinguished from
Natural rate of Unemployment
(NRU), 49; threat to money even
at NAIRU, 49–50

O.P.E.C, 19
over-accumulation problem of
capital, 170
own rate of interest, 83

peasantry: destroyed as a class in
the metropolis, 148; differential
treatment of by capitalism,
147–149; emigration to temperate
regions, 148; merchants and
middlemen take production
decisions of tropical peasantry,
149; not destroyed as a class in
tropical and sub-tropical regions
but suppressed, 148; in the
periphery carries over feudal
consciousness, 152; withdrawal
of state support to under neo-
liberalism, 103–104, 106
peasant suicides in India, 33, 104
perfect competition, 85; comparison
with free competition, 85
petty producers, 6, 7, 8, 10, 15, 23,
48, 86, 144, 147, 159; being
subjected to intolerable levels of
oppression, 153; emigration of
those displaced in the metropolis,
56–57, 148, 152; as price-takers,
53, 55
post-Bretton Woods system, 133;
hierarchy of currencies under, 135;
rests on cross-border capital
flows, 135; substantive differences

from Bretton Woods system less
significant than formal
differences, 133
post-colonial dirigiste regime, 31,
90, 145, 146, 155, 192, 202n4
(chap.6); support for peasantry
and petty production in India,
102–106
Poverty: "basket commanded"
measure of, 68, 69, 70, 71, 72,
202n3 (chap.5); estimating in two
possible ways, 113; evidence on
growth in absolute poverty in
periphery, 112–117; explanation
of divergence between the two
estimates, 115–117; false claims on
reduction in, 186; and income
inequality, 73–75; nutritional, 66;
relation between nutritional and
general, 66–72; spontaneous
tendency of capitalism to
keep aggravating in absolute
terms, 73
price-takers: absorb the impact of
autonomous wage or profit-
margin push, 53–55; attenuation
of stabilizing role of, 55; to be
found really in the periphery, 53;
behavior sustained by income
deflation, 59; Keynes saw workers
as, 52; labour reserves make
primary producers into, 52;
metropolitan workers reduced to
becoming under globalization, 55,
58; stabilize capitalist system, 52
profit-inflation, 15, 201n6 (chap.3);
explanation of, 40; and "forced
saving," 15; is secondary to
income deflation in periphery, 43;
underlying the Bengal Famine,
129, 149; within the periphery,
39–42, 65

inventories of goods produced on, 48; low weight in metropolitan demand of commodities produced on, 79; low weight of its products in metropolitan demand a result of social relations, 80–81, 145–146; "mainstream" trade theory has ignored the significance of, 11; more or less fully used up, 14–15, 28, 31; remarkable property of, 99; threat to value of money because of its fixity, 23, 27, 33, 45, 47, 48, 97; total output of, 63, 64; two kinds of metropolitan demand upon, 99

underconsumption: need for bubbles to thwart tendency towards, 77; tendency towards under globalization, 75–76, 90, 166
utility possibility curve, 13

value of money, 144, 145, 193, 197; claim that it is not threatened by inflation in tropical goods prices, 79–82, 145–146; its defence becomes even more necessary in more recent times, 147; threatened by profit inflation, 15; threat from increasing supply price to, 23, 27, 150, 173
Vietnam war, 19, 95
Von-Neumann rate of maximum balanced growth, 82

wage explosion of 1968, 130, 132; not the explanation for collapse of Bretton Woods; reasons behind, 131
Walras, Leon, 16, 87
Wittfogel, Karl, 162, 201n2 (chap.3)
worker-peasant alliance: advance to socialism remains fraught with difficulties, 152; not practicable at world level, 152; possible in particular countries, 152
world economy, segmentation of, 2, 3, 42, 90
WTO, 11, 13, 32, 159, 160, 161, 164, 171, 175, 183, 187